Real Fresh Gluten-free Food

Simple healthy meals for everyone

Real Fresh Gluten-free Food

Simple healthy meals for everyone

Anna & Roger Wilde
with photography by Daniel Allen

NEW HOLLAND

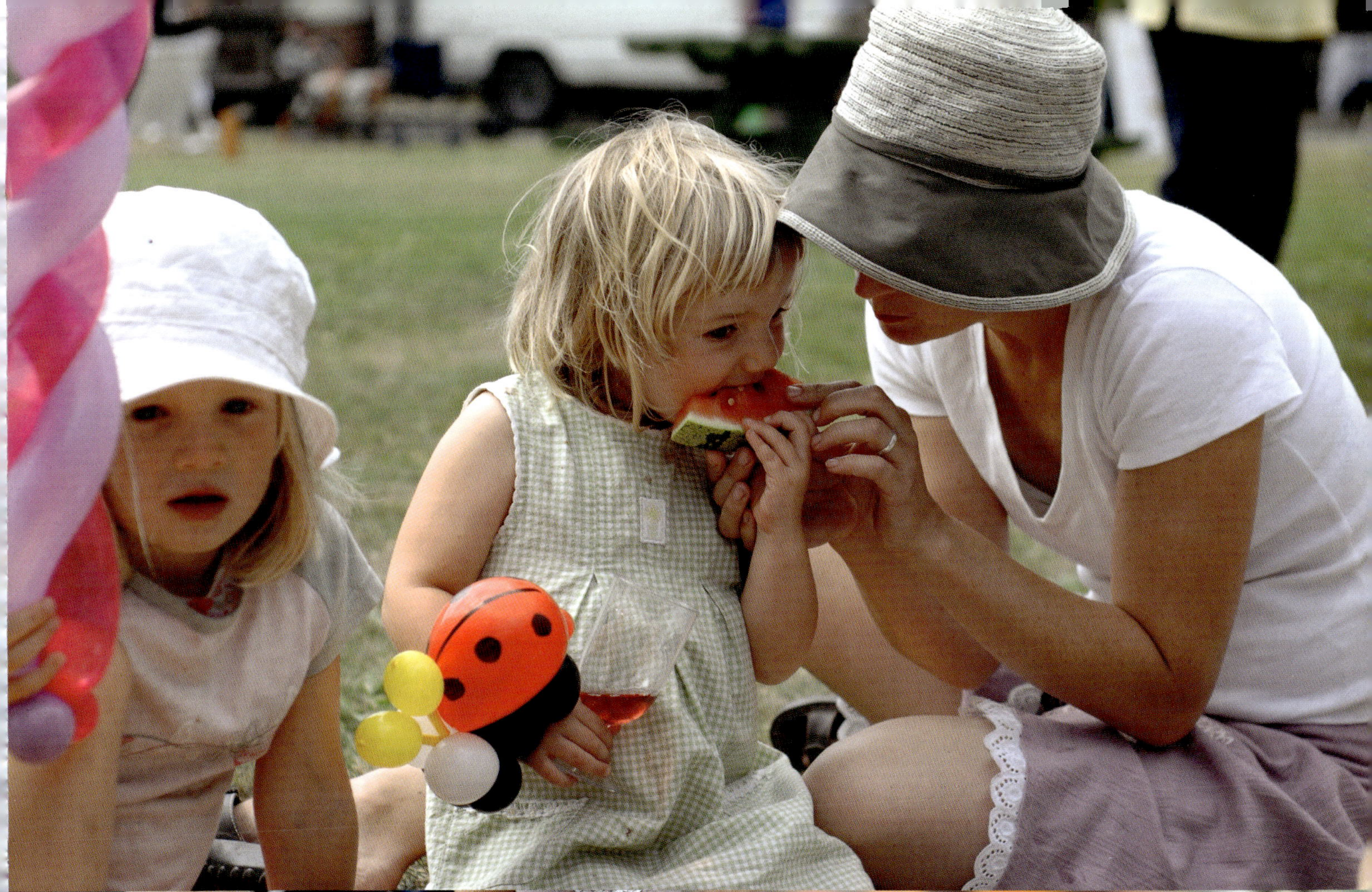

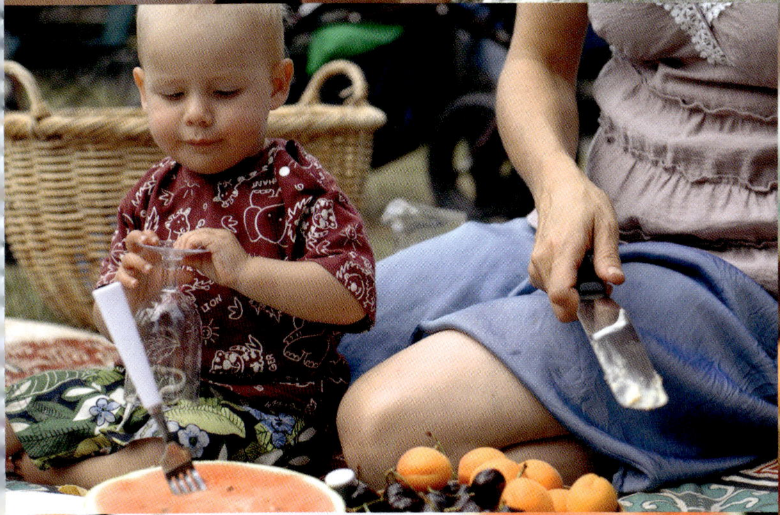

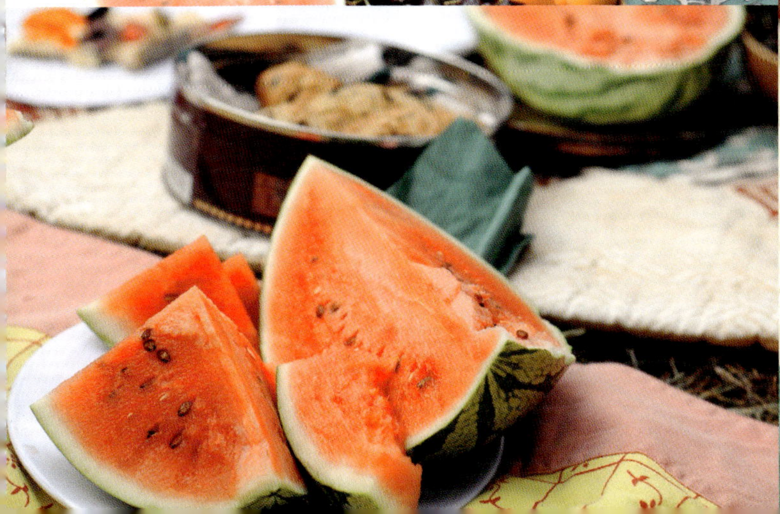

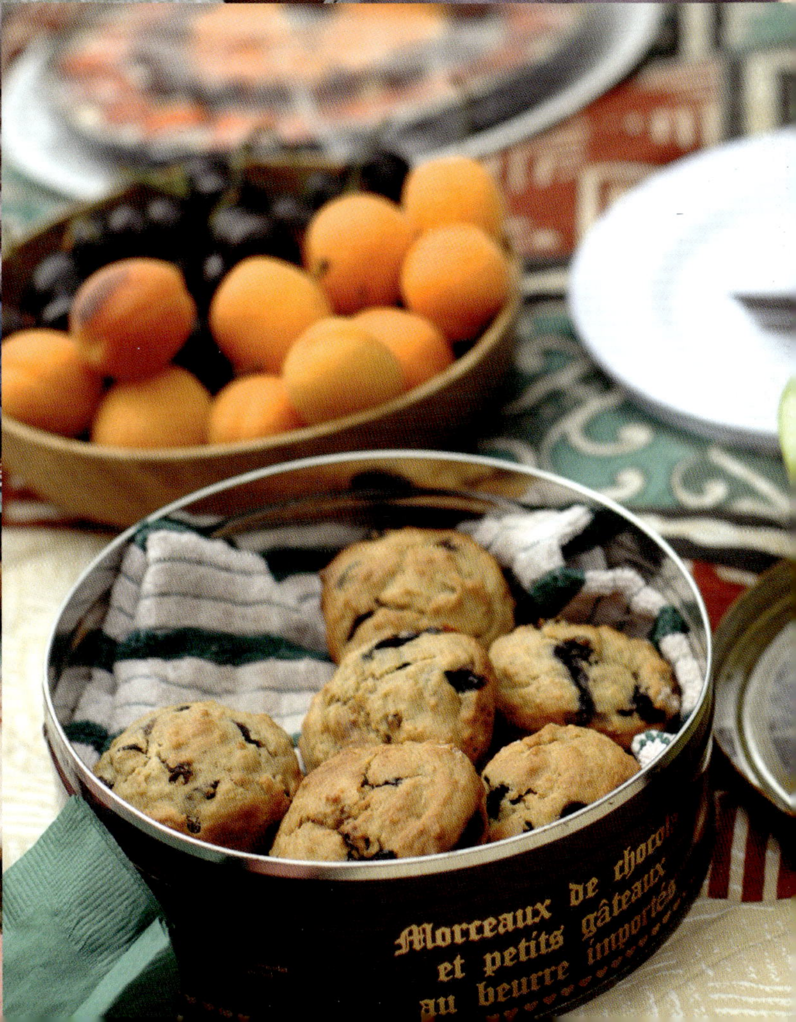
Morceaux de choco
et petits gâteaux
au beurre importés

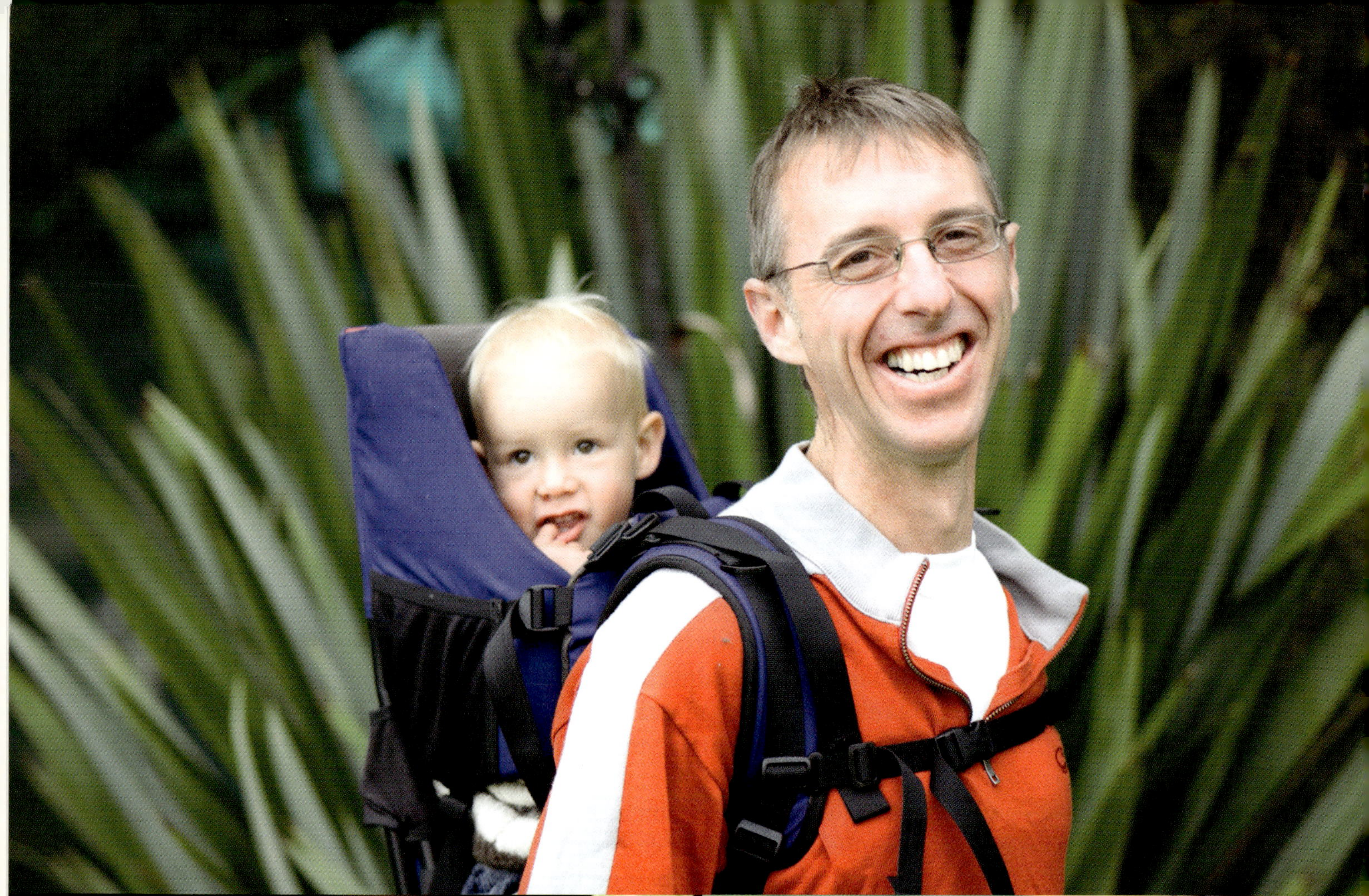
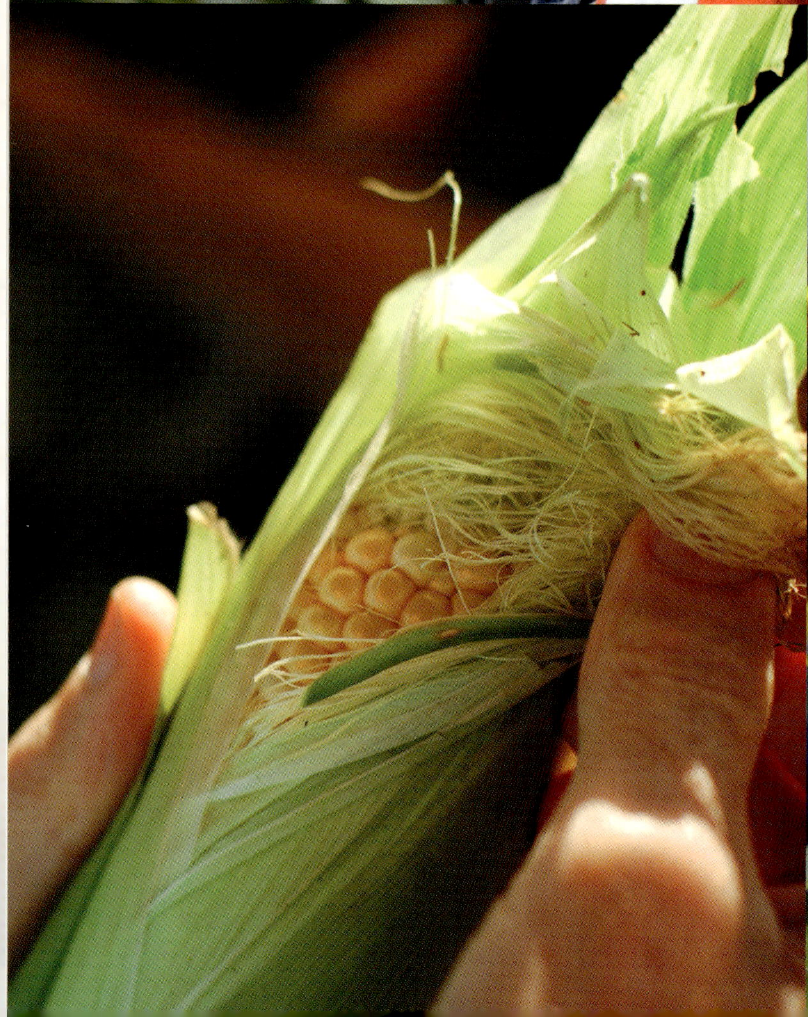
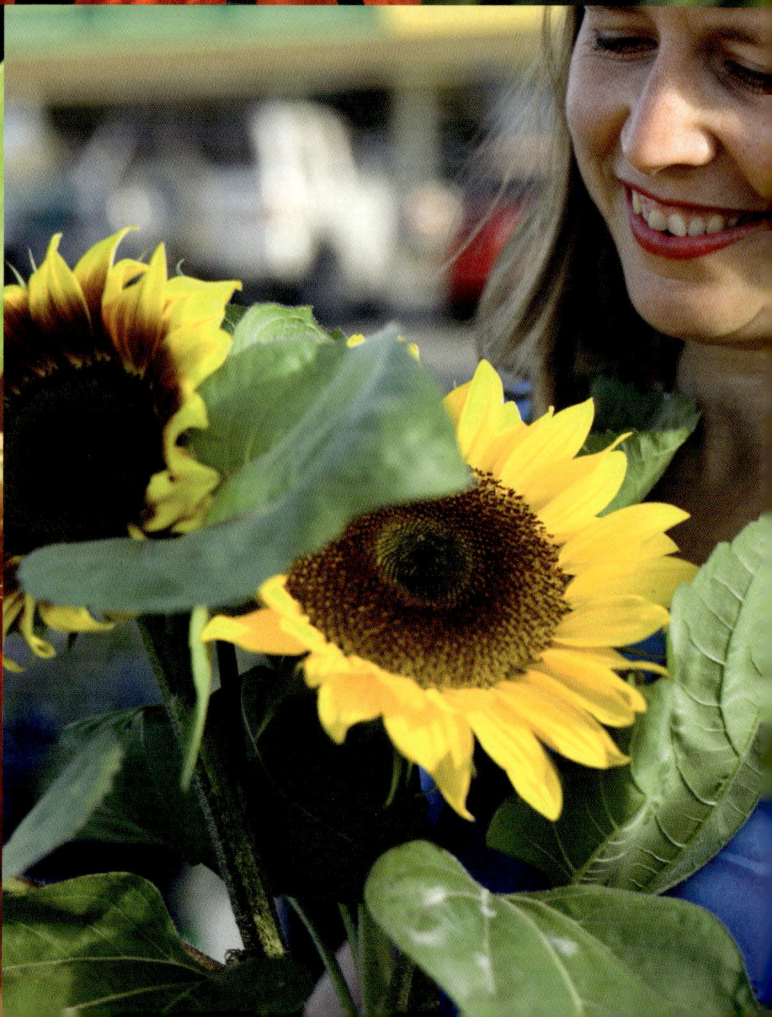

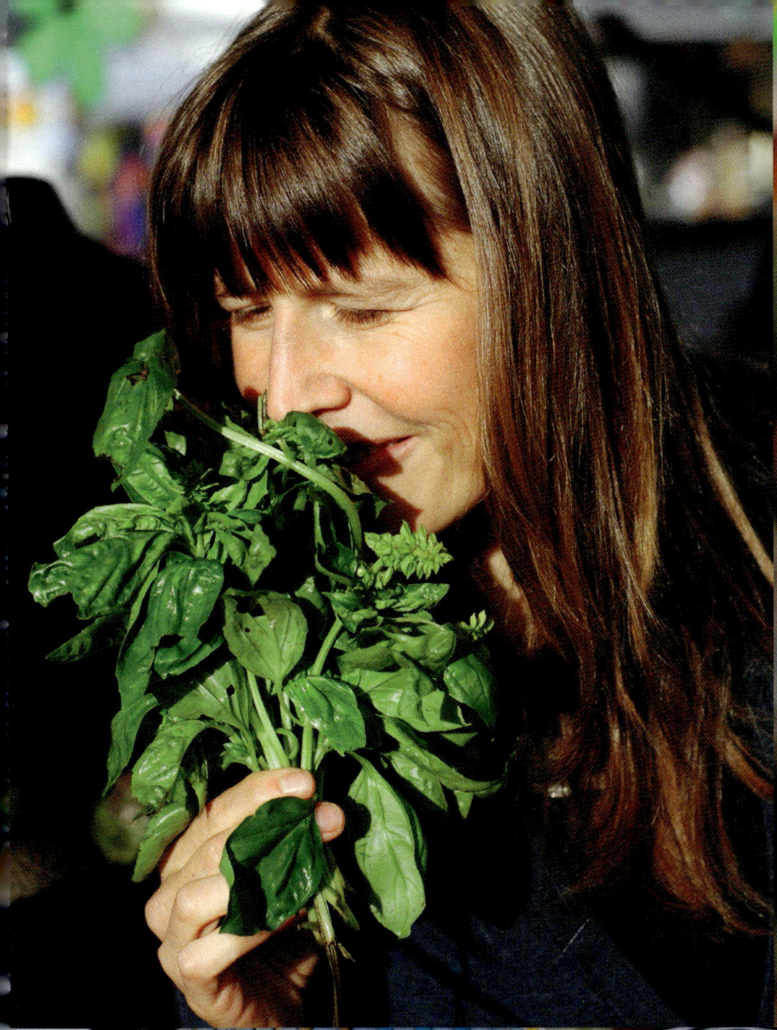

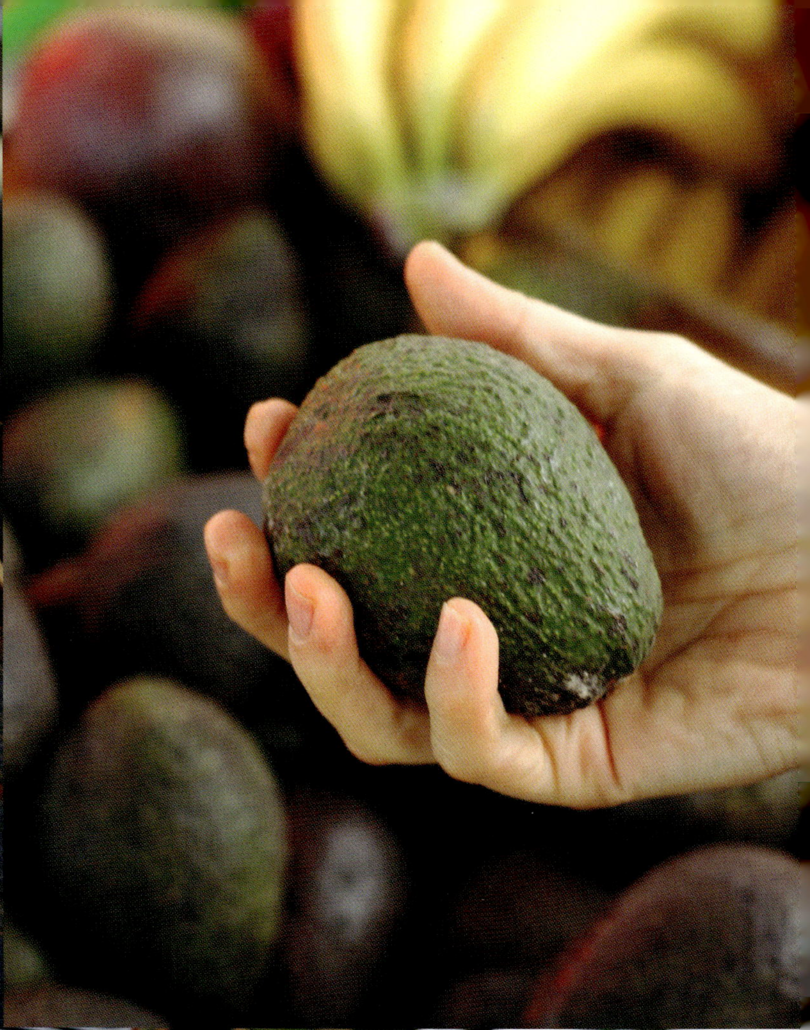

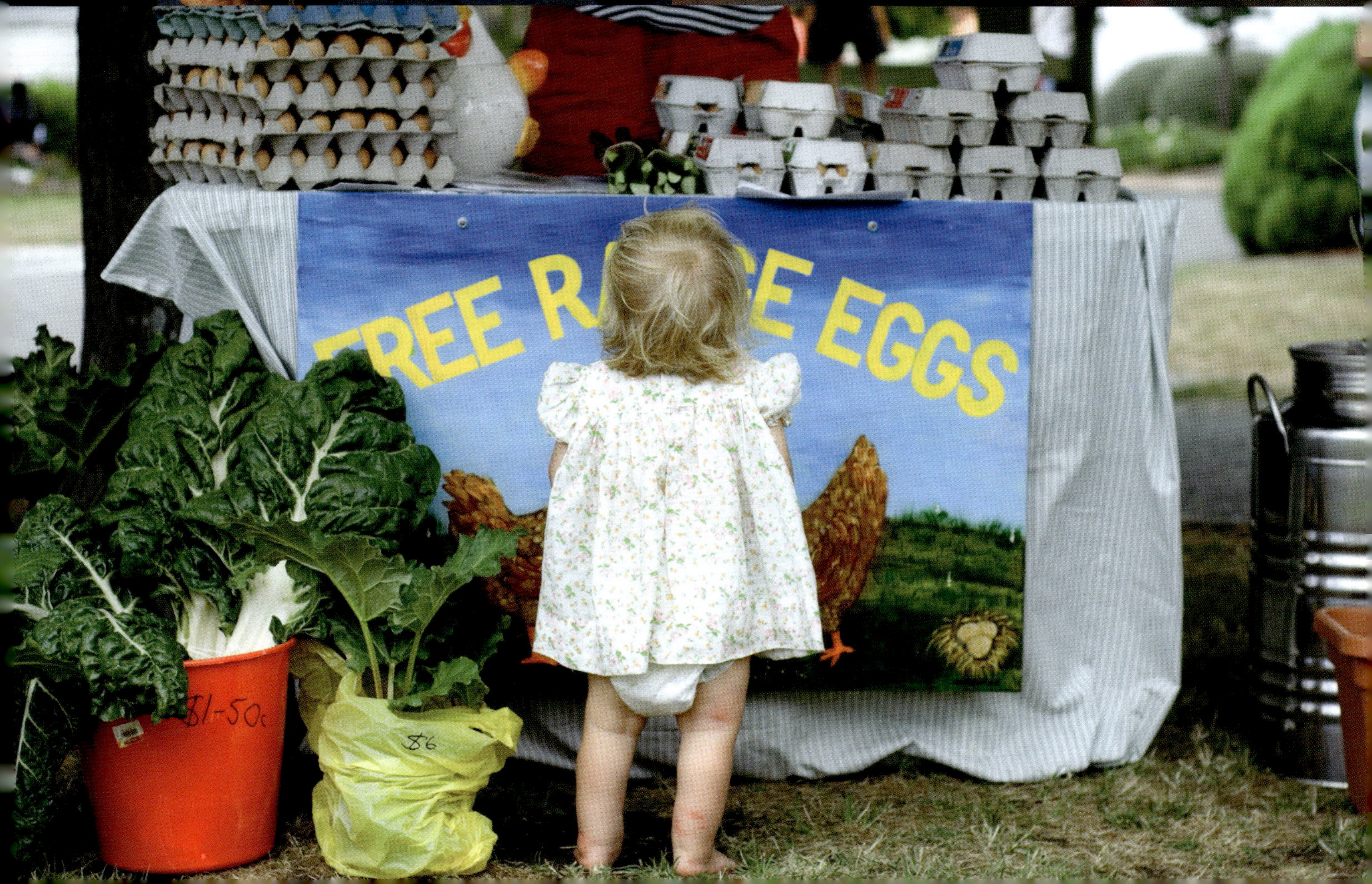
EGGS
$1-50c
$6

GLUTEN-FREE FLOUR BLEND

Our gluten-free flour blend is a mix that works for the recipes in this book. It rises well and is nicely moist in baking, with just a hint of sweetness. Find the ingredients at a good supermarket, organic food shop or bulk-bin store.

In a large bowl, mix together 2 cups brown rice flour, 2 cups buckwheat flour, 1 cup tapioca flour, 1 cup coconut flour and 2 teaspoons of xantham gum. Store in an airtight container.

SEASONING

Processed packaged foods generally have extreme flavours – usually salty or sweet – and are designed to stimulate cravings for more. Food made from natural ingredients, on the other hand, that have been carefully seasoned are nourishing and satisfying. Most well-loved traditional dishes are popular because they have a good balance of flavours.

When a dish tastes flat, it is likely to need a little sea salt. Add salt a pinch at a time and taste after each addition to ensure the flavours are just right.

Try any of the following natural seasonings in your cooking:
- Honey, sugar and dried fruit for added sweetness.
- Salt, miso and shoyu (soy sauce) for saltiness and to draw out existing flavours in the dish.
- Lemon zest and juice, vinegar and tamarind paste for a touch of piquancy.
- Black pepper, garlic, chilli and ginger for added spice.

NUTS AND SEEDS

Nuts and seeds are a wonderful source of protein, healthy fats and minerals. In their raw form, however, they are difficult to digest. Many of our recipes use nuts, seeds or grains that have been soaked in water for several hours or overnight. Rehydrating the nuts and seeds makes them more nutritious.

How to soak nuts:
- Place in a bowl, then cover with plenty of water.
- Leave larger nuts, such as almonds, hazelnuts and cashews, to soak overnight. Smaller seeds, such as sunflower seeds, may be ready to use after 3 or 4 hours.
- Drain and rinse the nuts or seeds before use.
- Surplus soaked and drained nuts will keep for several days in the refrigerator. They can be used in salads, as snacks or added to a lunchbox. Even small shoots can be used in salads. Soaked nuts and seeds can also be frozen and thawed in warm water, as required.

Something I've always loved about Anna is the way she can turn the simplest meal into a special occasion. She may put flowers on the table, light a candle, or pause to say some words of gratitude before eating. Nowadays, these little rituals help keep us sane amidst the chaos of feeding hungry boys. – **ROGER**

ENJOY YOUR MEAL

Eating in a relaxed atmosphere can aid digestion. By taking time to appreciate the colours, flavour and texture of the food you are eating, you are also more likely to know when you have eaten enough.

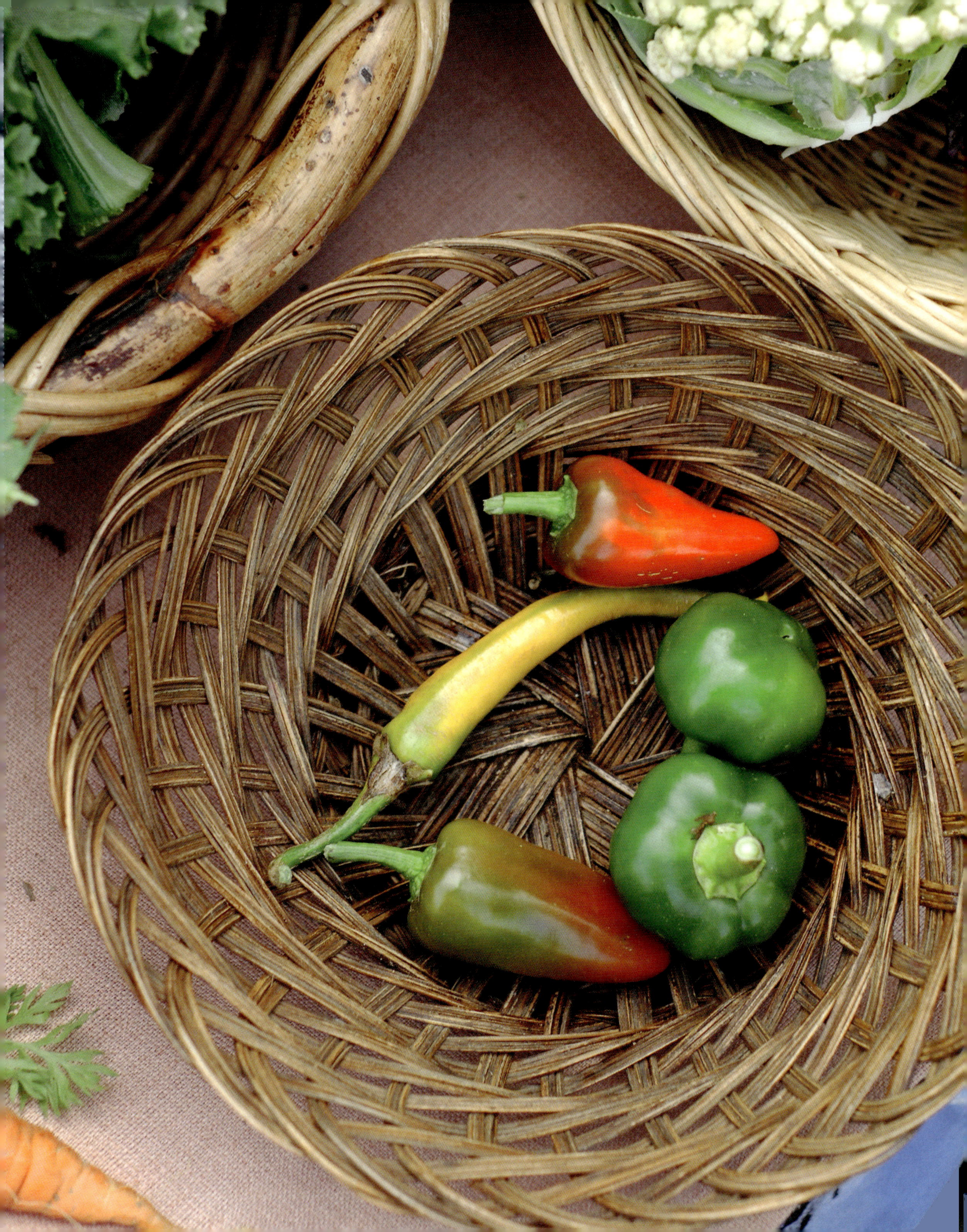

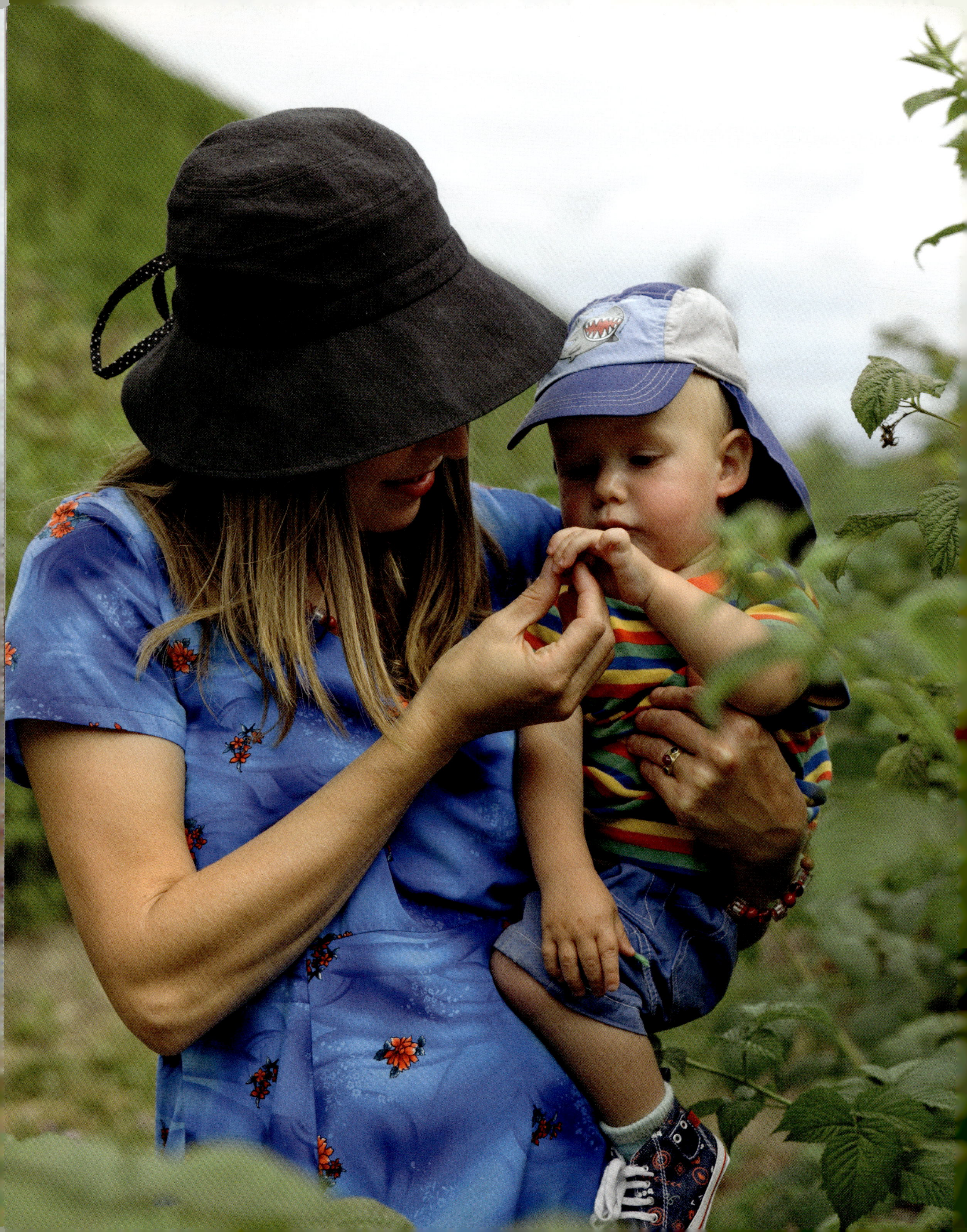

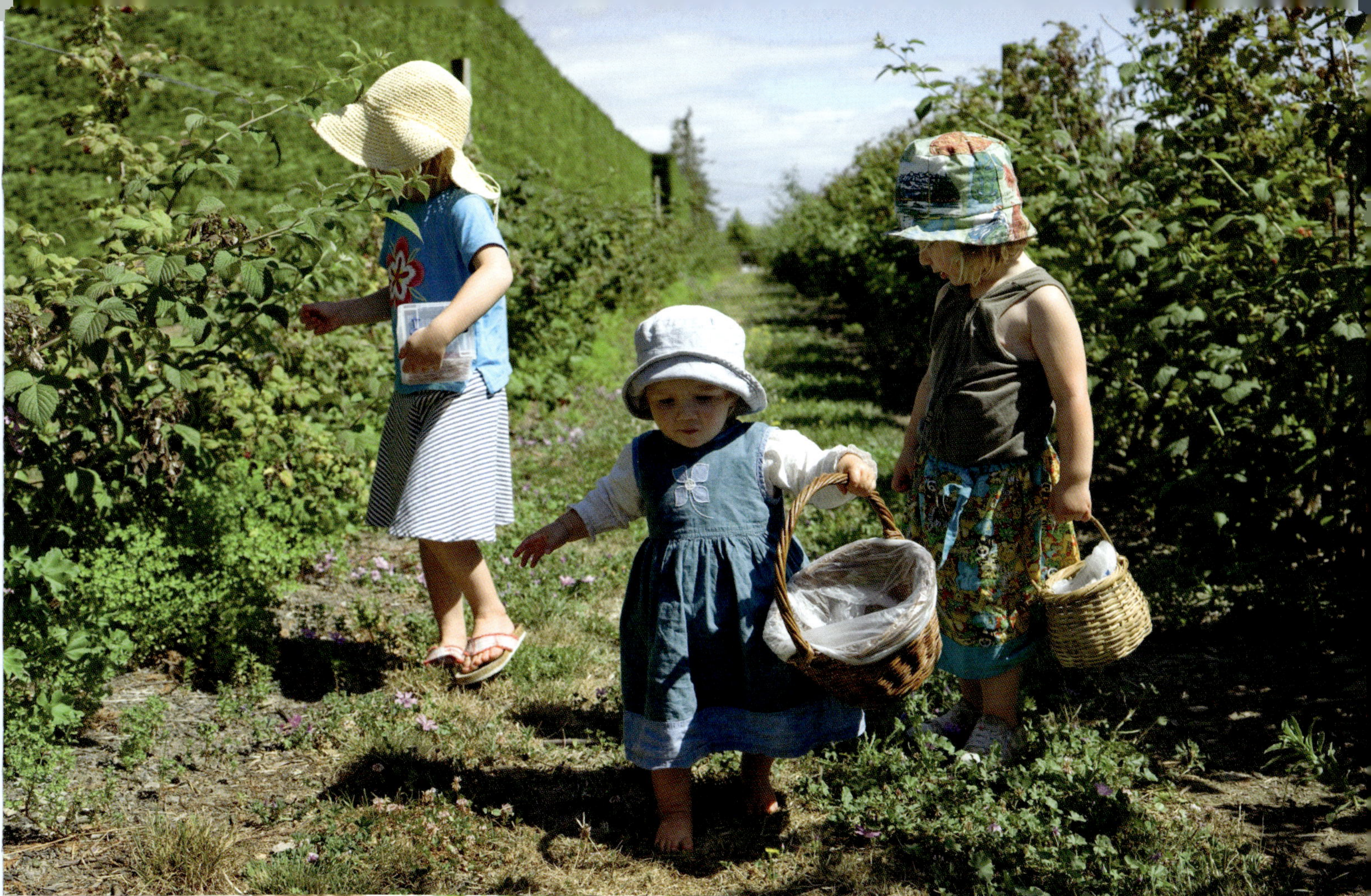

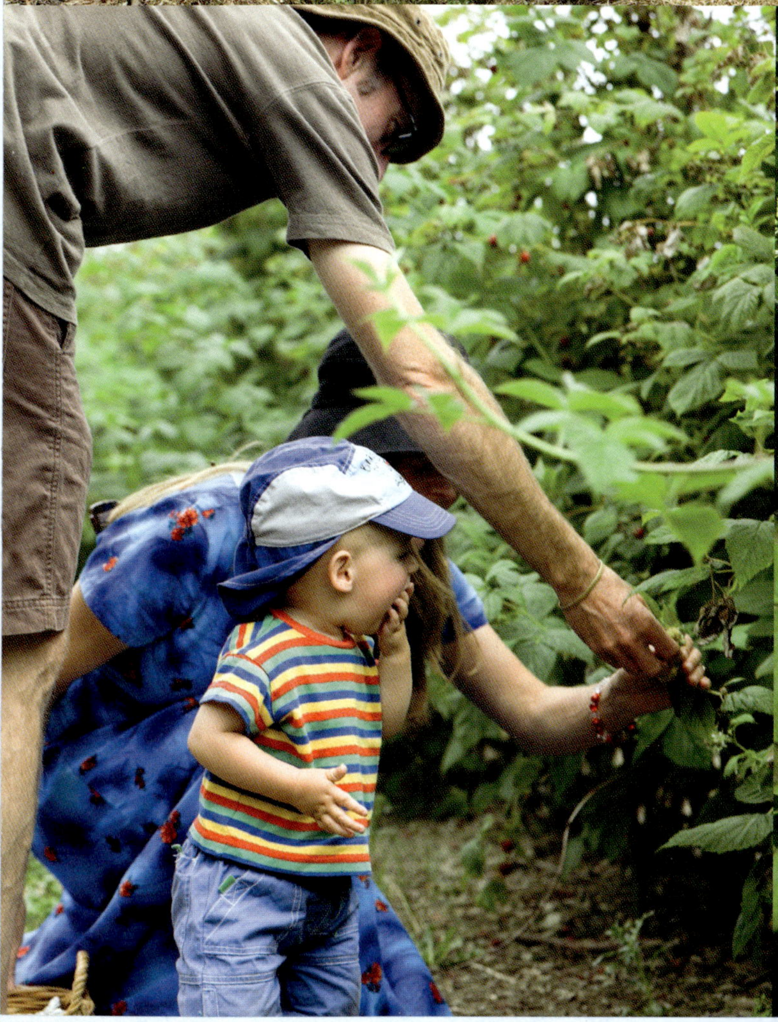

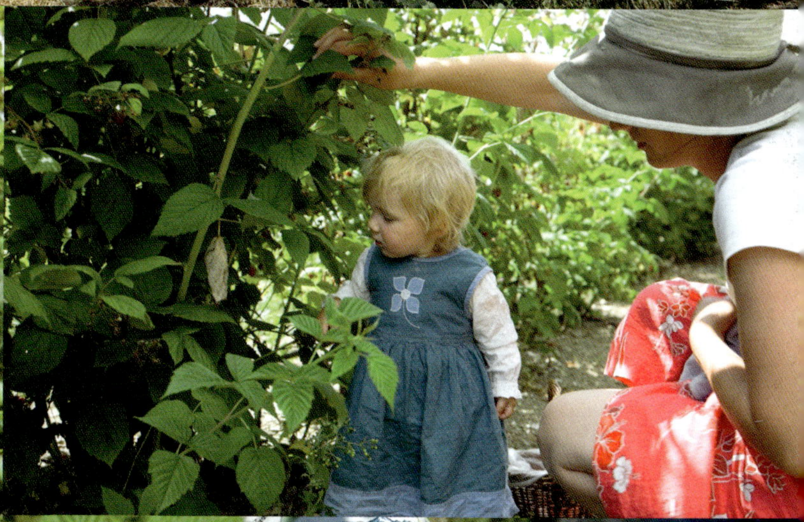

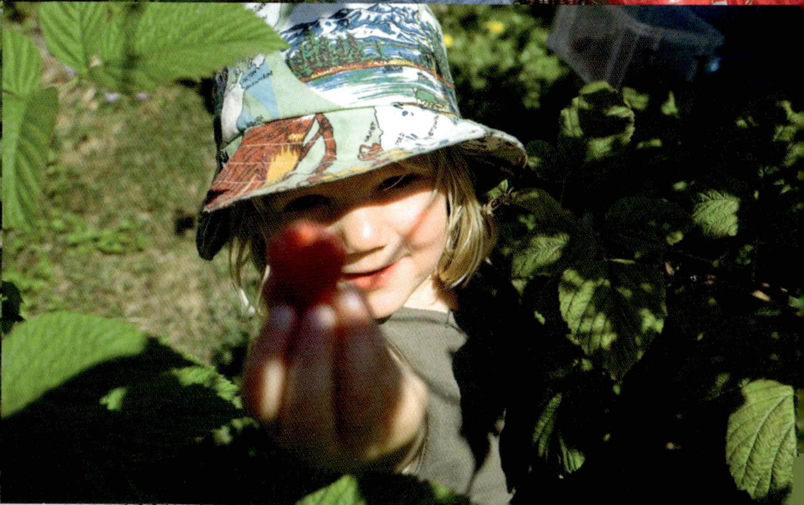

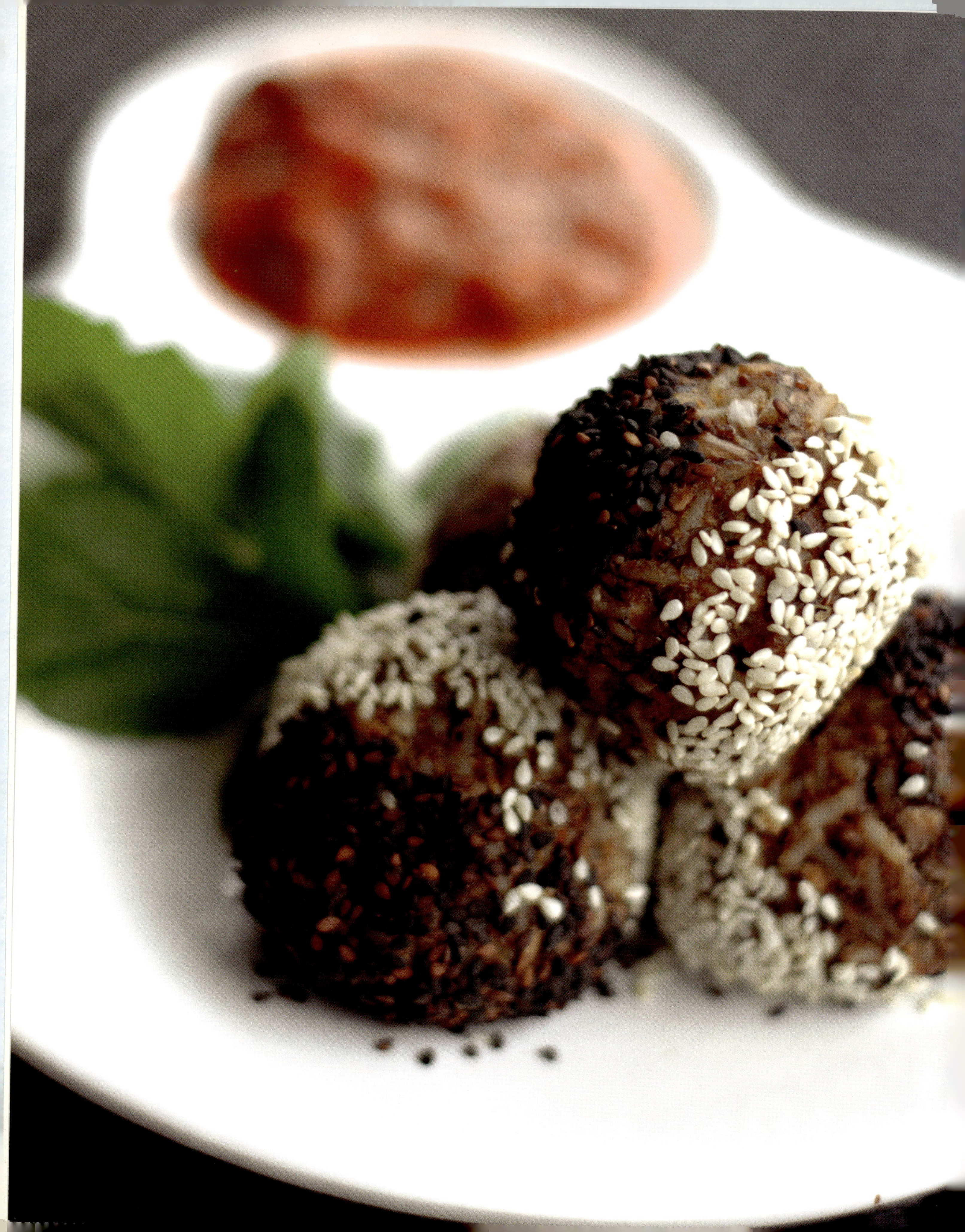

Tofu and mushroom rissoles

DF V

This is a handy way to use leftover rice. Easy finger-food and fine eaten cold, the mushroom balls look stunning decorated with black and white sesame seeds, but will taste as good with just one colour.

⅔ cup flaxseed
1 red onion, roughly chopped
1 tablespoon fresh thyme, chopped
300g mushrooms, roughly chopped
300g firm tofu
3 cups cooked rice (from 1 cup dry rice)
1 teaspoon sea salt
3 tablespoons shoyu
¼ cup white sesame seeds
¼ cup black sesame seeds

Grind flaxseed in a spice grinder until fine. You may need to do this in several batches.

Place red onion and thyme in a food processor (with S blade) and pulse until fine. Add mushroom and pulse-chop again for a few seconds until fine but not completely minced. Transfer mixture into a bowl.

Break up tofu and add to the bowl. Mash tofu by squeezing through fingers. Add cooked rice, ground flaxseed, salt and shoyu. Mix well. Form mixture into balls, a bit larger than golf-ball size, using your hands to press firmly into shape. Place balls on a tray.

Put black and white sesame seeds into two separate bowls. Dip one side of each ball into the white seeds, then turn over and dip into black. Place mushroom-tofu balls on an oven tray.

Bake at 180°C for 25 minutes or until firm.

Serve with a rich tomato-based pasta sauce.

(For a variation, add 6-8 chopped sun-dried tomatoes or ⅓ cup of pitted and sliced black olives.)

SERVES 6 AS A LUNCH WITH SALAD

Farinata

DF V

Our version of farinata (traditionally a thin, crispy pancake) is more like a frittata, but made with chickpea flour instead of egg. Delicious hot or cold, it's perfect for a picnic or packed in lunchboxes for school or work.

CHICKPEA BATTER
250g chickpea flour
3 cups warm water
1 teaspoon ground cumin
1 teaspoon sea salt
juice of 1 lemon
75ml olive oil

FILLING
1 large eggplant (400g), cut in 2cm cubes
3 tablespoons olive oil
½ teaspoon sea salt
1 red onion, diced in large pieces
3 zucchini (300g), cut in 2cm chunks
3 tomatoes, roughly diced
chopped parsley or other fresh herbs
½ teaspoon chilli flakes (optional)

To make batter, sift chickpea flour into the water while whisking. Add cumin, sea salt and lemon juice. Leave in a warm place for about 2 hours. (The batter thickens slightly while resting.)

For the filling, heat oven to 180°C. In a large roasting dish, toss cubed eggplant with olive oil and salt. Roast for about 15 minutes until soft. Add red onion and zucchini and roast for about 10 minutes until zucchini has softened slightly. Remove from oven and add diced tomato and herbs.

Add olive oil to the chickpea batter. Whisk well, then pour evenly over the vegetables in roasting dish. Sprinkle with chilli flakes.

Return dish to oven and bake for 20-25 minutes until the centre feels firm to touch. Remove from oven and allow to cool for 10 minutes.

Cut into large squares and serve.

SERVES 6

Tamari roasted seeds

DF V

Eat these seeds on their own as a snack, or sprinkle onto salads or soups.

1 tablespoon tamari
pinch of cayenne pepper (optional)
¼ teaspoon garlic powder (optional)
1 cup sunflower or pumpkin seeds

Measure tamari into a small cup and add spices, if using.

Heat a heavy-based frying pan over moderate heat. Toast seeds, stirring constantly with a wooden spoon, until fragrant and slightly browned. Pumpkin seeds will swell and pop when ready.

Remove pan from heat and sprinkle tamari over hot seeds. Continue stirring. The remaining heat will cause tamari to dry onto seeds. Return briefly to the heat if necessary.

Allow seeds to cool, then store in an airtight jar for up to 2 weeks.

MAKES 1 CUP

The low-fat mantra of recent years is gradually being replaced by a low-carb message. Both sugars and starches from sweet foods and refined grains contribute to elevated glucose levels in the bloodstream. Consistently excessive blood sugar is recognised as a key contributor to the most serious health problems of the modern world: heart disease, obesity and diabetes.

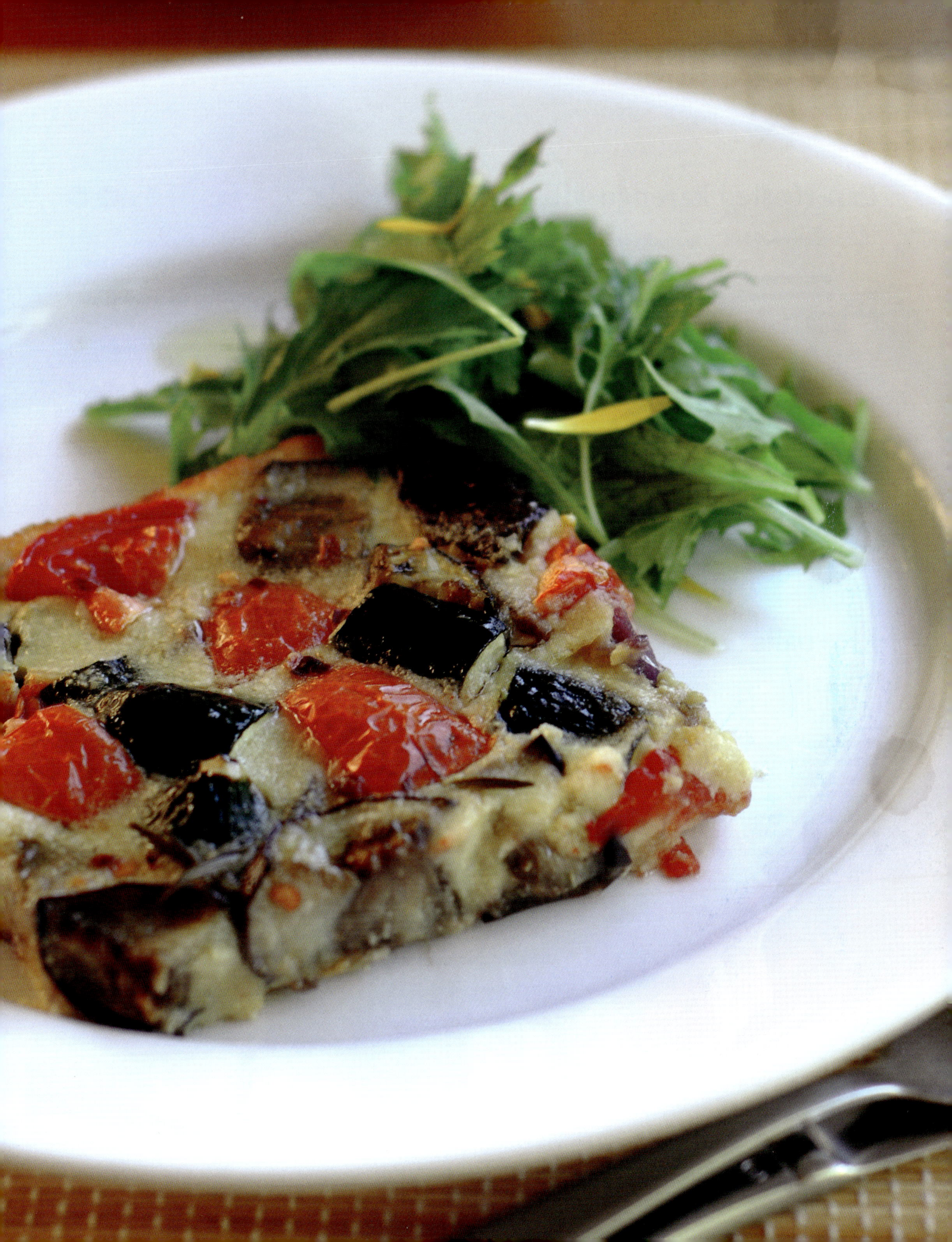

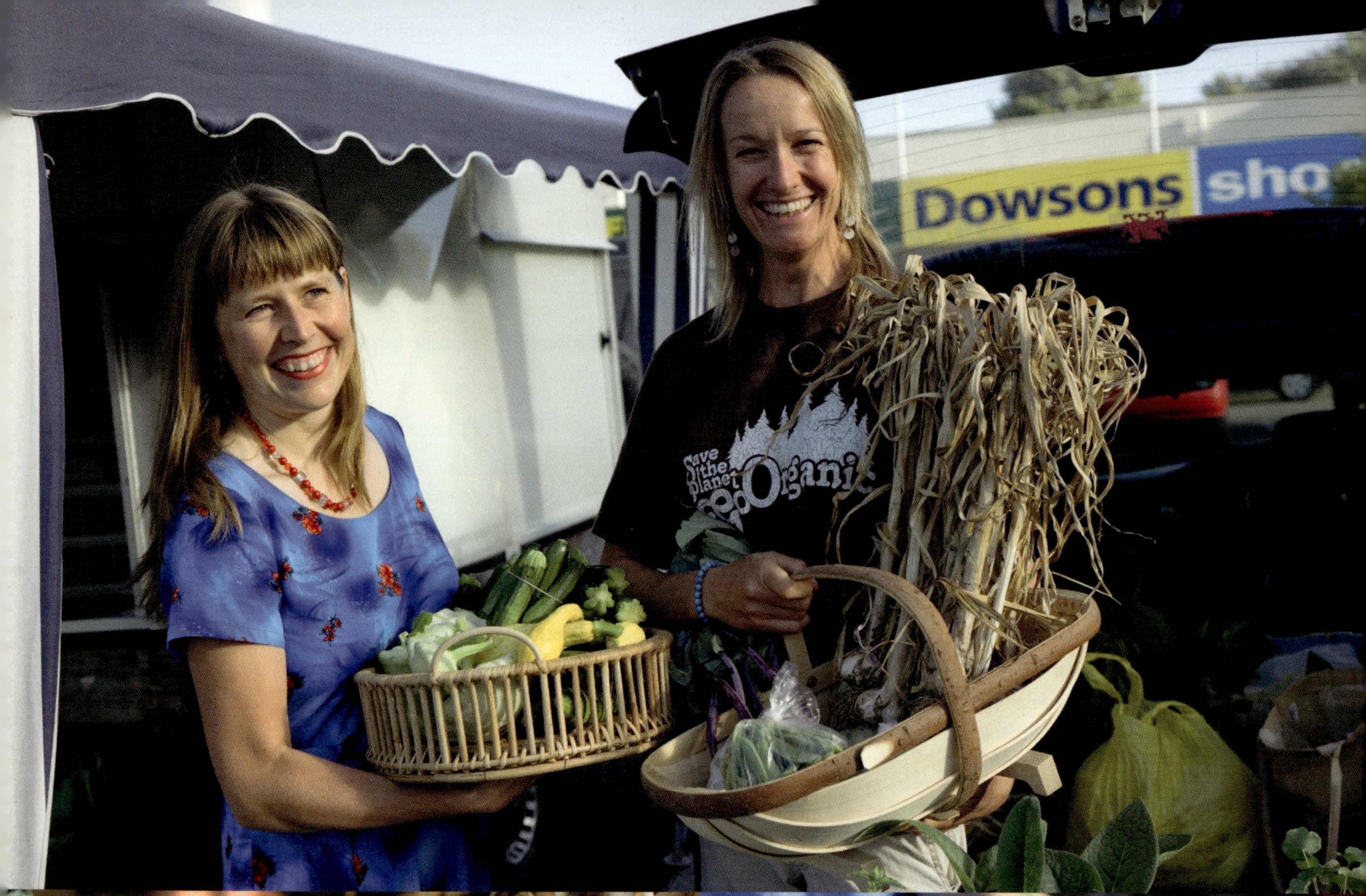
Dowsons
Organic
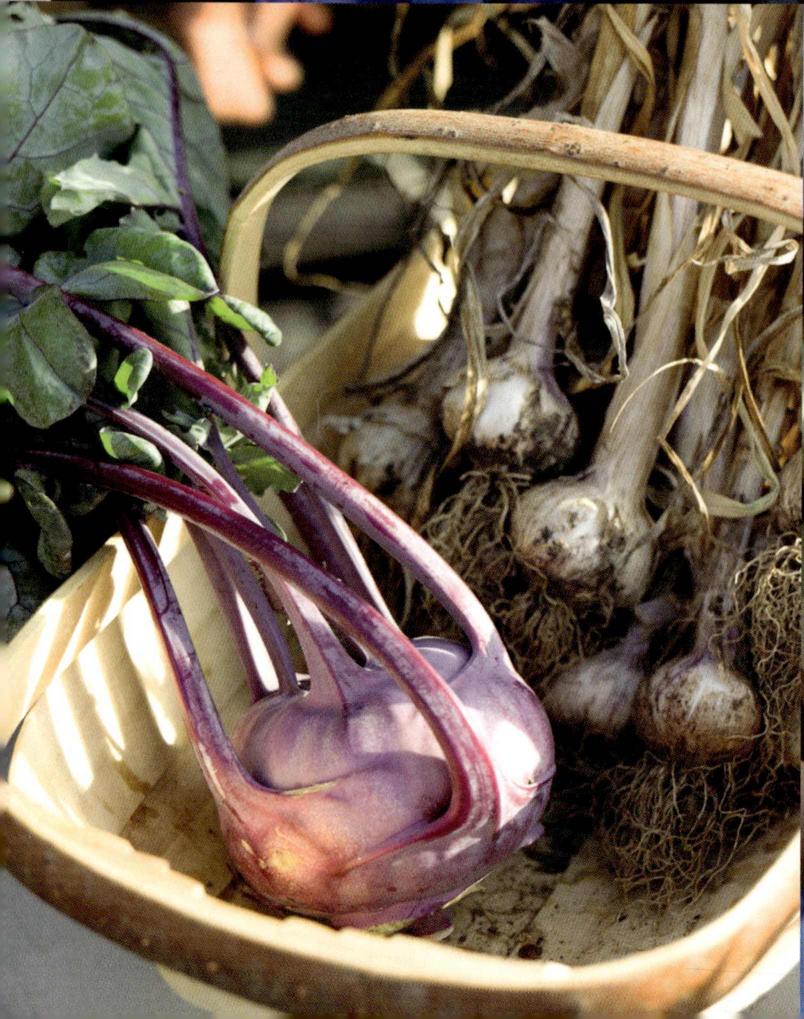
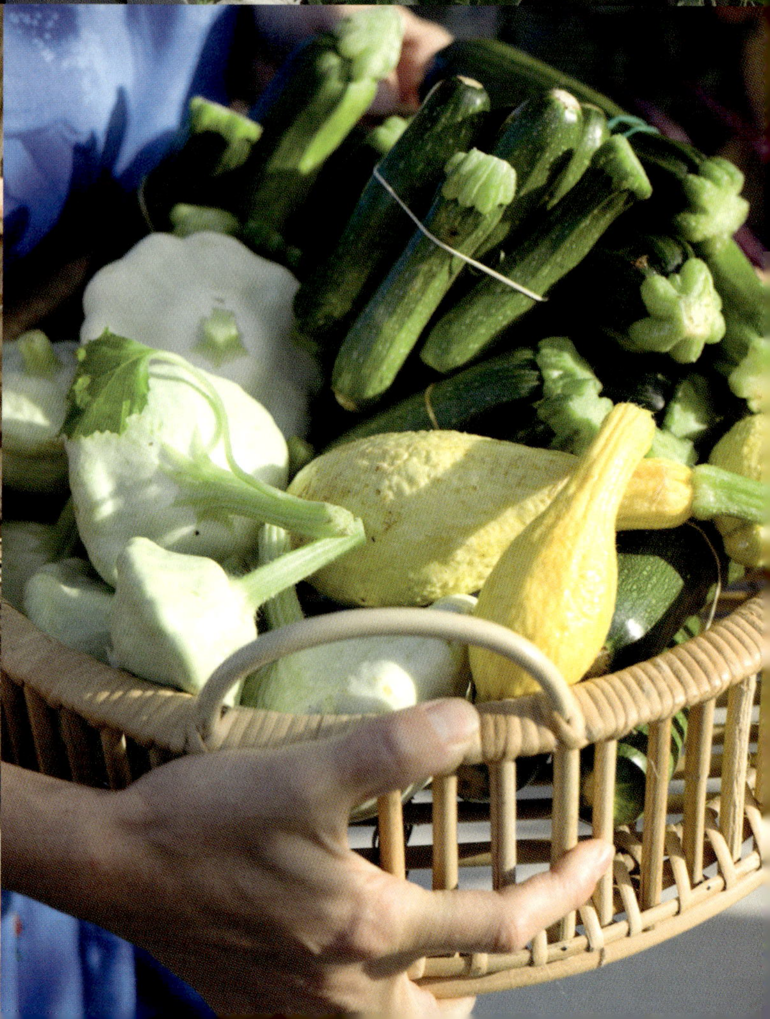

"easy peel"
Garlic
This seasons
$1.00 each

Pepinos
50¢ each

Beetroot
'chioggia'
$2 a bunch

ORGANIC

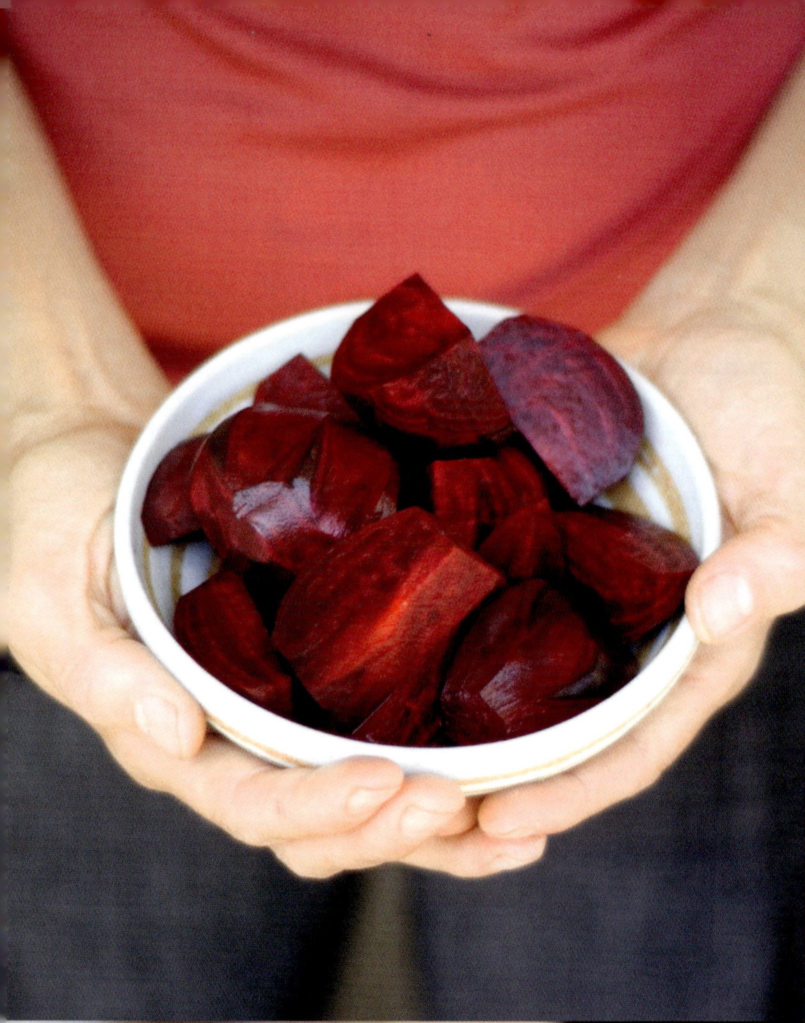

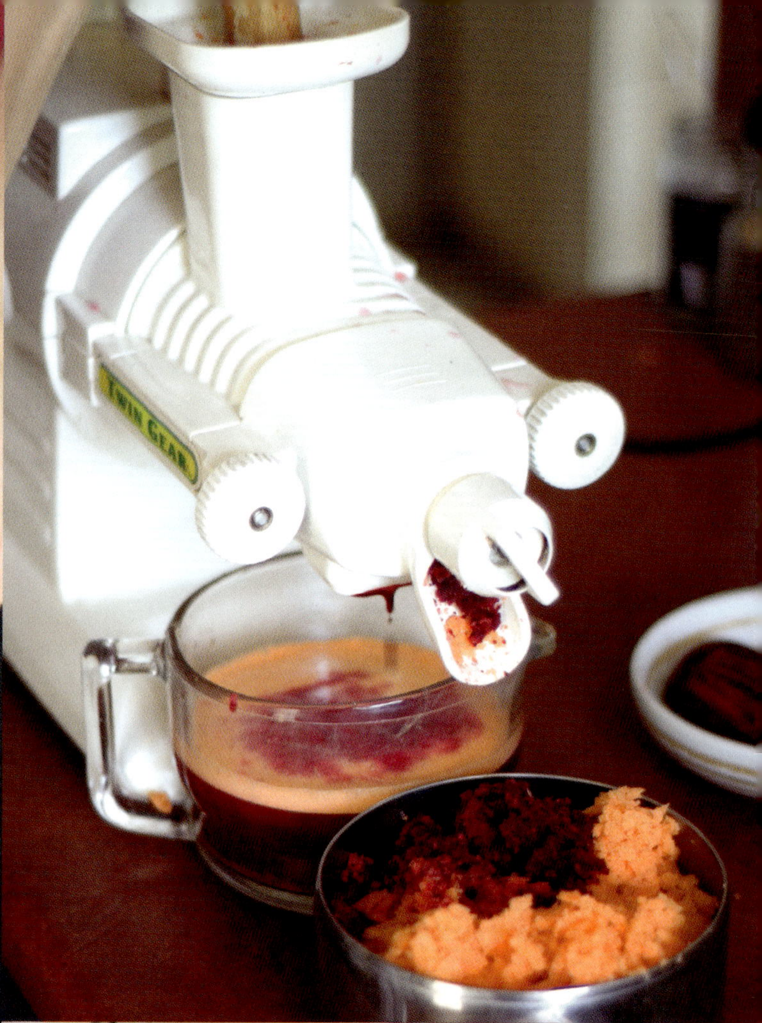
TWIN GEAR

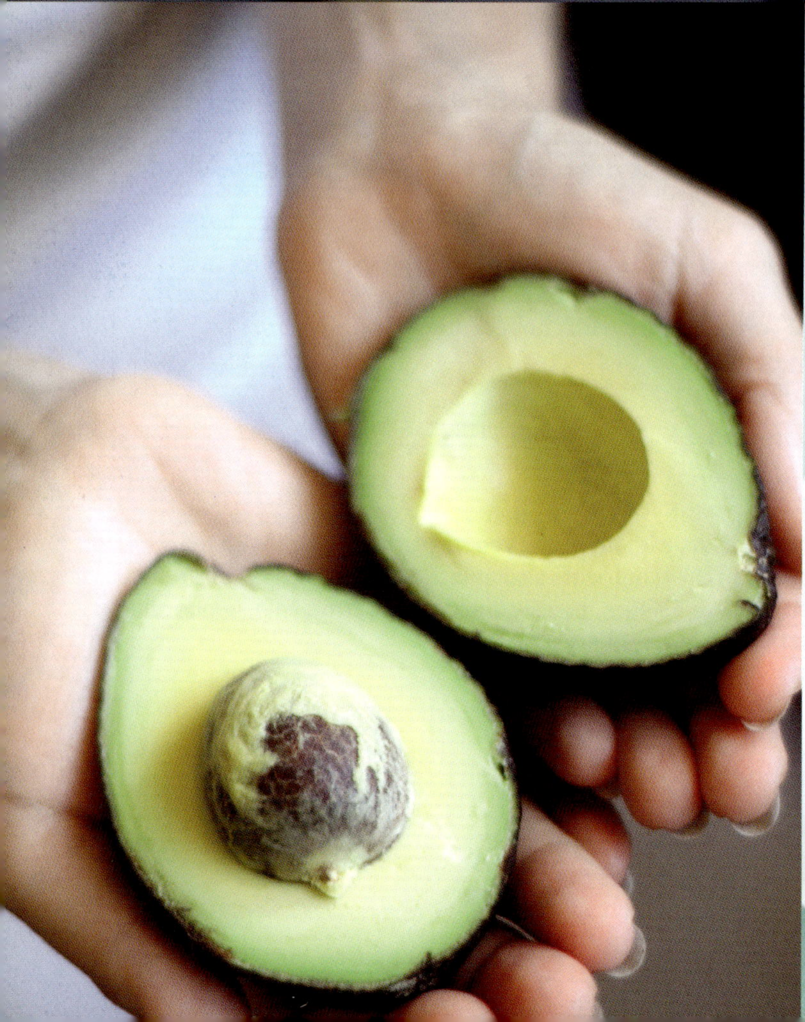

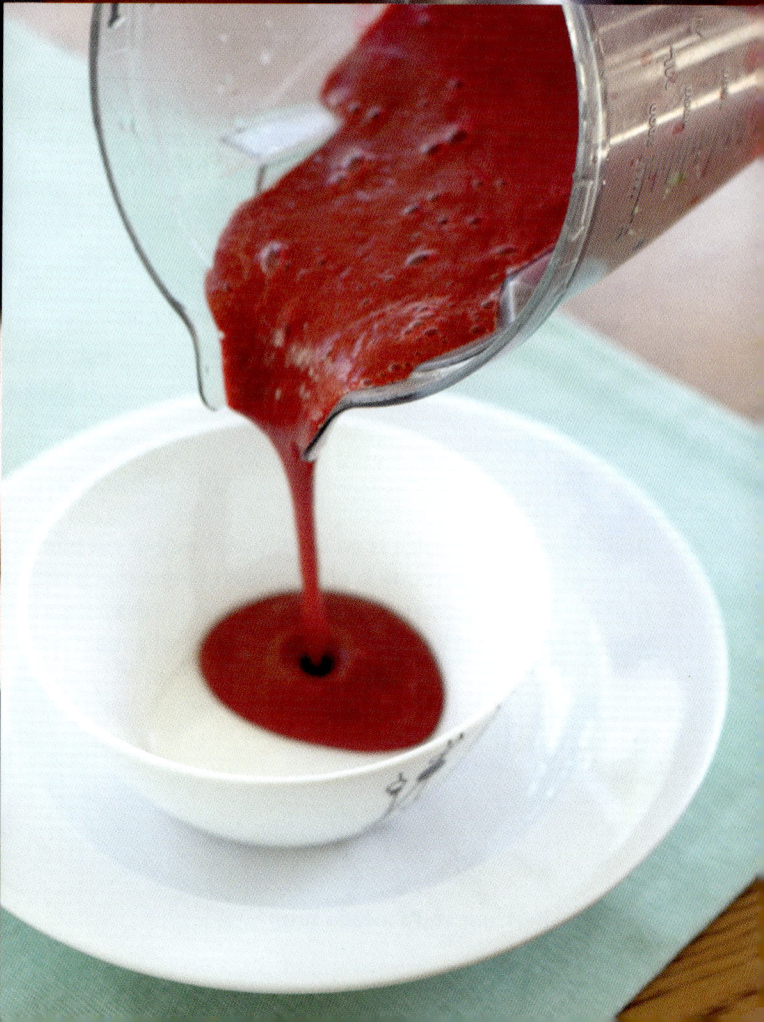

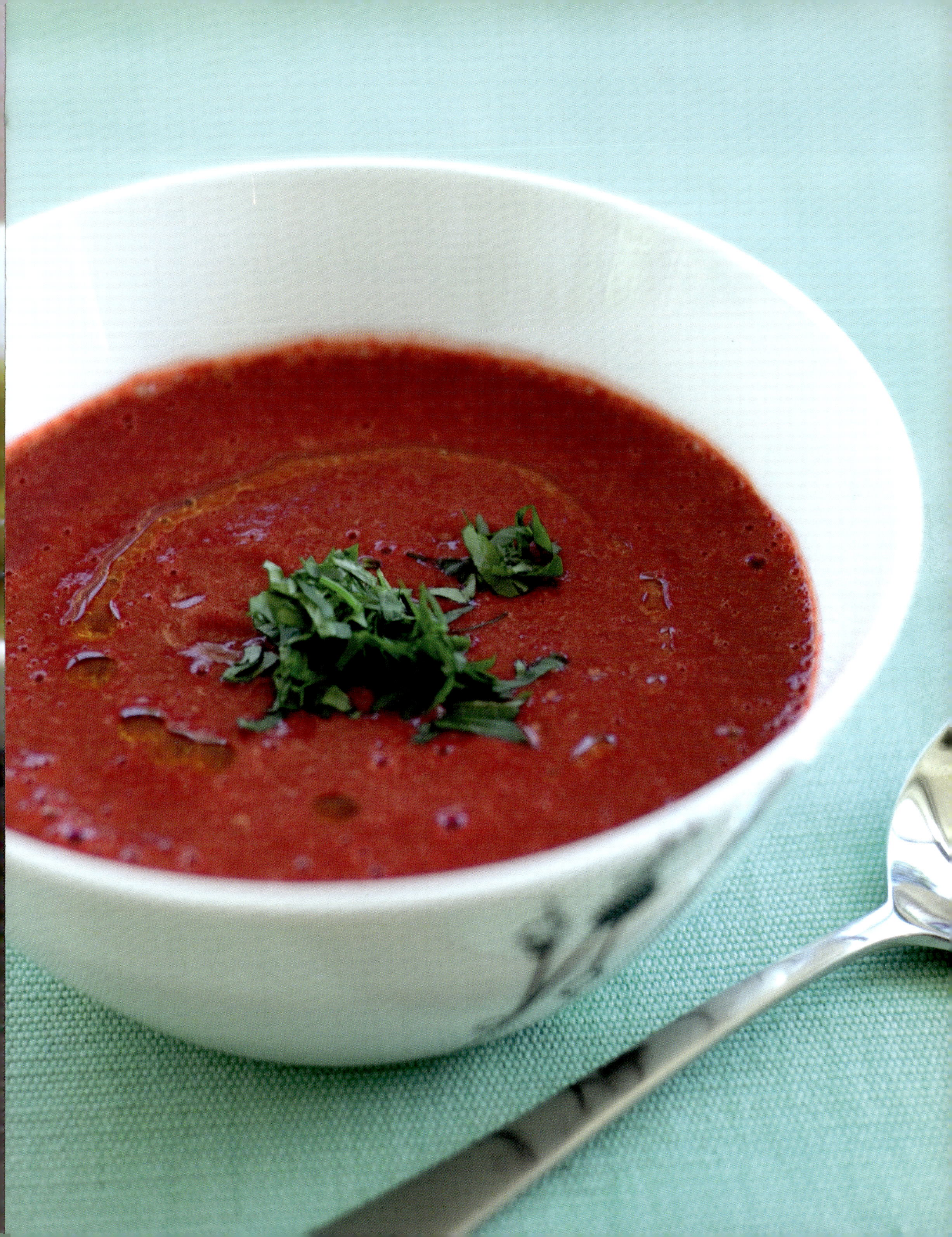

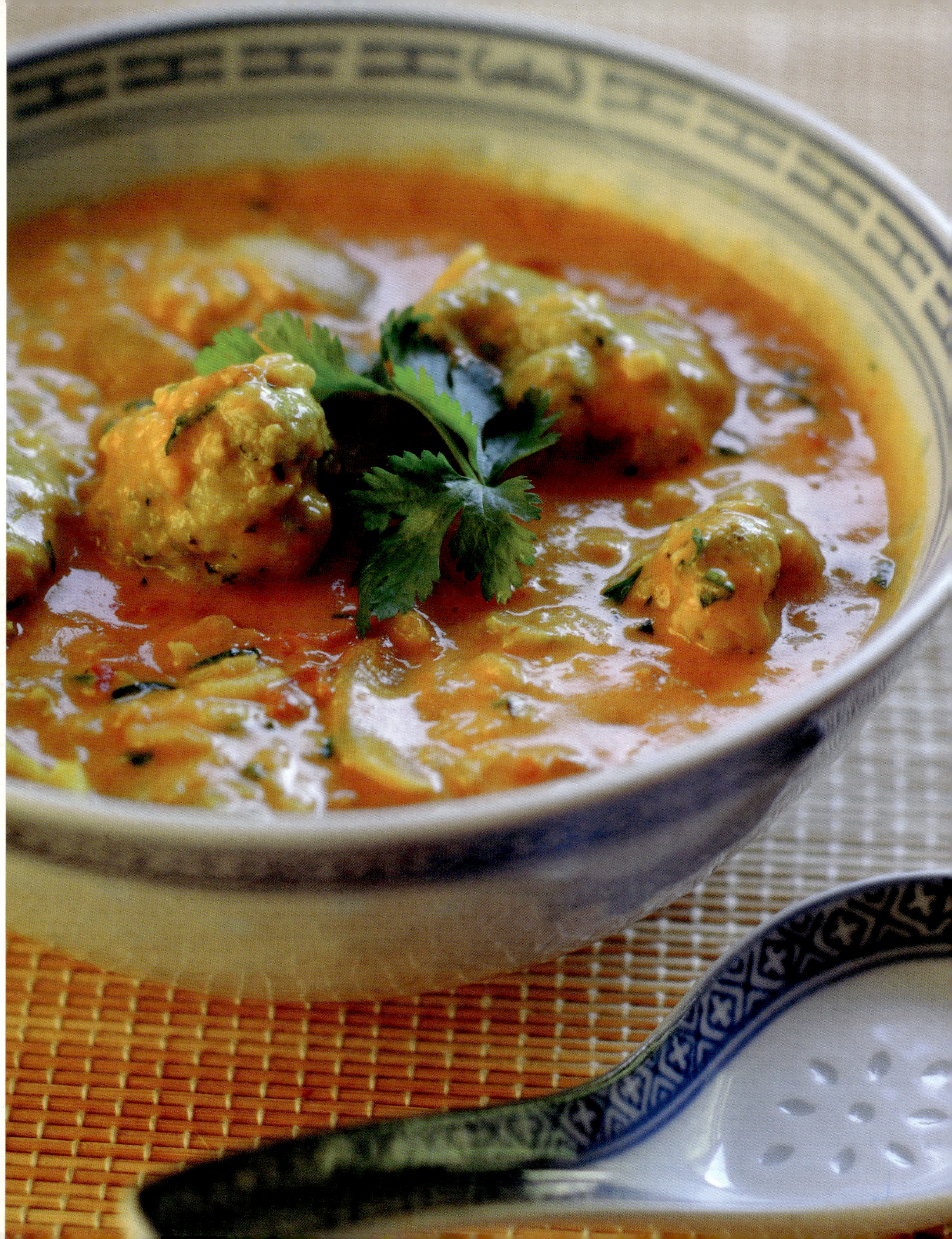

Tomato and coconut soup with fish dumplings

DF

A colourful, nourishing soup which warms the heart and belly, this is a genuine meal in a bowl! Add calamari, scallops or prawns if available.

SOUP
- 2 tablespoons sesame, coconut or olive oil
- 1 onion, sliced
- 1 tablespoon red curry paste
- ⅓ cup long-grain rice
- 400g can chopped tomatoes
- 1 teaspoon turmeric
- 2 cups water
- 400ml can coconut cream
- juice of 1 lemon
- 1 teaspoon sea salt
- chopped fresh coriander for garnish

DUMPLINGS
- 400g fresh, boneless, white-fleshed fish
- 1 egg
- 1 teaspoon fennel seeds, toasted (or 1 teaspoon ground cumin)
- small bunch coriander, chopped
- ½ teaspoon salt

Heat oil in a large heavy-based saucepan over medium heat. Sauté onion until softened slightly.

Add red curry paste and rice. Cook for several minutes. Add tomato, turmeric and water. Bring to a boil and simmer for about 15 minutes.

Meanwhile, make fish dumplings. Cut fish into small chunks and place in a food processor fitted with an S blade.

Add remaining ingredients and process for 20-30 seconds until well combined.

When rice in soup is well cooked, add coconut cream. Bring to a low boil. Using a dessertspoon, scoop some of the fish mixture, squeeze it gently in the hand to form a dumpling and add to soup. They can be any shape but a consistent size is best. Continue making dumplings, adding to soup as you go, until all the fish mixture is used up. Add lemon juice and sea salt. Simmer for about 5 minutes until dumplings are just cooked.

Serve in individual bowls, garnished with coriander.

SERVES 4-6

Vegetables & salads

One of the first meals Anna made for me featured a salad of purslane – a weed that was growing in the middle of her driveway! This lunch was my introduction to the world of edible wild plants and confirmation that I had, indeed, met a remarkable woman. – ROGER

If we had to simplify the message of this book down to just three words, this is what we would say: Eat more vegetables!

Vegetables are generally low in calories and fats, but high in fibre, vitamins and minerals. Numerous studies have shown that increased consumption of vegetables improves health and longevity, lowering the risk of major diseases such as cancer, heart disease, stroke, diabetes, arthritis and nervous-system disorders.

Eating 9-10 serves per day would put you in the top 10 per cent for vegetable and fruit consumption and you would be at lowest risk for degenerative diseases. That may seem like a lot, but it's easy to add vegetables to almost any meal. For example, serve steamed greens and mushrooms with poached eggs for breakfast, include a salad with lunch, and add plenty of diced vegetables and herbs to casseroles for dinner. Even snacks can be freshened up with crunchy sprouts, cucumber, carrot and celery.

EAT WITH THE SEASONS

Choosing to eat fruit and vegetables when they are in season will not only be good for your household budget, it will also ensure you're eating the best-quality, tastiest, freshest produce all year round. For instance, vine-ripened summer tomatoes are infinitely superior to glasshouse tomatoes in winter.

Cooking with the rhythms of the garden will make you appreciate foods with a limited growing season. You will also minimise your carbon footprint by eating only locally produced seasonal fruit and vegetables.

EAT PLENTY OF LEAFY GREENS

Of the hundreds of vegetables available, leafy greens are particularly nutrient-rich yet low in calories. The darker green leaves, such as spinach, kale and Chinese greens, are especially nutritious. Regularly eating greens helps build and maintain strong bones, cleanse the blood, strengthen the heart and boost the immune system. They are also easy to digest in combination with other food.

EAT PLENTY OF NON-STARCHY VEGETABLES

Non-starchy vegetables are dense in micronutrients and low in carbohydrates. Recent public health promotions recommend that half the food on a dinner plate should be non-starchy vegetables.

Non-starchy vegetables (listed from lowest to highest carbohydrate value) include: bean sprouts, leafy greens (spinach, silverbeet, kale, bok choy, puha, watercress and rocket), herbs (parsley, coriander, basil, etc.), celery, radishes, sea vegetables (nori, wakame, karengo), broccoli, cauliflower, cabbage (also as sauerkraut), mushrooms, avocado, cucumber, capsicums, zucchini, spring onions, asparagus, leeks, Brussels sprouts, snow peas, green beans, tomatoes, eggplant, fennel, onions and carrots. Starchy vegetables include corn, potatoes, sweet potatoes, yams, pumpkin, butternut, taro and cassava.

Eat more serves of non-starchy vegetables than starchy ones. A useful guide is to imagine your plate half-filled with non-starchy vegetables, quarter-filled with starchy vegetables or grains, and quarter-filled with a protein food.

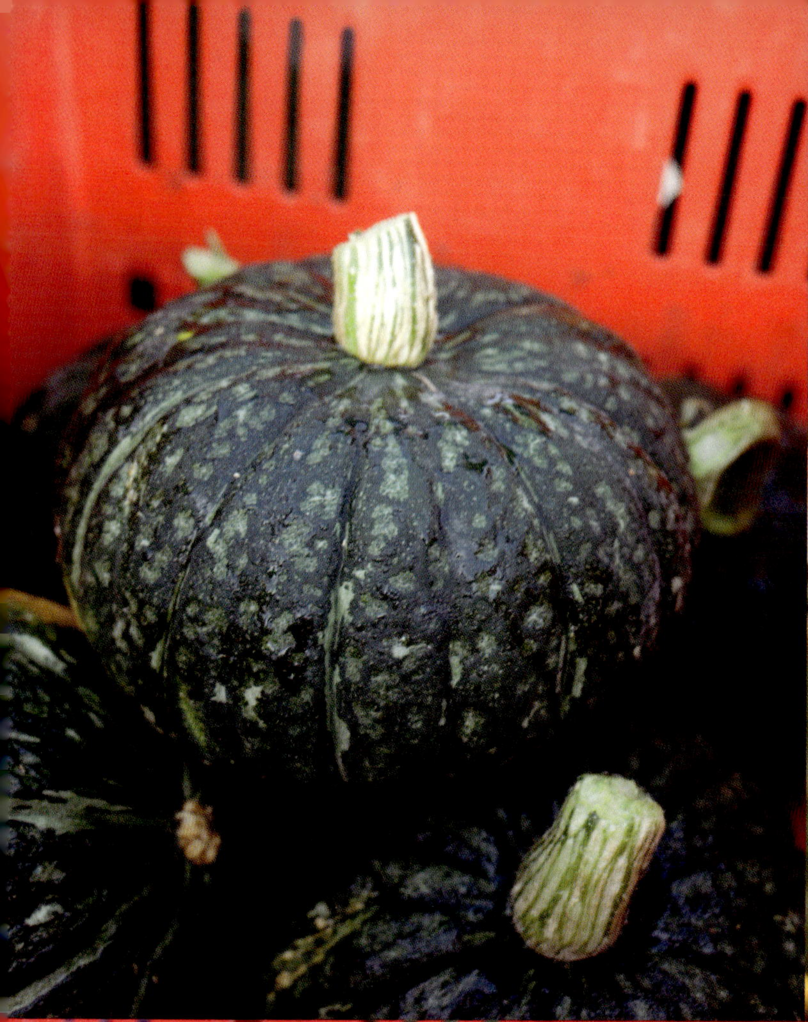
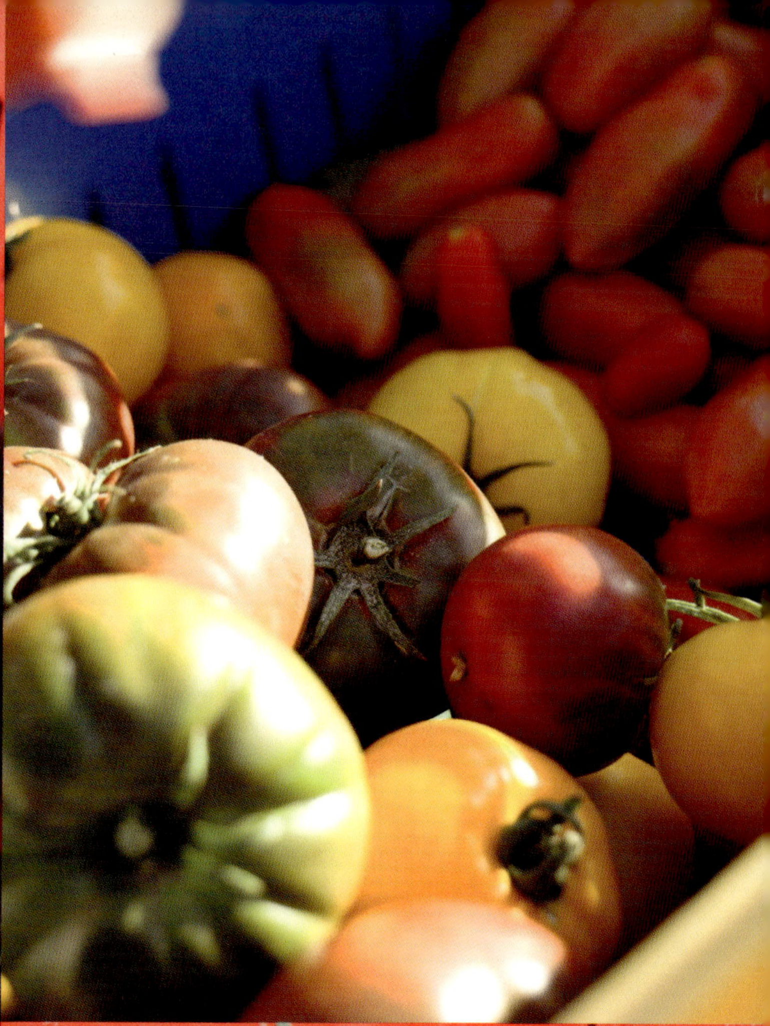
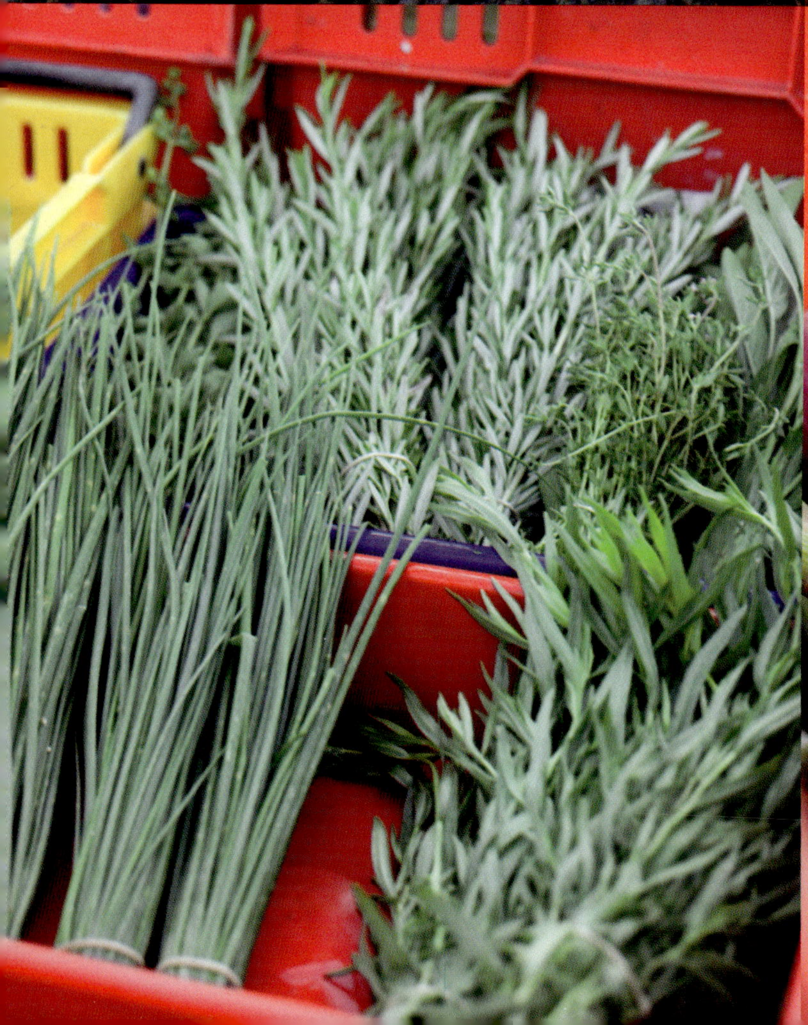
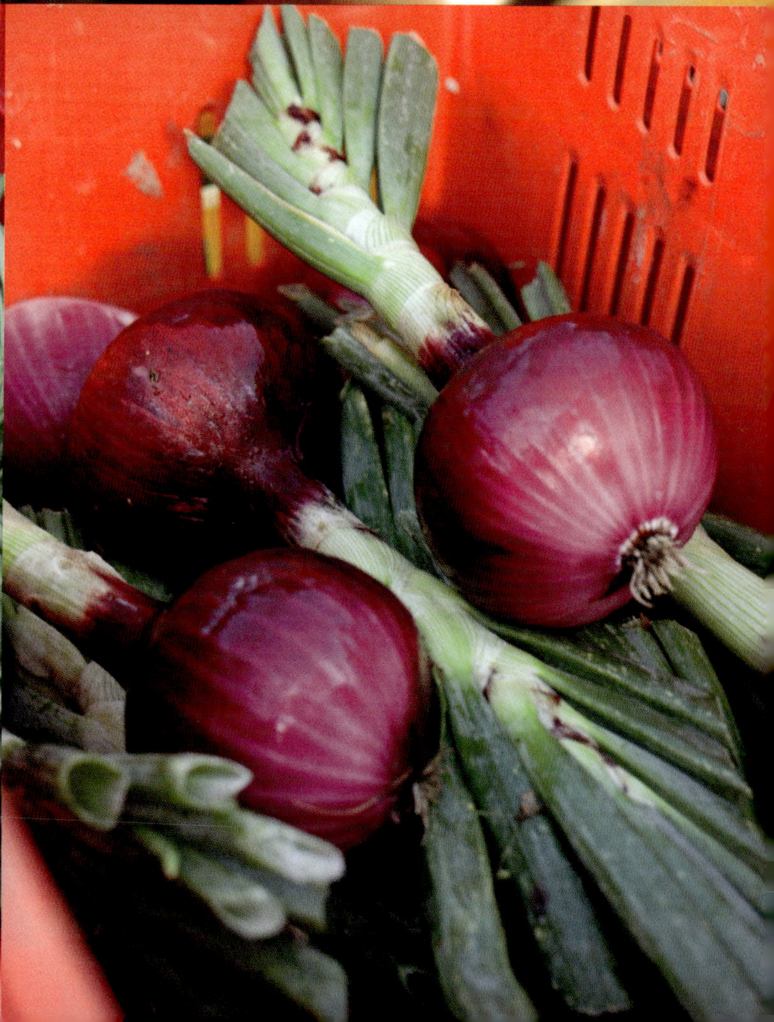

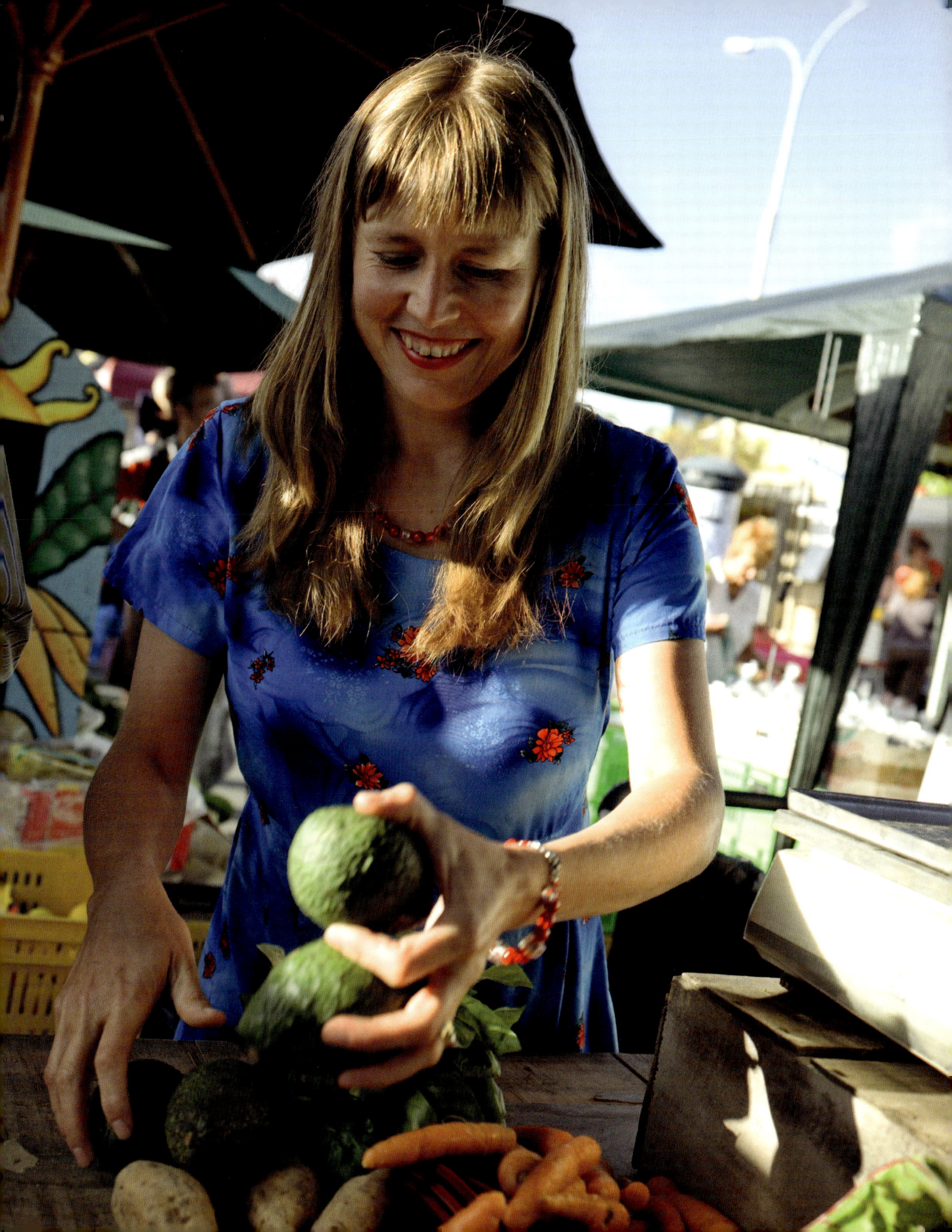

Balsamic-roasted beetroot with goat's cheese and rocket

We buy a wonderful, locally produced, organic goat's-milk cheese from our local farmers' market and simply shave it fine for this salad. A soft creamy feta would also work well with the concentrated sweetness of the roasted beetroot.

6–8 small beetroots (500g)
olive oil
pinch of sea salt
1 tablespoon balsamic vinegar
300g rocket leaves (including flowers, if available), washed and drained
100–200g goat's cheese, finely shaved or cut into small cubes
extra virgin olive oil for drizzling

Place whole, unpeeled beets in a small saucepan, cover with cold water and bring to a boil. After about 15 or 20 minutes check whether they are soft right through by piercing them with a skewer or sharp knife. When soft, drain and allow to cool for 10 minutes. Under cold running water, peel beets using your fingers. The tough outer skins should just rub off, but if this isn't working, peel them with a small knife.

Heat oven to 190°C. Slice beets into bite-sized segments. Place in a roasting dish and toss with about 1 tablespoon of olive oil and a pinch of salt. Roast for about 15 minutes, turning segments once or twice, until they start to shrink and caramelise.

Remove dish from oven and immediately sprinkle with balsamic vinegar, tossing slices to coat evenly.

When cool, arrange on 4 individual plates with the rocket leaves and goat's cheese. Drizzle with a little extra virgin olive oil before serving.

SERVES 4

Bok choy stir-fry

DF **V**

Spicy white pepper highlights the earthy/sweet flavour of bok choy. This method works with other Chinese greens too, including gui larn and choi sum or any other variety with thick but tender stems.

1 bunch bok choy (about 400g)
1 teaspoon coconut oil
½ teaspoon toasted sesame oil
small pinch of ground white pepper
2–3 teaspoons shoyu

Trim base off bok choy to separate leaves. Slice stalks and leaves into 3cm lengths. Wash thoroughly and drain in a colander.

Heat a wok or large frying pan over high heat. Add the oils. When the oils are very hot, add the bok choy. Keep heat high and stir for 2–3 minutes until greens and stems have wilted. (The water on the leaves should be sufficient to create enough steam and prevent burning, but you can add a little extra water if necessary.)

Season bok choy with pepper and shoyu, toss for another 30 seconds and transfer into a serving dish. Serve immediately.

SERVES 4 AS A SIDE DISH

Stir-frying requires fast intense heat. Moisture on the leaves creates steam which rapidly wilts the greens. For successful stir-frying, use an oil that can be safely heated, such as coconut or sesame oil, and follow these simple steps:
1. Cut everything into even, small or thin pieces.
2. Heat the wok or frying pan before adding the oil, but do not let the oil smoke.
3. Keep the heat high. Unless cooking relatively small amounts, fry each vegetable (or meat or tofu) separately.
4. Keep cooked ingredients warm in a covered bowl. Mix together at the end and heat through briefly.
5. For an extra healthy stir-fry, add water to half-steam/half-fry the vegetables.
6. Season each batch of vegetables with a little salt. This will draw out moisture and add to the steaming effect. Add shoyu towards the end of the cooking process to prevent it burning.

Balsamic-roasted beetroot with goat's cheese and rocket

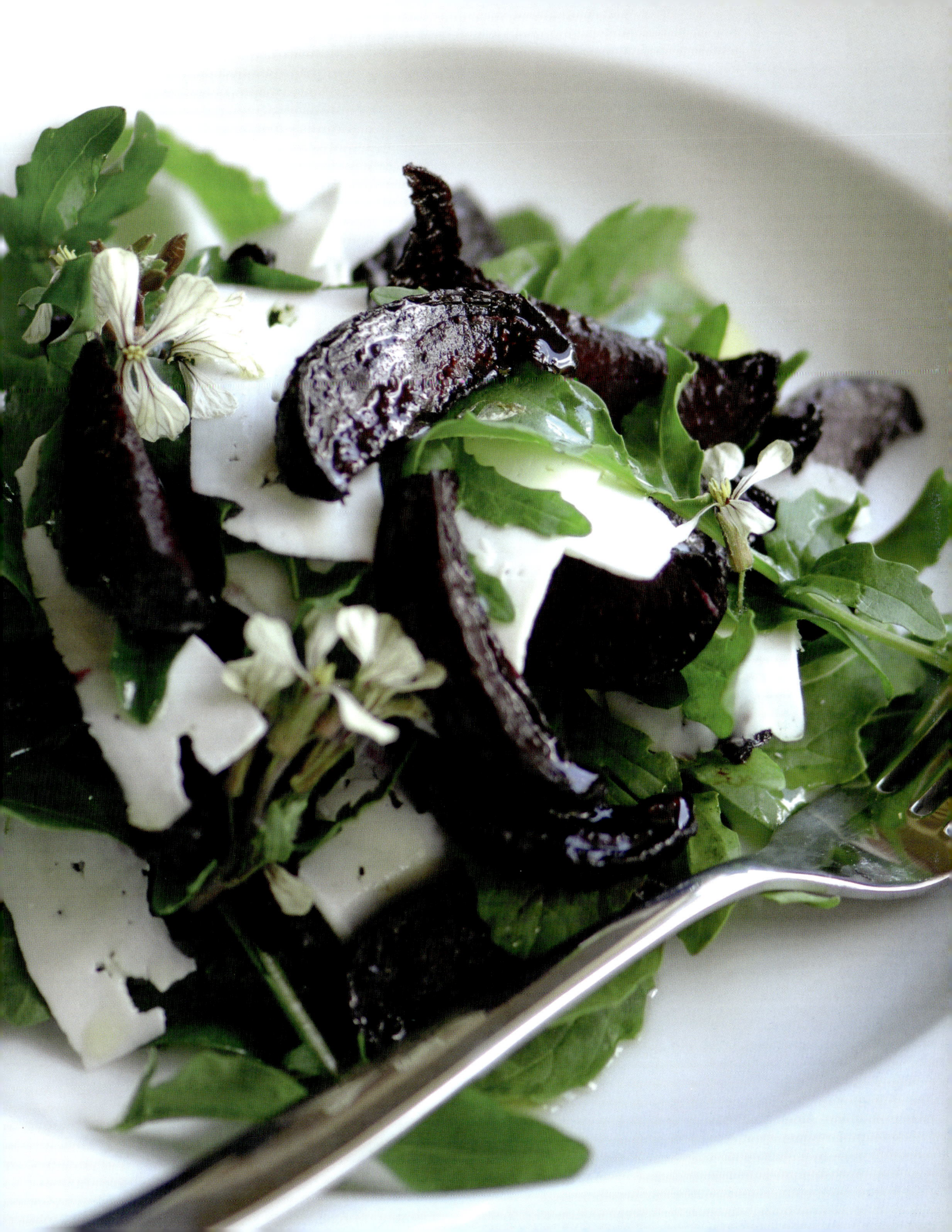

Cauliflower mash   DF V

A light and flavourful alternative to mashed potatoes, this tastes best when the cauliflower is only just cooked through – perhaps even slightly underdone.

1 medium-sized cauliflower (800g with leaves removed)
3 tablespoons olive oil
rind and juice of 1 small lemon
½ teaspoon sea salt
ground pepper

Cut cauliflower into chunks. Remove only tough parts of stem. Put about 2cm of water in a large saucepan and bring to a boil. Add cauliflower and cover. Steam over a high heat for several minutes until cauliflower is only just cooked. Test by poking a piece of the stalk with a small sharp knife. (It should be easily pierced.)

Place drained, hot cauliflower in a food processor or high-speed blender. Add olive oil, lemon rind, juice and salt and process on high speed until smooth.

Season with salt and pepper and serve immediately.

SERVES 4–6 AS A SIDE DISH

To maximise nutrient retention in your produce, buy local, refrigerate if required and eat as soon as possible. Don't wash vegetables before putting in the refrigerator, as too much moisture can damage them and cause browning. Most green vegetables keep best stored loose in the vegetable-conditioning drawer in your refrigerator. This moderates humidity and sustains the crunch in green leaves for up to 5 days. Root vegetables store well in the refrigerator for 1–2 weeks. Store mushrooms in a paper bag in the refrigerator for up to 7 days.

Oven-baked savoury wedges   DF V

Appease that craving for deep-fried chips with these tasty wedges. Enjoy them with a bowl of guacamole, or serve with a green salad and grilled fish or organic steak. Alternatively, try using different herb and spice combinations, and kumara (sweet potato) instead of potato.

1½ teaspoons organic vegetable stock powder (or ½ teaspoon sea salt)
½ teaspoon ground cumin
1 teaspoon dried rosemary
½ teaspoon curry powder
4 medium-sized (500g) roasting potatoes
2 tablespoons olive oil

Preheat a large oven tray in oven preheated to 200°C.

Mix together stock powder or salt, cumin, rosemary and curry powder.

Scrub potatoes, leaving skin on. Slice into even-sized wedges and place in a large bowl.

Pour oil onto wedges and tumble with your hands. Sprinkle herb-spice mix over wedges and stir gently until evenly coated.

Spread wedges evenly on the preheated oven tray. Bake until crispy on the outside and soft on the inside (about 15–25 minutes).

SERVES 2–4

Potato varieties suitable for roasting include Agria, Ilam Hardy, Red Rascal and Desiree. We prefer to use Agria which are firm and well-flavoured and have an appealing golden colour when cooked.

Broccoli and cauliflower salad

DF V

Blanching the broccoli and cauliflower creates a beautiful bright salad that is easy to digest.

sea salt
300g broccoli, cut into bite-sized florets
300g cauliflower, cut into florets slightly smaller than the broccoli
2 tablespoons sesame seeds
150g mung bean sprouts
1 red capsicum, deseeded and thinly sliced (optional)
segments from 1 orange, all pith removed (optional)
Orange soy dressing (see page 76)

Bring a large saucepan of water to a boil and add a couple of teaspoons of salt.

Keep heat high and add broccoli and cauliflower. After several minutes test a piece. Drain when cooked but still firm and crunchy to bite.

Immediately transfer vegetables to a large bowl. Put the bowl in the sink and cover vegetables with cold water. Leave them in the water until they feel cool.

Put a small frying pan over a low heat and toast the sesame seeds until fragrant and lightly coloured.

Combine all ingredients in a bowl and dress with plenty of orange soy dressing. Transfer to a serving dish.

SERVES 6

Sweet and sour kumara with shiitake

DF V

Shiitake mushrooms have long been used in Chinese medicine for their immunity-enhancing properties. Combined with the gorgeous sweet and sour kumara (sweet potato), this dish makes the perfect accompaniment to meat or fish.

6 dried shiitake mushrooms (25g)
2 tablespoons rice or cider vinegar
3 tablespoons shoyu
2 tablespoons arrowroot
1 teaspoon sesame oil
1 medium red onion, sliced
400g can pineapple pieces in juice
1½ cups water, or chicken or vegetable stock
500g kumara, sliced in big chunks about 0.5cm thick
honey for sweetness (optional)
spring onions, finely sliced for garnish (optional)

Soak mushrooms in water for at least 2 hours.

Drain mushrooms. Remove stems (discard) and slice caps into strips.

Mix rice vinegar, shoyu and arrowroot together in a small bowl.

Heat sesame oil in a large wide frying pan. Add mushroom and sauté for 2–3 minutes.

Add red onion and sauté for 1–2 minutes further.

Add pineapple pieces with juice. Add water or stock.

Arrange kumara slices on top. Cover the pan and boil hard for about 5–7 minutes until kumara is cooked through.

Turn heat down very low. Stir the vinegar/soy/arrowroot mixture and add to the pan. Stir everything immediately, as the sauce will quickly thicken. (Add honey for a sweeter taste if required.) Continue to cook on low heat, while gently stirring for 2 more minutes. Serve immediately garnished with the spring onions.

SERVES 6 AS A SIDE DISH

Shiitake are not only a delectable addition to Asian meals, they are also a dynamic healing food. Shiitake contain a powerful immunity-enhancing compound called lentinan that helps fight infection and also has anti-tumour properties. Soak shiitake mushrooms for at least 2 hours before adding to miso soup, noodle dishes and stir-fries.

Tempeh, corn and green bean salad DF V

Some of these ingredients may be unfamiliar to you, but it's worth trying to find them to give this recipe a try. Salads are fun to play with, so if you can't find everything on the list, feel free to experiment. Canned corn works well too.

¼ cup arame (dried seaweed)
sea salt
1 cob fresh corn
150g fresh green beans, trimmed and cut in 3cm lengths
½ block tempeh (125g)
2 teaspoons olive oil
Umeboshi dressing (see page 76)

Cover arame with about 1 cup of water. Leave to soak while preparing other ingredients.

Bring a large saucepan of water to a boil and add a couple of teaspoons of salt. Keep the heat high and add the corn. When cooked but still firm and crunchy to bite, use a slotted spoon to lift corn from water and transfer it to a large bowl. Put bowl in the sink and cover corn with cold water. Leave it in the water until it feels cool.

Repeat with beans.

Drain cooled vegetables. Cut corn cob in half.

One at a time, stand corn halves on end on a chopping board, then slice off kernels using downward cuts, close to the core. Place corn in a bowl and use fingers to break apart the kernels.

Slice tempeh in half to make two thin, flat pieces.

Heat oil in a small frying pan over a moderate heat. Fry tempeh on each side until golden brown. When cool, slice into thin strips.

Drain arame and discard soaking water.

Mix corn, beans, tempeh and arame in a bowl. Add about 5 tablespoons of dressing to taste. Mix everything well and serve.

SERVES 4

Wild greens with sesame DF V

Eating the fresh shoots of certain herbs stimulates the liver, helping to cleanse the body of toxins built up by rich winter food. This is an easy, delicious recipe that suits strong-tasting weeds such as sow thistle (puha), but also dark, leafy greens such as spinach, silverbeet or bok choy.

1 large bunch leafy greens
¼ cup freshly ground sesame seeds
1½ tablespoons shoyu

Two-thirds fill a large saucepan with water and bring to a boil.

Trim, wash and drain greens. Cut into 2–3cm lengths.

Drop greens into the boiling water and blanch briefly. (Most greens will need less than 1 minute.) Drain immediately.

When cool enough to handle, squeeze gently and transfer to a large bowl. Mix ground sesame seeds and shoyu with the greens. Check seasoning and adjust if necessary.

SERVES 4–6

Tempeh, corn and green bean salad

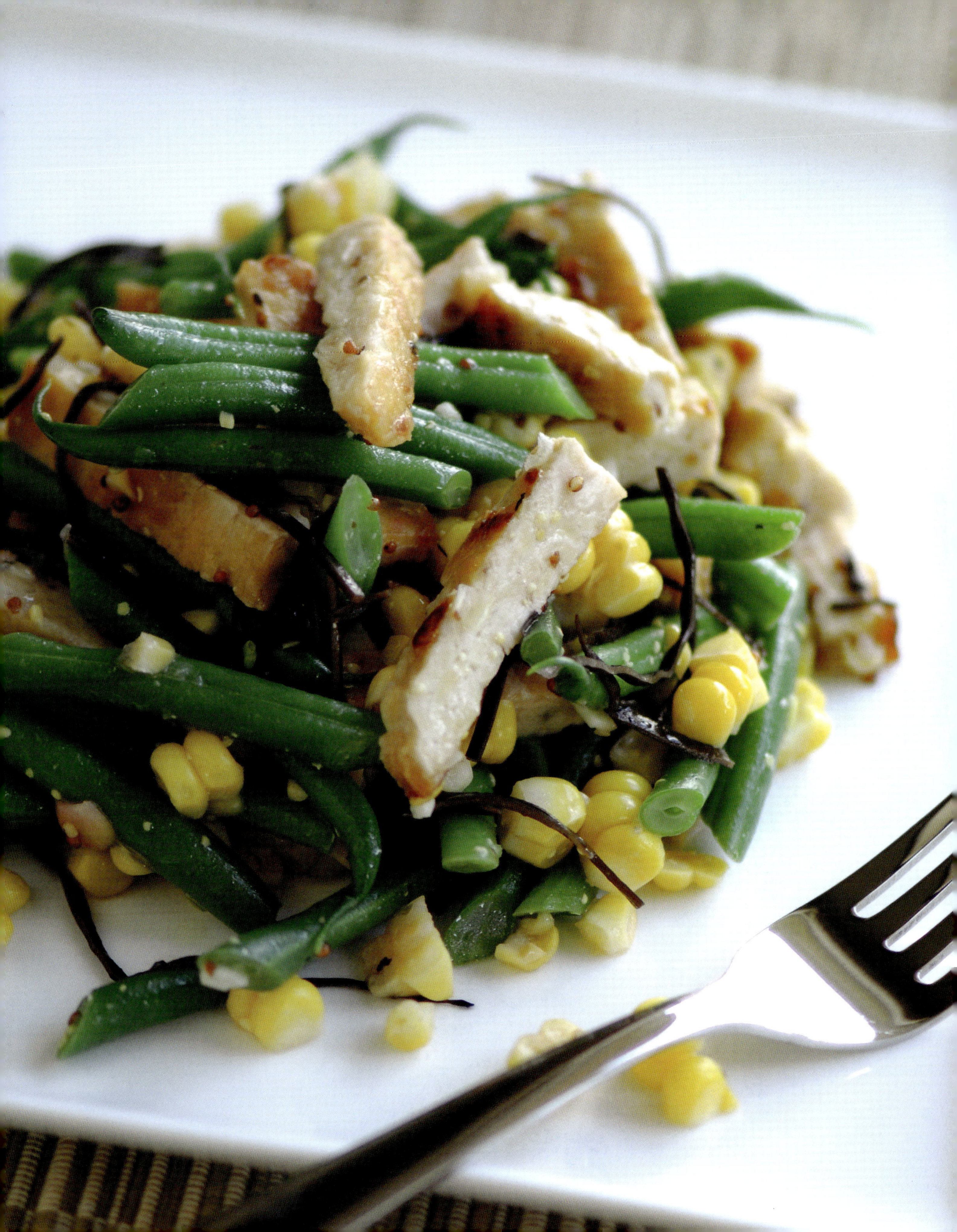

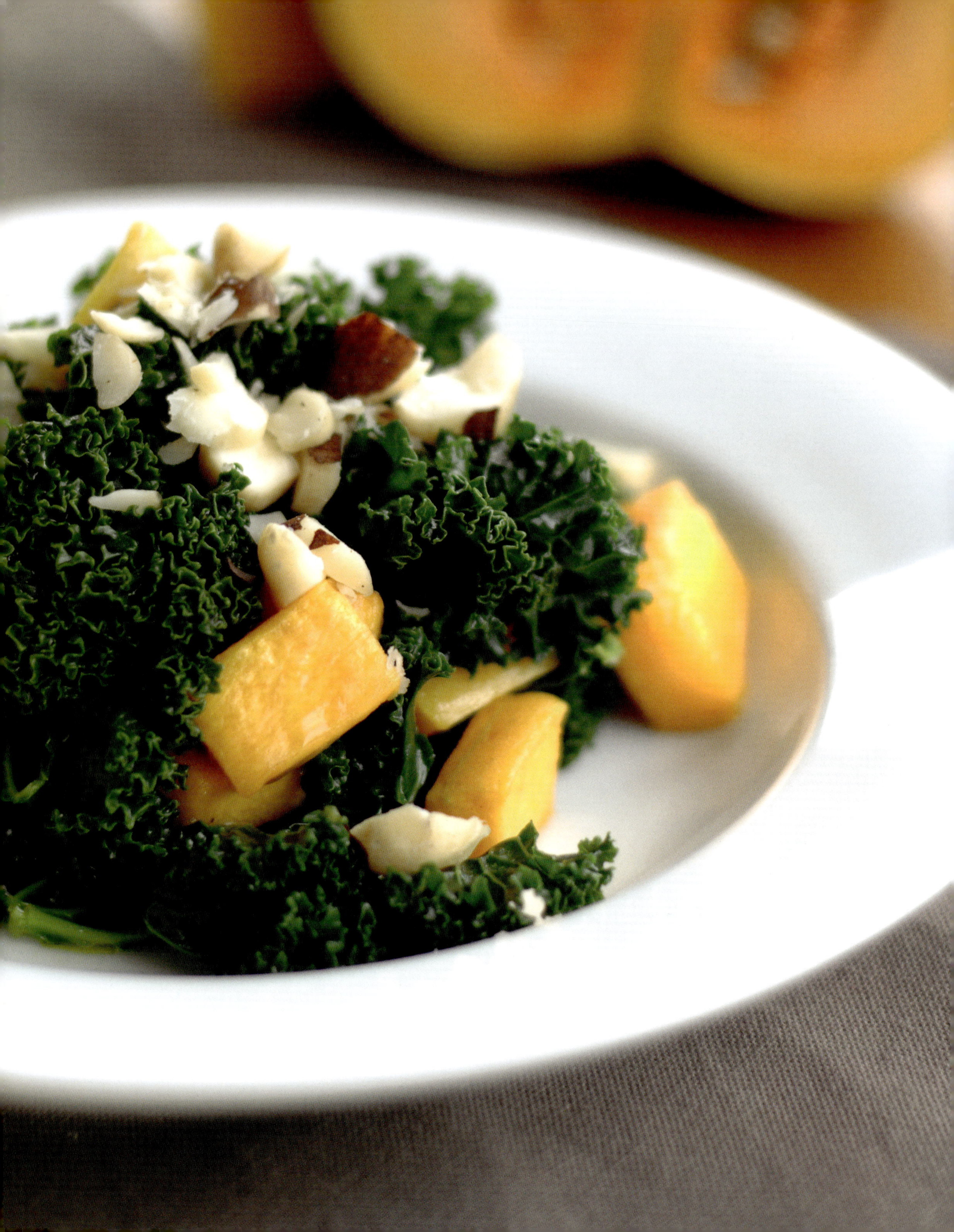

Kale and roasted pumpkin salad

DF V

Curly kale retains a good texture when cooked, holding its own in dishes where other greens would wilt into insignificance. Steamed kale has a wonderful earthy-green flavour that combines well with sweet pumpkin.

500g pumpkin, chopped into bite-sized chunks
2 tablespoons olive oil
½ teaspoon sea salt
several large kale leaves (250g)
2 tablespoons shoyu
8 Brazil nuts, chopped

Heat oven to 175°C.

Place pumpkin in a roasting dish with the olive oil and salt. Mix well. Roast for 20 minutes or until just cooked.

Wash and drain kale leaves. Strip leaves by hand, discarding hard stems. Chop leaves into large pieces.

Place kale in a saucepan with about 0.5cm water in the bottom, then cover. Steam over a high heat until softened. Remove from heat and drain off excess water.

Tip steamed kale onto roast pumpkin in roasting dish. Add shoyu and mix well.

Transfer vegetables into a serving dish and garnish with chopped nuts.

SERVES 6

The beautiful curly leaves of kale provide more nutritional value for fewer calories than almost any food. Like broccoli, kale also belongs to the Brassica family, a group of vegetables that has gained recent widespread attention due to their health-promoting and cancer-preventing phytochemicals. Kale is an excellent source of calcium and vitamin C. Just 1 cup supplies almost 90 per cent of the recommended daily intake for vitamin C. Try kale steamed and mashed into potato Dutch style, with gravy and sausages, or use in soups, stews and stir-fries.

Spinach salad with walnut pesto dressing

DF V

3 packed cups spinach leaves, washed and drained
½ cup walnuts, pine nuts or cashew pieces
1 cup basil leaves
4 tablespoons olive oil
1 tablespoon lemon juice
1-2 cloves garlic, roughly chopped
½ teaspoon sea salt
freshly ground black pepper

Chop the spinach leaves and stems into bite-sized pieces and place in a large bowl.

Place all remaining ingredients in a food processor. Pulse for 20-30 seconds until well combined but keeping some of the nuts fairly chunky.

Add to the spinach and mix by hand, ensuring all the leaves are well-coated.

Serve immediately.

SERVES 4

Kale and roasted pumpkin salad

Zucchini and olive pasta sauce DF V

Zucchini grow like crazy over summer – sometimes they just can't be picked fast enough! When plump and cheap, use them as the base for this super-quick pasta sauce. To serve, simply pour the blended sauce onto cooked gluten-free pasta and add the sliced olives. Top with feta or parmesan cheese if desired.

400g zucchini, chopped into rough chunks
¼ red onion, chopped
1 tablespoon tomato paste
¼ cup olive oil
1 tablespoon organic powdered vegetable stock
1 tablespoon lemon juice
freshly ground black pepper
⅓ cup pitted kalamata olives, sliced

Place all ingredients except the sliced olives in food processor. Blend at high speed for 1-2 minutes until smooth.

Store in the refrigerator until required. Add olives just before serving.

SERVES 4

Roast Jerusalem artichokes DF V

Jerusalem artichokes are easy to grow and delicious as part of a winter meal. They can be eaten raw in a salad, boiled in water or roasted. Coconut oil and butter combine to give a wonderful nutty coat to this earthy vegetable.

1 kg Jerusalem artichokes
1 tablespoon butter or olive oil
1 tablespoon cold-pressed coconut oil
½ teaspoon sea salt
freshly ground black pepper

Heat oven to 180°C.

Carefully scrub artichokes, pulling bulbs apart to remove dirt.

With a small knife, remove any tough, dry or discoloured parts and discard. Chop remainder into bite-sized chunks. Place in a roasting tray and add the butter, coconut oil, salt and pepper.

Place dish in oven. After 10 minutes, give artichokes a good stir to coat with melted oils and seasoning.

Bake for a further 20 minutes or so until artichokes are soft inside.

SERVES 4

Fresh vegetables and fruit straight from the garden or farmers' market are best, but for variety and convenience we occasionally buy frozen berries and vegetables. Although there is loss of nutrients in the freezing process, fresh produce in the supermarket has also suffered degradation during transport and in storage. At least frozen foods have been picked and packed at peak quality. Frozen vegetables require minimal cooking because they have been blanched briefly before packing.

Cabbage and bacon stir-fry

DF

Steaming or stir-frying brings out the best in cabbage. The trick is to cook it hot and quick, adding the minimum amount of liquid, so it remains slightly crunchy.

100g free-range shoulder or middle bacon, cut into small slices
1 teaspoon fennel seeds
1 medium-sized onion, cut into long strips
300g cabbage, cut into bite-sized pieces
¼ cup white wine
½ teaspoon sea salt

Place a large, deep frying pan over a low-medium heat and sauté bacon and fennel seeds for 1-2 minutes until the bacon releases a little fat.

Add onion and sauté for several minutes further until softened.

Add cabbage, white wine and salt and give everything a good stir. Cover pan with a lid and turn up heat to medium-high. After 3 or 4 minutes stir again and check liquid. Add a little water if necessary. Continue to cook until cabbage is softened, but still slightly crunchy.

Serve immediately.

SERVES 4

Mango and avocado salsa

DF V

The tropical combination of mango and avocado is a party on a plate, brightening even the dreariest mood. This salsa can be served atop pan-fried fish or grilled chicken, or rolled up with feta and salad leaves for a lunchtime wrap.

1 avocado
1 mango
small handful of fresh mint, finely sliced
½ small red onion, finely sliced
2 tablespoons olive oil
juice of 1 lemon
½ teaspoon sea salt
freshly ground black pepper

Remove flesh from avocado and mango. Cut into small cubes and put in a bowl.

Add mint, red onion, olive oil, lemon juice, salt and pepper and mix gently to combine.

SERVES 4

Pear and walnut salad

DF V

Freshly shelled walnuts give a big lift to this salad. The pears need to be ripe but firm. Locally grown, shelled walnuts are now available in many supermarkets. For a well-balanced lunch, add a large slice of grilled haloumi cheese.

½ frilly green lettuce or 3–4 cups salad leaf mix
small bunch red radishes, trimmed and sliced into wedges
1–2 spring onions, finely sliced
2–3 pears, quartered, cored and sliced
½ cup (75g) walnuts, chopped into large pieces
Toasted sesame dressing (see page 76)

Wash lettuce leaves in plenty of water. Dry in a salad spinner or drain well. Tear into bite-sized pieces.

Place lettuce leaves, radish, spring onion, pear and walnut pieces in a large bowl.

To serve, add several tablespoons of dressing and gently toss to coat.

SERVES 4

Bulk-bin walnut pieces are generally slightly rancid and may have a bitter flavour. This can be improved by soaking them. Place the walnut pieces in a bowl, cover with cold water and add juice of half a lemon. After a couple of hours, drain and rinse before adding to the salad.

Asparagus and mushroom salad

DF V

Marinating the mushrooms in the dressing gives them a luscious silky texture, providing a lovely contrast to the crunchy raw asparagus and radishes. When asparagus is not in season try using blanched green beans or raw courgettes.

DRESSING
1 tablespoon lemon juice
1 tablespoon cider vinegar
2 teaspoons wholegrain mustard
¼ cup olive oil
½ teaspoon sea salt
ground black pepper

SALAD
1 bunch watercress
250g asparagus, trimmed
2–3 red radishes, trimmed
150g white button mushrooms, thinly sliced
roasted seeds (optional)
shaved sheep's feta (optional)

Combine dressing ingredients in a small bowl and whisk together. Place mushrooms in a bowl, pour on dressing and mix well. Leave to marinate overnight, or, if pushed for time, for as long as it takes you to prepare the rest of the salad.

Pick through watercress, removing any tough stems. Wash and drain in a salad spinner. Arrange picked watercress in a flat serving bowl. Slice asparagus on the diagonal, long and thin. Slice in half lengthwise, then in thin pieces.

Add sliced asparagus and radishes to the mushrooms. Toss to combine. Spread salad on top of watercress. Garnish with roasted seeds or shaved feta, if using.

SERVES 4

It's easy to consume plenty of salad greens in summer, but in winter, when we are more inclined to eat heavier, richer, cooked foods, it is especially important to remember to eat a proportion of raw and lightly cooked greens. There are many green vegetables available through the winter months, such as kale, broccoli and Chinese greens.

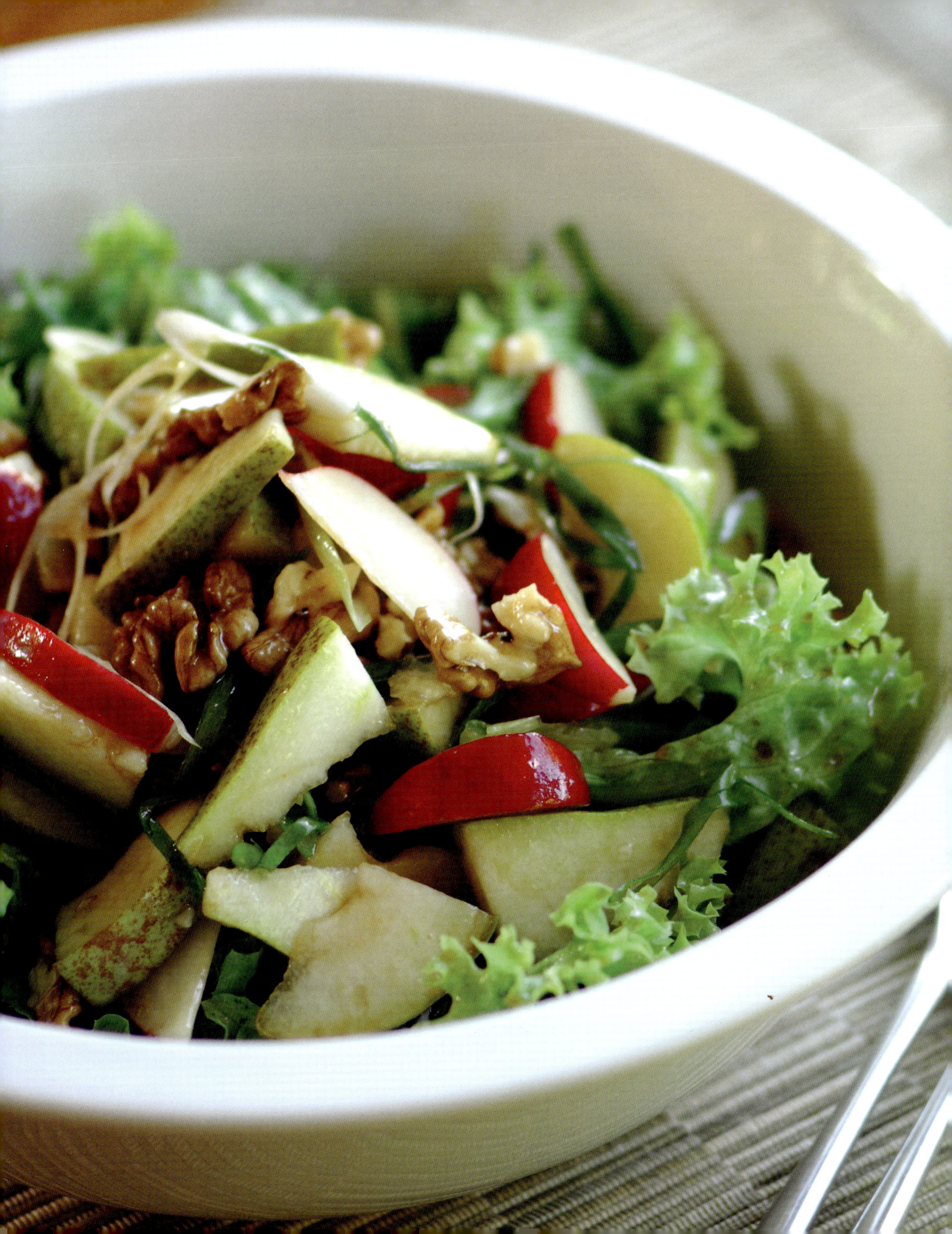

Cauliflower salad with anchovy dressing

Anchovy fans will love this salad. Cauliflower is a good match for the rich dressing, which is loaded with healthy fats. It's great for lunchboxes and keeps well in the refrigerator for up to 3 days. If anchovies are not popular, use sun-dried tomatoes instead.

1 medium-sized cauliflower, cut into bite-sized florets
⅓ cup olives
100g goat's feta, cut into small cubes
3 tablespoons capers
4 handfuls of leafy greens (spinach or mesclun mix)

DRESSING
¼ cup olive oil
½ cup thick, natural yoghurt (Greek-style is best)
4 anchovies or sun-dried tomatoes
1–2 cloves garlic, sliced
2 tablespoons white balsamic vinegar
1 organic free-range egg

Put a large saucepan of salted water over a high heat and bring to a boil. Add cauliflower and cook briefly until just cooked but still a bit crunchy. Pour into a colander, cool under cold running water and leave to drain.

Put dressing ingredients in a small blender and process until smooth.

In a large bowl, combine cauliflower, olives, feta and capers. Pour dressing on top and mix well. Leave to marinate for at least 20 minutes, if time allows.

When ready to serve, add leafy greens and toss gently.

SERVES 4–6

Wakame cucumber salad with ponzu

DF V

Ponzu sauce is a simple, oil-free dressing that also makes a zesty dipping sauce for grilled fish and other seafood.

⅓ cup wakame
⅓ telegraph cucumber, cut into quarters lengthwise, deseeded and finely sliced
½ teaspoon sea salt

PONZU SAUCE
1 tablespoon lemon juice
1 tablespoon shoyu
2 tablespoons rice wine or cider vinegar

Soak wakame for 20 minutes in cold water.

Drain wakame, and if not already cut fine, remove any hard stems and chop leaves into small pieces.

Place cucumber in a bowl and rub in the salt. Leave for 15 minutes and squeeze out excess moisture.

Combine drained wakame and cucumber in a bowl.

Put sauce ingredients in another bowl and stir to combine.

SERVES 4 AS A SMALL SIDE DISH

Wakame is an edible seaweed that can be purchased in several forms. The easiest to use is fueru wakame, which has no hard stems and is already cut into little pieces. Most large supermarkets and Asian stores now stock this product.

Rice noodle and watercress salad

DF V

This easy and substantial side dish pairs well with a simple piece of grilled fish. Rice noodles come in a range of thicknesses; we prefer to make this salad using a medium-sized noodle, similar to linguine. The noodles and dressing can be prepared and combined well in advance of eating, leaving just the greens to add at the last minute.

250g packet rice noodles
½ cup *Toasted sesame dressing* (see page 76)
1 large orange, peel removed and sliced
1 large bunch watercress or rocket leaves

Boil noodles according to instructions on packet. Check regularly by pulling out a strand. When only just cooked, drain and rinse under cold running water.

Transfer noodles to a large bowl. If the noodles are very long, chop them in the bowl using a pair of cooking scissors or a sharp knife. Add orange pieces and Toasted sesame dressing, and then use your hands to combine. Cover and leave in refrigerator until ready to serve.

Pick through watercress, removing any tough stems. Chop into 6-7cm lengths. Wash in plenty of water and drain well.

Just before serving, add watercress to bowl and toss gently to combine. Transfer to serving dish.

SERVES 4

Red radish pickles

DF V

These brightly coloured pickles keep for weeks in the refrigerator. They come in handy as a cheerful garnish for a salad or snack.

100ml red wine vinegar
1½ teaspoons sea salt
100ml water
1 bunch red radishes

Put vinegar, salt and water in a 375g jar. Cover and shake well to dissolve the salt.

Wash radishes and trim off tops and tails. Halve each radish, then slice as thinly as possible.

Pack radish slices into the jar. There needs to be just enough liquid to cover radishes when they are packed down. Add more vinegar if required.

Cover and refrigerate. Leave for at least 1 week before eating.

MAKES 1 JAR

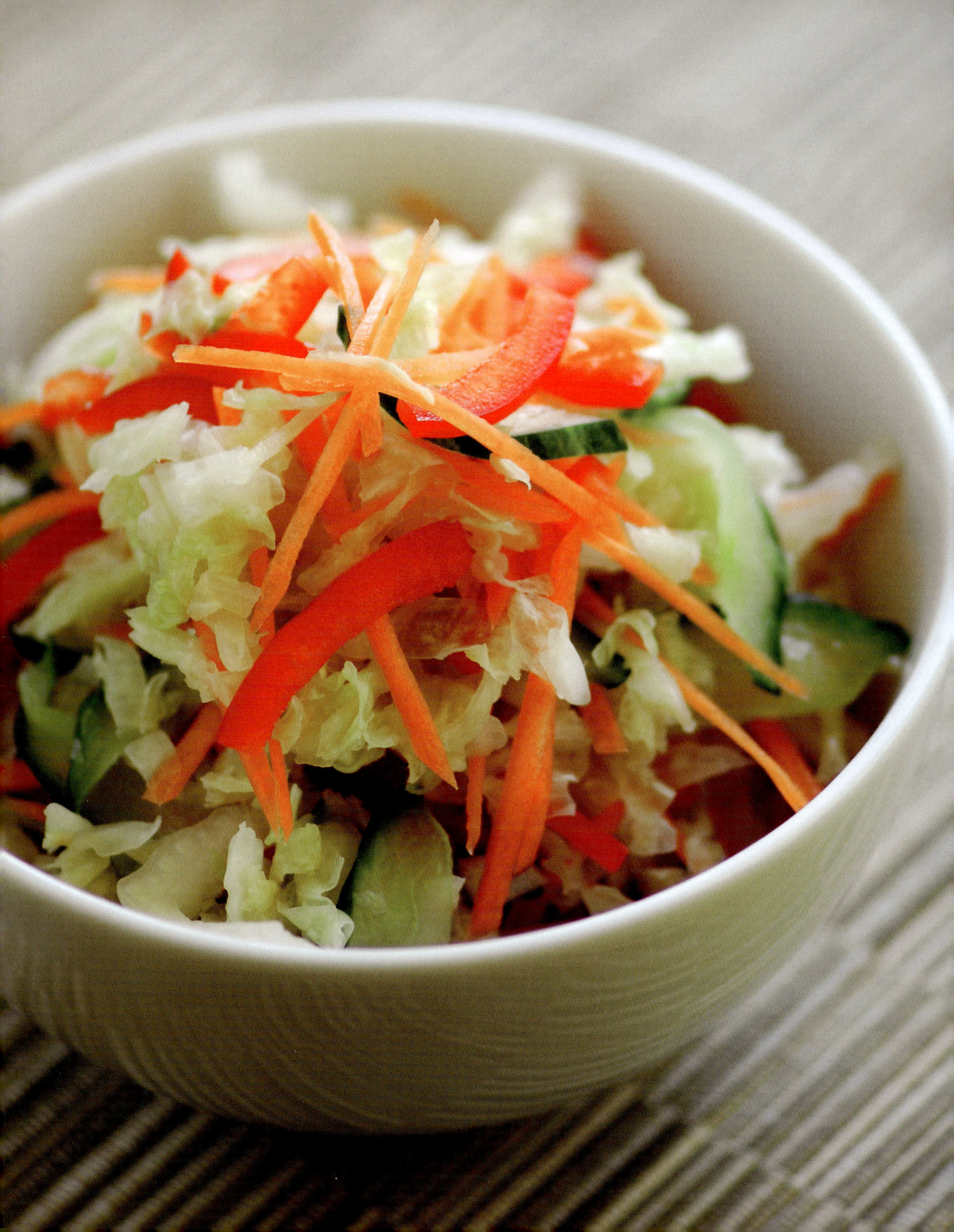

Simple pressed salad

DF V

Salting and pressing makes vegetables more digestible, breaking down the cell structure without losing valuable food enzymes (as would happen if we cooked it). This method can be used for a large variety of vegetables, but works particularly well with cabbages.

500g red or green cabbage (or a mixture), finely sliced
2 teaspoons sea salt
300g pumpkin or carrot, peeled and grated
6 red radishes, finely sliced
1 bunch rocket (or other salad greens)
olive oil (optional, to dress)
vinegar (optional, to dress)

Place cabbage in a large bowl and rub in 1 teaspoon of salt. The cabbage will become glossy and moist as the salt begins to draw out moisture. Transfer to a smaller bowl, pack the cabbage down and place a plate and a heavy weight on top.

Place pumpkin and radishes in another bowl and rub in remaining salt. Place a plate and a heavy weight on top.

Leave everything to pickle for 2–3 hours.

When ready to eat, drain off any excess liquid and either mix the vegetables and rocket together or arrange side by side in a bowl.

Serve as is or lightly dressed with a little olive oil and vinegar.

SERVES 6 WITH LEFTOVERS FOR THE REST OF THE WEEK

Korean kimchi salad

DF V

Here's another light, clean-tasting salad that keeps well for several days. Salting the vegetables helps with digestion and also retards spoiling when not refrigerated. This is a perfect salad for a picnic!

1 small Chinese cabbage (500g), finely sliced
½ cucumber, cut into quarters lengthwise, deseeded and finely sliced
1½ teaspoon sea salt
2 garlic cloves, finely chopped
2cm piece of fresh ginger, finely sliced, minced or grated
1 fresh red chilli, seeds removed, finely chopped
1 red capsicum, deseeded and sliced
1 carrot, finely sliced or grated
2 tablespoon cider vinegar

Place cabbage and cucumber in a large bowl and rub with sea salt. The vegetables will start to go glossy as the salt draws out moisture. Leave for 15 minutes while preparing remaining ingredients.

Place garlic, ginger, chilli, capsicum, carrot and cider vinegar in a separate bowl.

Drain cabbage and cucumber in a colander or sieve. Take handfuls of cabbage and cucumber, lightly squeeze to remove excess moisture and add to the other ingredients. Mix to combine.

SERVES 6 WITH LEFTOVERS FOR THE REST OF THE WEEK

Salt is vital for life, balancing electrolytes in blood and body tissue. We recommend using sea salt harvested from evaporated sea water. Sea salt contains a range of valuable minerals but lacks iodine, so be sure to eat plenty of seafood and sea vegetables for your necessary iodine intake. Unprocessed sea salt brings a more subtle, complex flavour to food.

The cheapest, most common cooking salts are refined – stripped of nutrients – and contain anti-caking agents. Most people consume too much refined salt from processed products, fast food and over-seasoning. This is a well recognised contributing factor to heart disease.

Korean kimchi salad

Fresh mustard

DF V

Use this as a substitute for wholegrain mustard in dressings and sauces. It will keep in the refrigerator for at least 2 months.

½ cup yellow mustard seeds
½ cup water
¼ cup apple cider vinegar
½ teaspoon sea salt
½ small apple, grated
1 tablespoon raw honey

☀ Soak mustard seeds in the water overnight. The seeds will absorb all the water.

Drain soaked mustard seeds. Place in a blender along with other ingredients. Blend until well combined.

MAKES 1 JAR

Toasted sesame dressing

DF V

¼ cup mild olive oil
2 teaspoons toasted sesame oil
2 teaspoons cider vinegar
2 teaspoons shoyu

Put all ingredients in a small jar and shake well to combine before use.

MAKES ⅓ CUP

Umeboshi dressing

DF V

½ cup olive oil
2 tablespoons umeboshi or red wine vinegar
1 tablespoon wholegrain mustard
1 clove garlic, chopped fine
black pepper

Put all ingredients in a small jar and shake well to combine before use.

MAKES ⅔ CUP

Orange soy dressing

DF V

juice of 2 oranges
½ cup olive oil
½ teaspoon mustard powder
2 cloves garlic, chopped
2 teaspoons honey
1½ tablespoons shoyu
1½ tablespoons cider vinegar

Put all ingredients in a small jar and shake well to combine before use.

MAKES ABOUT 1 CUP

Some oils are better than others. Here is the good oil from us:
- For salad dressings, dips and spreads, use cold-pressed olive, flaxseed, walnut or avocado oil.
- For moderate-temperature cooking, such as baking and sautéeing, use olive oil, butter or coconut oil.
- For high-temperature cooking, such as pan-frying, stir-frying and roasting, use sesame or coconut oil, or clarified butter.
- Please note that very high heat, for example when grilling and frying, may damage even the most stable cooking fats creating dangerous free-radicals.

Lemon tahini dressing

DF V

2 tablespoons lemon juice
1 tablespoon tahini
1 tablespoon honey
1 tablespoon Dijon mustard
½ cup olive oil
sea salt and freshly ground black pepper

Blend or whisk all ingredients together to form a thick, smooth consistency. Check seasoning and adjust, if required.

MAKES ABOUT ¾ CUP

Green goddess creamy dressing

DF V

½ avocado
½ orange with rind removed
¼ cup olive oil
1 tablespoon cider vinegar
½ cup chopped green herbs
1 teaspoon curry powder
sea salt and ground black pepper
water if necessary

Put avocado flesh and all other ingredients in a blender. Blend together until smooth. Adjust consistency with water.

MAKES 1½ CUPS

Apple ginger dressing

DF V

1 apple, cored and chopped
3 tablespoons olive oil
juice of 1 small lemon
1 teaspoon ginger powder
2 teaspoons cider vinegar
1 teaspoon wholegrain mustard
3 tablespoons water
½ teaspoon sea salt
ground black pepper (to taste)

Put all ingredients in a blender. Blend together until smooth.

MAKES 1 CUP

Polyunsaturated oils like nut and seed oils are fragile and degrade easily when exposed to heat and light. We recommend avoiding cheap oils from the supermarket, such as canola, safflower, soya, sunflower and corn oil. They are highly processed and will cause oxidative damage to cells, speeding up the ageing process and contributing to disease.

Pulses & grains

Our enthusiasm for raw foods once led to a nasty run-in with kidney beans. We sprouted them and ate a whole lot, resulting in explosive gas and stomach cramps. We learnt the hard way that smaller pulses and seeds are best for sprouting while the big ones, such as chickpeas and kidney beans, are best cooked. – ANNA

Pulses are the edible seeds of the legume family, including peas, beans and lentils. Regular consumption of pulses significantly increases life expectancy and positively benefits the digestive system and heart, while helping stabilise blood-sugar levels.

Grains come from the grass family. Gluten-free whole grains provide plenty of starchy carbohydrates, minerals and vitamins for regular energy production.

Beans and whole grains are relatively inexpensive, easy to store and can be used in a variety of ways to form an important and tasty part of a healthy, balanced diet.

HERE ARE OUR TOP TIPS TO HELP YOU GET THE MOST FROM GRAINS:

- Eat whole grains. Processed grains like white rice and white rice flour have been stripped of the bran – the valuable outer layer.
- Soak whole grains for several hours or overnight before cooking. They will be quicker to cook and you'll end up with a creamier texture.
- Buy organically grown grains that are free from added chemicals.
- If you can tolerate small amounts of gluten you may wish to use ancient wheat varieties, such as spelt and kamut. Modern hybridised strains of wheat are more likely to cause digestive problems; this is one reason why many people feel better going gluten-free.
- Reduce consumption of all flour products, even gluten-free flours and pasta. Enjoy cakes and pastries as occasional treats.

HOW TO COOK DRIED BEANS

1. Look for beans that appear plump and fairly uniform in size and colour. Remove any discoloured, broken, cracked or shrivelled beans as they won't cook properly.
2. Place beans in a large bowl, cover with water and soak overnight. (Only lentils and split peas can be cooked without prior soaking.)
3. Drain and rinse the soaked beans.
4. Place in a saucepan and cover with plenty of water – approximately 1 cup beans to 3 cups water. Do not add salt to the cooking water – this stops the beans from softening.
5. Bring to a rolling boil with the lid off and continue to boil rapidly.
6. Check occasionally and add more water if required – the beans need to be covered throughout the cooking process.
7. Continue to cook until the beans are soft.

HOW TO COOK WHOLE GRAINS

1. Rinse the grains briefly in a fine-mesh sieve under running cold water.
2. Transfer grains to a small saucepan. Add water (1 cup grains to 2 cups water) and sea salt.
3. Bring to a boil over medium heat and turn heat down very low.
4. Cover with a lid and simmer until all the water has been absorbed. Check all the water is gone by using a spoon to pull the grains aside at the bottom of the pot.
5. If time allows, fluff with a fork, cover and leave to stand for 10 minutes before serving.

COOKING TIMES

Brown rice	45 minutes	Green lentils	30-45 minutes
Buckwheat	20 minutes	Red lentils	20-30 minutes
Millet	20-25 minutes	Puy lentils	20-30 minutes
Quinoa	20 minutes	Amaranth	25-30 minutes
Adzuki beans	1 hour	Mung beans	1-1½ hours
Black beans	1-1½ hours	Pinto beans	1-1½ hours
Fava beans	45-60 minutes	Soya beans	3 hours
Kidney beans	1-1½ hours	Split peas	30-45 minutes
Lima beans	1-1½ hours	Chickpeas	1½-2½ hours

BEING GLUTEN FREE

Many people find they feel better after simply reducing their consumption of wheat products. Some may have a wheat intolerance because they lack the enzymes needed to digest wheat proteins such as gluten efficiently. We personally recommend that everyone tries a two-week abstinence from wheat or gluten products. There is a range of mild to severe health symptoms that can evaporate with this one simple dietary change.

Please note: people with coeliac disease are allergic to gluten and should cut it out of their diet forever.

Mexican chilli beans

DF V

These beans make a quick lunch on their own or may be served wrapped in a tortilla, with a bowl of corn chips, or poured over a baked potato. Ring the changes further with a wide range of accompaniments.

1 tablespoon olive oil
1 onion, diced
2 cloves garlic, minced
½ red capsicum, deseeded and chopped
1½ cups or 400g can cooked kidney beans or black beans
2 cups chopped fresh tomatoes or 400g can chopped tomatoes
1 teaspoon ground cumin
1 teaspoon dried oregano
1 teaspoon paprika
pinch of cayenne pepper (more or less)
½ teaspoon sea salt

Heat oil in a large heavy-based frying pan.

Add onion and sauté for several minutes until starting to soften.

Add garlic and capsicum and sauté for 1 minute more.

Add all remaining ingredients. Bring to a boil and turn heat down low. Cover saucepan with a lid and simmer for 20-30 minutes.

Serve accompanied by any or all of the following: sour cream, diced avocado, sliced tomato, fresh salsa, chopped fresh coriander and/or sliced jalapeño peppers.

SERVES 4 AS A SIDE DISH

Tempeh and kumara curry

DF V

The nutty flavour and chewy texture of the tempeh combined with the creaminess of the kumara (sweet potato) work well in this dish. The vegetables can be varied according to the season. If you're not a fan of tempeh, try an extra cup of cooked chickpeas instead.

1 tablespoon sesame or coconut oil
2 medium-sized onions, chopped
1 teaspoon cumin seeds
2cm piece fresh ginger, minced
1-2 tablespoons Thai red curry paste
½ cup water
200g carrots (or daikon)
500g kumara (or pumpkin), chopped into chunks
2 cups cooked chickpeas
400g block tempeh, cubed
1 tablespoon shoyu
½ teaspoon sea salt
400g can coconut milk
2 tablespoons tamarind paste or 1 tablespoon lemon juice
fresh chopped coriander or sliced spring onions to garnish

Heat oil in a large heavy-based saucepan.

Add onion and cumin and sauté for several minutes.

Add ginger and curry paste (be cautious if using a hot variety) and sauté for 1 minute further.

Add water, carrot (or daikon), pumpkin (or kumara), chickpeas, tempeh, shoyu, salt and coconut milk, and bring to a boil. Turn the heat down low. Cover and cook for 30 minutes or until vegetables are very soft.

Add tamarind paste (or lemon juice) and gently mix the curry.

Serve garnished with coriander or sliced spring onion with brown or basmati rice.

SERVES 4

Tempeh is one of the most nutritious ways to eat soya beans. Try grilled tempeh with *Satay sauce* (see page 82) in a burger, or crumbled up into a bolognaise sauce instead of mince.

Pressure-cooked brown rice   DF V

Pressure cookers are not as common as they once were but perhaps, as the world becomes more energy-conscious, they will make a comeback. They are both time and energy efficient. We use ours regularly for cooking everything, but find it is especially good for cooking brown rice.

Cooked under pressure, brown rice becomes satisfyingly rich and full tasting, with a wonderful sticky texture. The cooked rice keeps well in the refrigerator and we always cook enough for at least two meals. You will need to begin cooking the rice at least an hour before serving time.

1½ cups brown rice
2 cups water
pinch of sea salt

Wash rice thoroughly in a fine-mesh sieve under cold running water.

Put rice, water and salt in the pressure cooker. Secure lid. Place over medium heat and bring gradually up to pressure. When there is a good strong hiss of steam from the cooker, turn heat down low. Adjust heat to maintain pressure – a steady gentle hiss. Cook for 30 minutes.

Turn off heat and allow rice to cool. Once pressure has dropped enough to open cooker, gently mix rice with a wooden spoon before serving.

(For a variation, add ⅓ cup soaked dried soya beans, chickpeas or adzuki beans, or 1 cup chopped kumara or pumpkin to the cooker with the rice. No extra water is required.)

SERVES 6

Millet with pumpkin and nori   DF V

Novice seaweed-eaters can reduce the amount of nori or use freshly chopped parsley and garlic instead.

1 cup millet
2 cups water
½ teaspoon sea salt
2 sheets nori seaweed
1½ cups (200g) pumpkin, peeled, deseeded and cut into bite-sized pieces
Tamari roasted seeds (see page 42)

Wash millet in a fine-mesh sieve under cold running water. Put millet in a saucepan with water and salt.

Cut nori sheets into small pieces with scissors and sprinkle evenly on top of the water. Spread pumpkin on top of the nori and cover saucepan with a lid.

Bring to a boil, then turn heat down very low. Leave to simmer for about 20 minutes until all the water has been absorbed.

Turn off heat and leave to stand for a few more minutes. Mix gently with a wooden spoon before serving.

Serve sprinkled with *Tamari roasted seeds*.

SERVES 4

A pressure cooker can turn dried beans and grains into fast food, reducing cooking time by more than one-third. Pressure-cook large beans like chickpeas and kidney beans for 15–20 minutes. Smaller pulses, like lentils or mung beans, will cook in 10 minutes or less.

Gado-gado

DF V

This exotic-tasting dish is a well-balanced and satisfying meal. To avoid cooking, try making the salad with sliced tomatoes and cucumbers instead of beans or broccoli and carrots.

4 free-range organic eggs (optional)
150g green beans or broccoli, cut into bite-sized florets
250g carrots, cut into batons
150g cabbage, sliced
½ red capsicum, deseeded and sliced
100g mung bean sprouts
200g tempeh or tofu, sliced into rectangular strips about 0.5cm thick
Satay sauce (see below)

Hard-boil the eggs. (It will take about 8 minutes from when they come to a boil.)

In a separate saucepan of boiling salted water, blanch green beans and carrots in two separate batches.

Mix blanched green beans and carrots with the cabbage, capsicum and mung bean sprouts.

Pan-fry tempeh or tofu slices in a little coconut or sesame oil until golden. Slice when cool.

Peel and cut eggs in quarters lengthwise.

Divide mixed vegetables between 4 individual plates. On top of each, arrange tofu slices and egg quarters. Drizzle on plenty of *Satay sauce*, served warm or at room temperature.

SERVES 4

We usually have sprouts in the refrigerator where they will keep for a week or so. Our favourites are lentils and mung beans. Here's how to sprout beans:
1. SORT: Check the beans before use and remove any obviously malformed or discoloured beans.
2. SOAK: Place beans in a bowl and cover with plenty of water. Leave overnight.
3. DRAIN: Rinse sprouts at least once a day and drain thoroughly.
4. EAT: As a general rule, wait until the sprout tail is about as long as the seed itself. When the tips of the sprouts are starting to go green, transfer them to an airtight container and store in the refrigerator.

Satay sauce

DF V

Our version of satay sauce is made simply in a blender without cooking. In addition to its starring role in *Gado-gado*, try serving this sauce over grilled fish or with chicken skewers.

1 tablespoon red curry paste (more or less)
100ml coconut milk
1 tablespoon shoyu
1 tablespoon lemon juice
4 tablespoons (60g) peanut butter
2 tablespoons grated palm sugar or whole cane sugar

Put all ingredients in a blender and process until smooth.

Adjust seasoning to taste. Add more curry paste if you want extra spiciness.

MAKES 1 CUP

Some nutritionists believe soy products are a wonderful source of low-fat protein while others consider them unsuitable due to high levels of substances that interfere with protein digestion. However, proper fermentation prevents this problem. We recommend you moderate your intake of unfermented soy products, such as tofu and soy milk, and products with added soy protein. Fermented soy products, including tamari, miso, natto and tempeh, can be safely consumed on a regular basis. Cheaper brands of shoyu are not fermented – check labels carefully before buying.

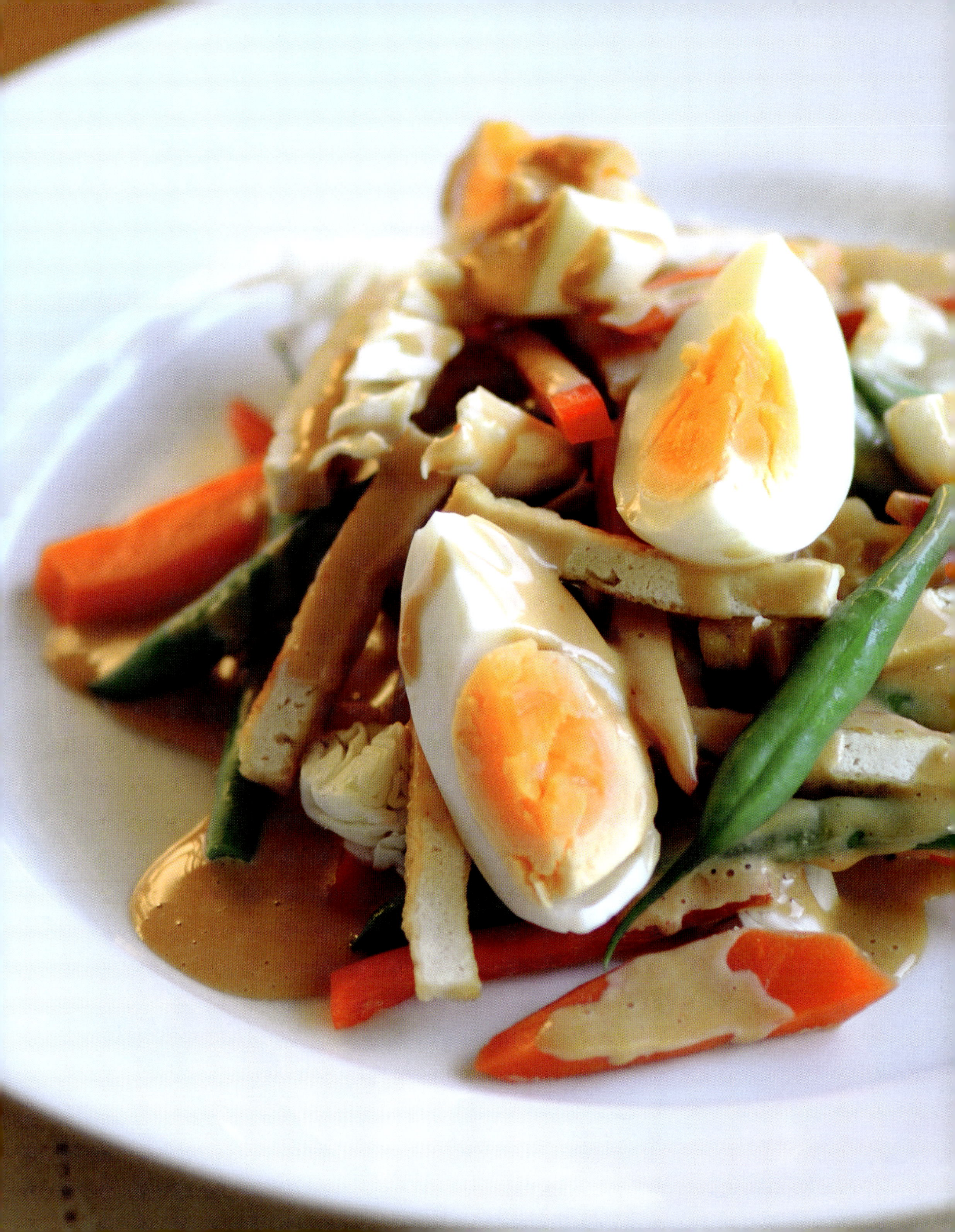

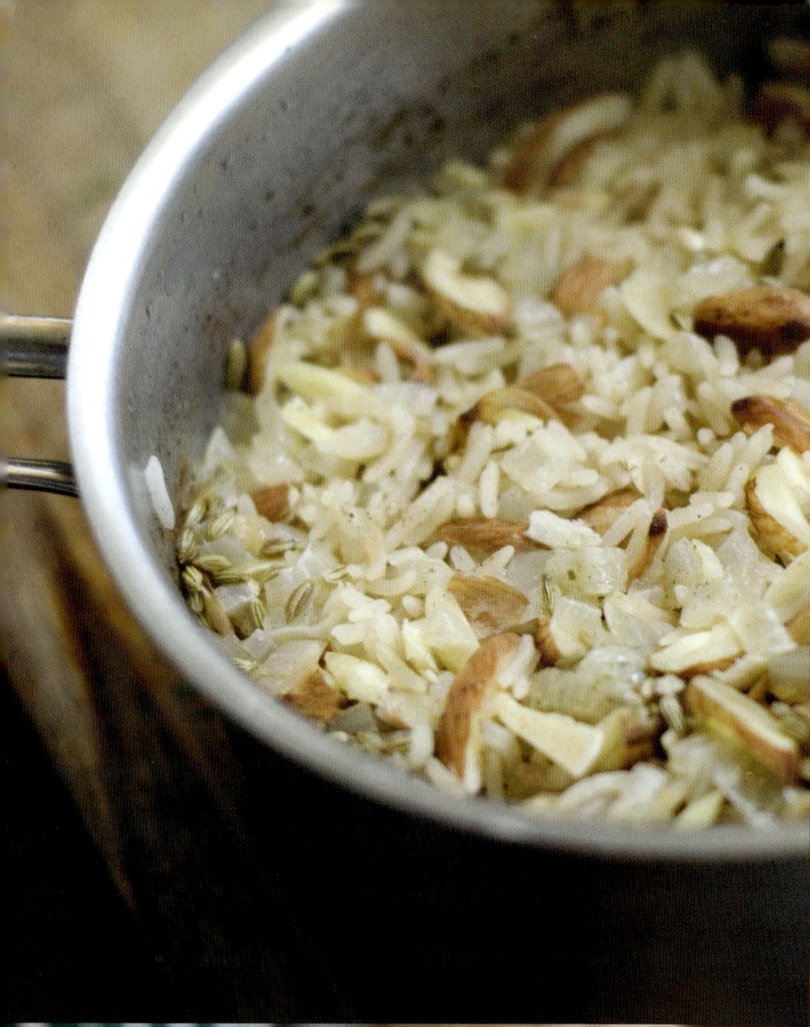
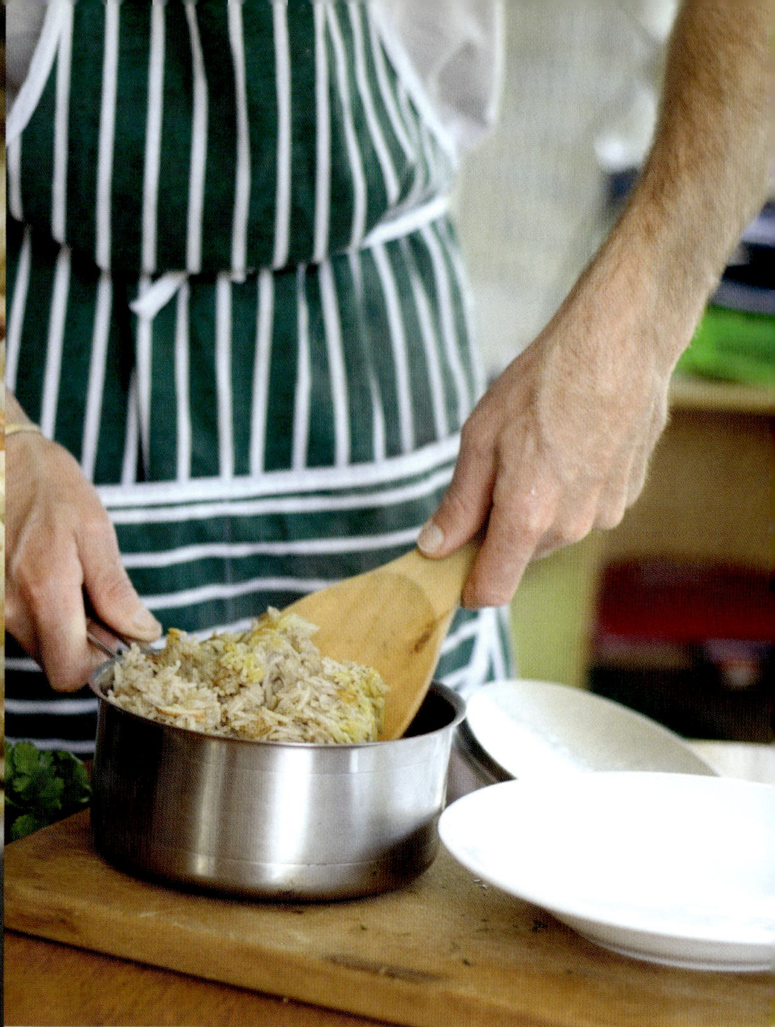
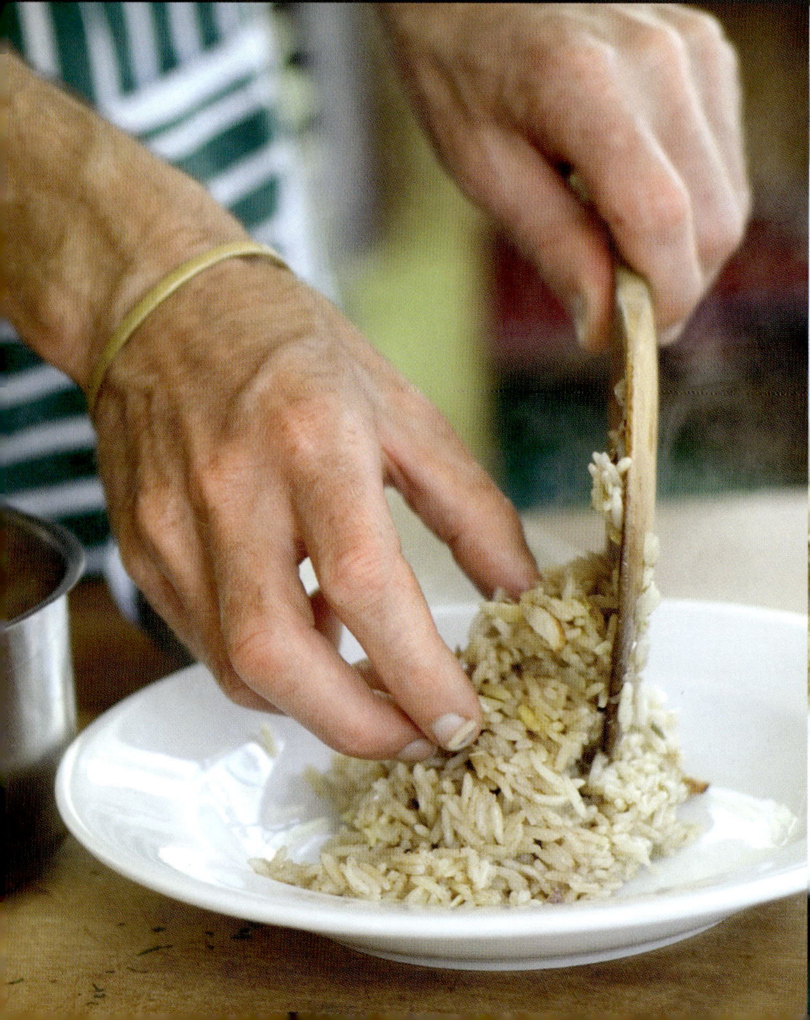
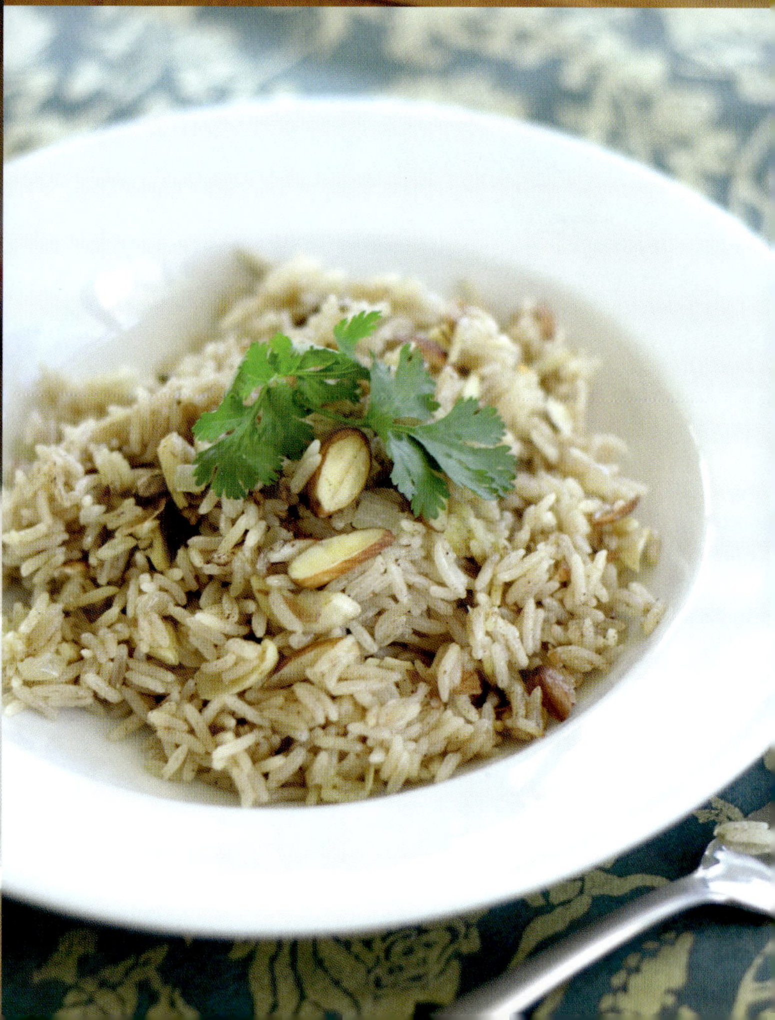

Buckwheat kasha

DF

Here is a traditional Slavic method of preparing buckwheat. The chicken stock makes this a robust and nutritious dish. If you use water instead of stock you will need to add sea salt.

1 cup buckwheat
1 egg, lightly beaten
2 cups chicken or vegetable stock or water
2 tablespoons butter or olive oil
freshly ground black pepper to taste
sea salt to taste
1–2 spring onions, finely sliced

Heat a heavy-based saucepan over medium heat and add buckwheat. Toast buckwheat, stirring often with a wooden spoon, for 3-4 minutes until fragrant and slightly browned. Remove pan from heat and leave to cool for at least 5 minutes.

Pour egg onto buckwheat in the pan. Return to heat and stir constantly until egg is cooked but grains are separated. This may happen very quickly if pan is still quite warm!

Add stock and butter and season with pepper and salt. Bring to a boil, cover and cook for 20-25 minutes.

Leave to cool for 10 minutes then gently fold in the spring onion.

Serve immediately with a salad for lunch or as part of a main meal.

SERVES 4

Almond pilaf

DF V

Pilaf is a traditional Middle-Eastern rice dish, flavoured with aromatic spices. In some cultures, pilaf is baked in an oven. However, this version can be quickly assembled and cooked on the stovetop, using the same absorption method as for steamed rice.

2 tablespoons olive oil or clarified butter
1 onion, finely diced
½ teaspoon fennel seeds
1 cup basmati rice
1 teaspoon ground cinnamon
1 tablespoon vegetable stock powder
¼ cup almonds, chopped
2 cups cold water

Put oil or butter in a saucepan over moderate heat. When butter has melted, add onion and fennel seeds and sauté until onion is soft.

Add remaining ingredients to pan, including water, and cover. Bring to a boil and turn heat down low. Simmer for 15-20 minutes.

Turn heat off and leave pilaf to stand for about 10 minutes. Mix gently with a wooden spoon before serving.

SERVES 6

Be careful when it comes to storing and eating leftover foods, particularly grains and meats. Cool and refrigerate or freeze in clean containers as soon as possible after dinner. Cooked grains in particular can quickly attract yeast and bacteria, so eat within 2 days.

Almond pilaf

Red quinoa salad with pears and feta

Red quinoa – although more maroon than red – has all the wonderful nutritional properties of regular quinoa and a dramatic bright colour. If preferred, use cow's feta or blue cheese instead of goat's feta. It will still be delicious.

1 cup red quinoa
2 cups water
½ teaspoon sea salt
2 tablespoons sliced almonds
2–3 firm but ripe pears
2 tablespoons olive oil
lemon juice to taste
1 tablespoon fresh chives or spring onions, finely sliced
110g goat's feta

Rinse quinoa thoroughly in a fine-mesh strainer under cold running water, then drain.

Place quinoa in a large saucepan, add water and salt and bring to a boil. Cover and leave to simmer for about 15 minutes until all the water has been absorbed.

Toast sliced almonds in a small saucepan over low heat until just starting to colour.

Slice pears into quarters, remove core and slice flesh into long thin strips.

Place quinoa, pears, almonds, olive oil, lemon juice and chives or spring onions in a bowl and toss to combine.

To serve, crumble feta on top and gently mix to combine.

SERVES 6

Goat's feta is a staple ingredient in our household. Goat's milk and goat's milk products are beneficial because goat's milk:
- has a similar chemical structure to human milk
- is lower in fat and has much smaller fat molecules than cow's milk, making it easier to digest
- has been found to soothe problems in the digestive tract
- products are not mucus-forming
- is less allergenic than cow's milk.

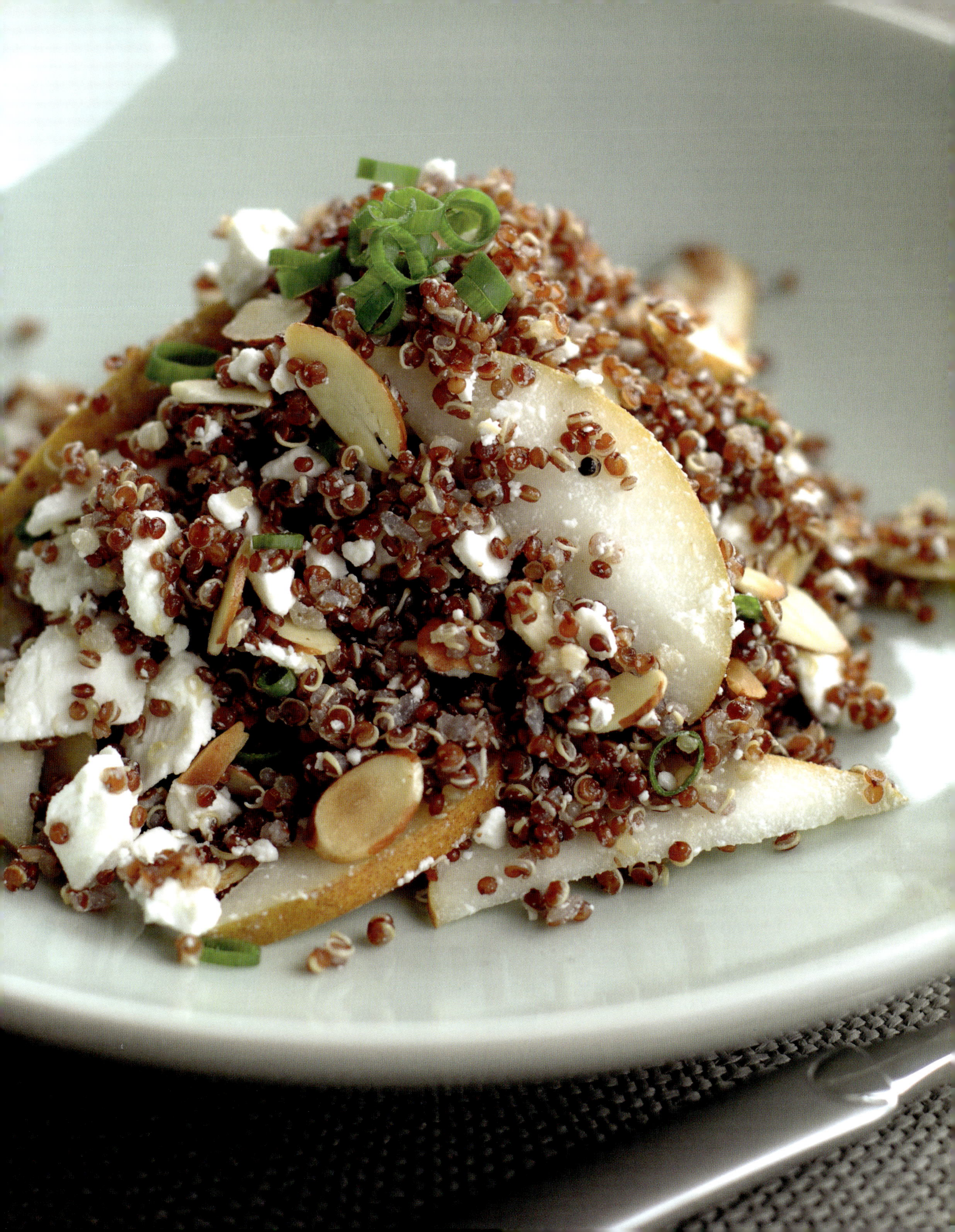

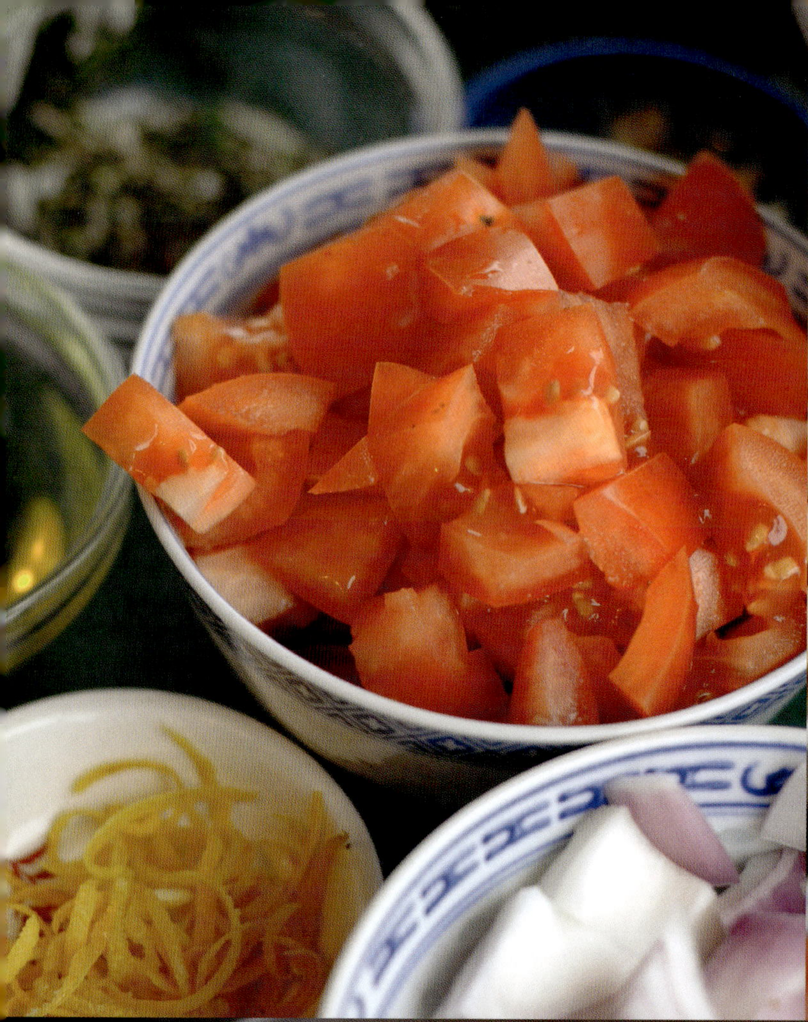
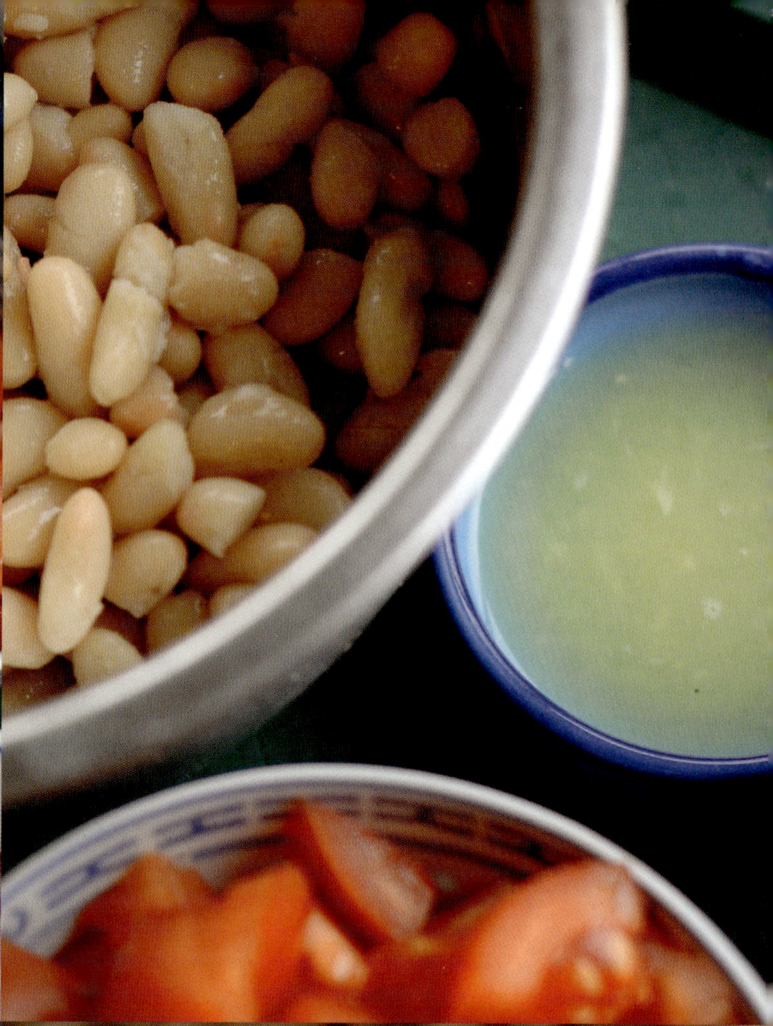
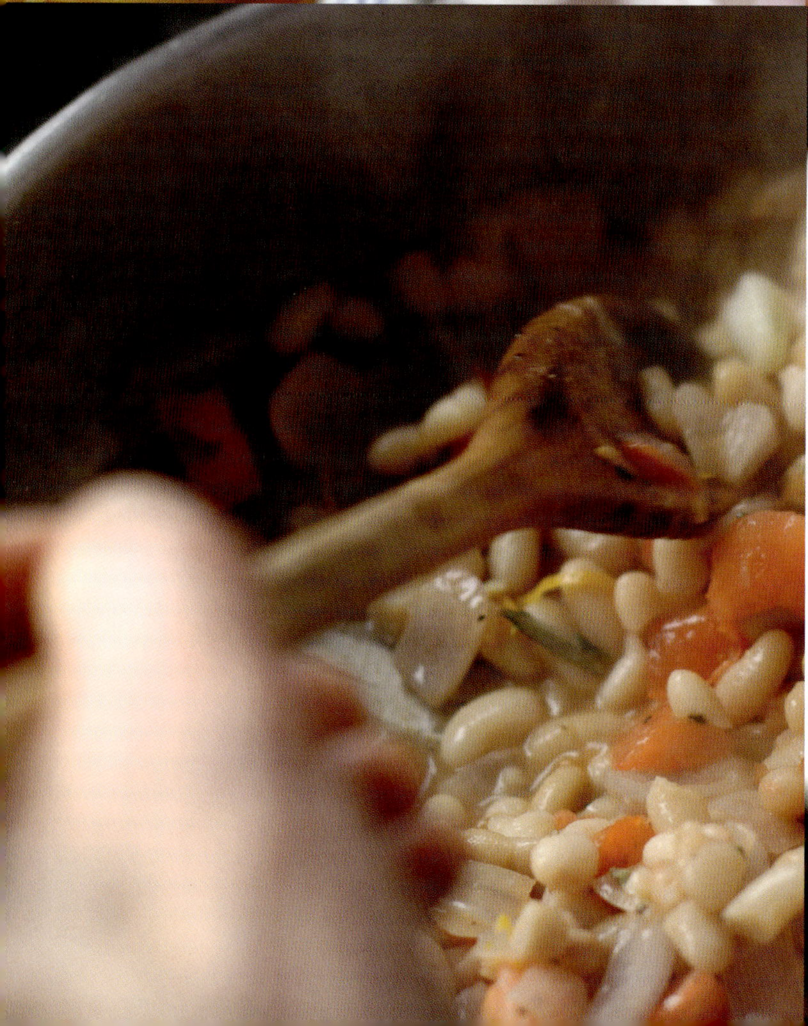
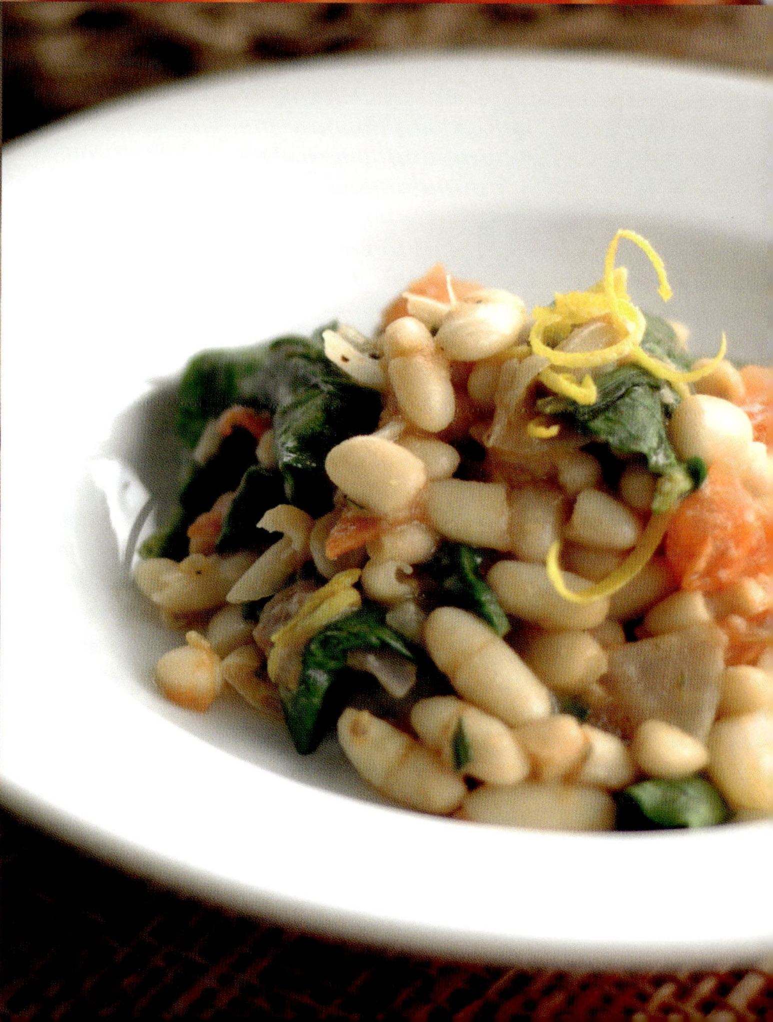

Warm cannellini and spinach salad

DF V

Serve these creamy white beans and Mediterranean vegetables on toast for a nourishing lunch. Alternatively, use them as a base for grilled or pan-fried fish.

3 tablespoons extra virgin olive oil
1 large red onion, chopped
4 cloves garlic, minced
2 x 400g cans cannellini beans, drained
100g spinach leaves (small bunch), washed and roughly chopped
2 large tomatoes, chopped
zest and juice of 1 lemon
½ teaspoon sea salt
freshly ground black pepper
¼ cup chopped fresh parsley or basil

Heat a large saucepan on a moderate heat. Add olive oil, onions and garlic, and gently sauté until onions are starting to soften.

Add cannellini beans and heat through. Add spinach and tomatoes. Continue heating until the spinach wilts slightly. Remove from heat.

Add lemon juice and zest, salt, pepper and fresh herbs. Mix gently to combine. Serve immediately.

SERVES 6

Red lentil stew

DF V

Humble and often maligned, lentils are actually nutritional superstars! This simple stew has a wonderful earthy flavour, perfect for autumn and winter. Eat this dish on its own for lunch or with fish and greens for a hearty dinner.

2 cups brown or green lentils
1 tablespoon olive oil
1 onion, sliced
3 cloves garlic, chopped
2 carrots, roughly chopped
500g pumpkin, peeled, deseeded and roughly chopped
4 bay leaves
2 tablespoons miso
1½ teaspoons sea salt
ground black pepper to taste
small bunch parsley, chopped

☀ Soak lentils in water overnight.

Drain and rinse lentils, then set aside until required.

Heat a large heavy-based casserole dish over medium heat. Add oil, onion and garlic and sauté for a few minutes.

Add lentils, carrot, pumpkin and bay leaves. Cover with water to about 2cm above contents and bring to a boil.

Skim off any foam and turn heat down to maintain a low boil. After 20 minutes check that there is still sufficient water. (You want to have just a little liquid remaining after the lentils are cooked.) Continue cooking for 30 minutes or until lentils are soft.

Dissolve miso in a little of the liquid from stew and add to dish. Add sea salt and pepper.

To serve, mix in freshly chopped parsley.

SERVES 6–8

Pulses are an excellent source of dietary fibre, protein, B vitamins, iron, magnesium and several other important minerals. Look for beans that appear plump and fairly uniform in size and colour. There should be few, if any, cracked, broken or discoloured beans. Buy from a retailer that is likely to have a high turnover of stock to avoid buying old, over-dry beans that won't cook or sprout uniformly.

Warm cannellini and spinach salad

Lentil and grapefruit salad with mint dressing

DF V

Leftovers can result in strange and wonderful combinations, such as this salad that Anna created the day after a dinner party. Try it for lunch with a slice or two of fresh bread, or with grilled fish or chicken for a substantial dinner.

⅔ cup brown or green lentils
1 sweet grapefruit
2 large handfuls fresh salad greens (e.g. lettuce, rocket or spinach)
1 medium-sized avocado, cut into small cubes
1 small fennel bulb, core removed and finely sliced

DRESSING
50ml olive oil
1 tablespoon pomegranate molasses or honey
1 tablespoon cider vinegar
½ cup fresh mint leaves, chopped
½ teaspoon sea salt

Boil lentils in 4 cups of water for 20 minutes or until cooked. Drain and leave to cool.

Remove skin and white pith from outside of grapefruit. Cut into thin segments or slices, removing any seeds or tough core.

If salad greens have large leaves, chop into short lengths.

Place lentils, grapefruit, avocado, fennel and greens in a bowl.

To make the dressing, whisk ingredients together in a separate bowl.

When ready to serve, pour dressing over lentil salad and mix gently to combine.

SERVES 4

Adzuki pumpkin casserole

DF V

Dried adzuki beans look like small kidney beans and are available at health-food stores and some supermarkets. This is a good dish to eat regularly if you suffer from blood-sugar imbalances.

1 cup dried adzuki beans
1 tablespoon sesame or rice bran oil
1 large onion, chopped
2cm piece fresh ginger, sliced fine or grated
2½ cups water
800g pumpkin, peeled, deseeded and cut in bite-sized pieces
1½ tablespoons shoyu or 2 tablespoons miso
1 spring onion, finely sliced

※ Soak adzuki beans in water overnight.

Drain and rinse adzuki beans.

Put oil in a large saucepan over medium heat and sauté onion until it begins to soften.

Add the ginger and cook for several more minutes. Add adzuki beans and water. On top of beans, spread pumpkin pieces. Finally, add shoyu or miso.

Bring to a boil, turn heat down to medium (beans need a fairly strong boil to cook properly) and cover.

Check after about 20 minutes that there is still plenty of liquid around the beans. After about 30 minutes of cooking, beans and pumpkin should be cooked.

Gently mix stew to combine and serve garnished with spring onions.

SERVES 4–6

Here are our best time-saving tips for using beans:
※ Cook a large batch of beans and freeze in several small containers – this works especially well for larger beans such as chickpeas and kidney beans. Thaw them in boiling water or add directly to soups or stews.
※ Canned beans are not as nutritious or tasty as home-cooked, but they are a handy standby when you are in a hurry. Organic varieties are worth the small extra cost.

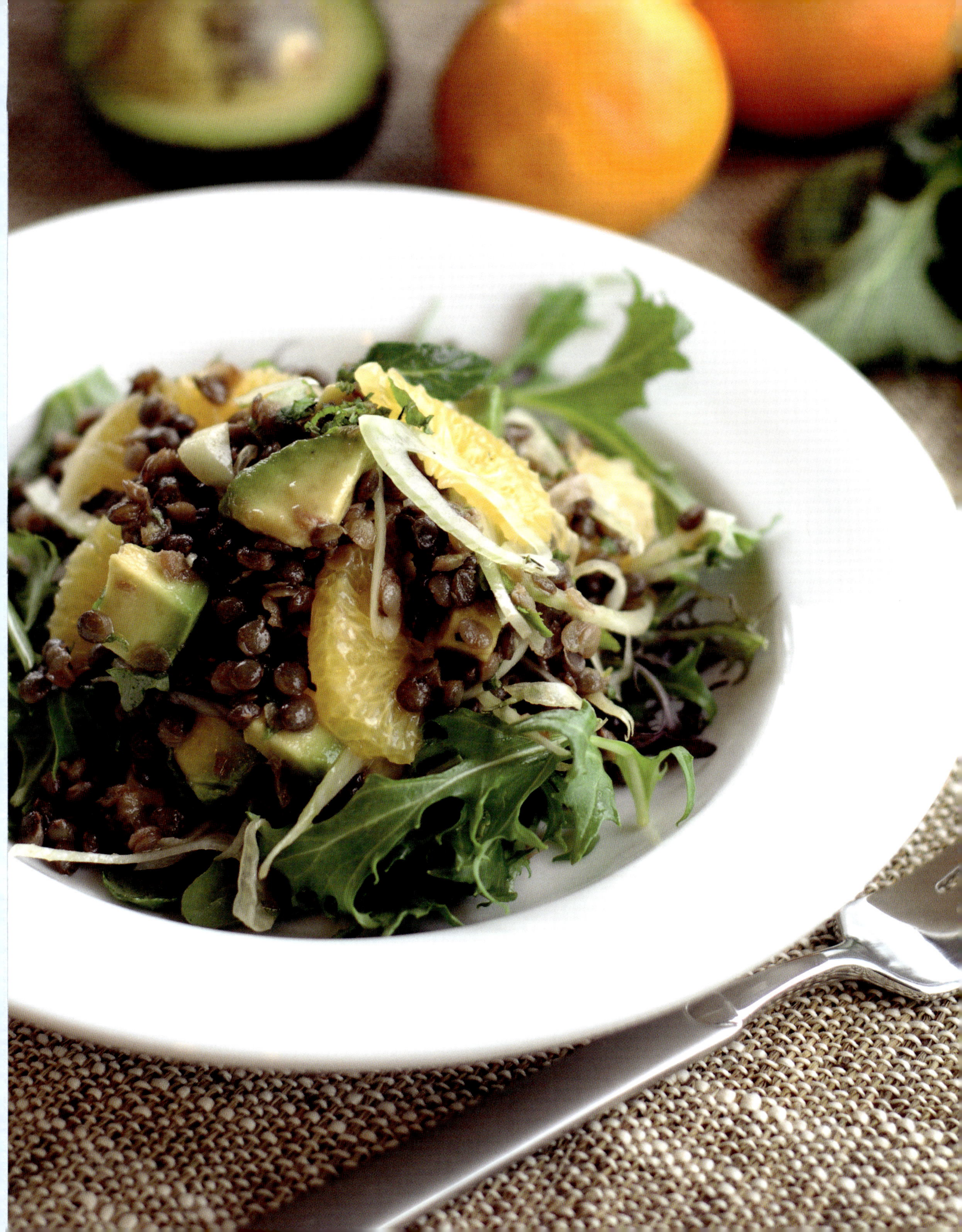

Indonesian fish cakes

Authentic South-East Asian food is alive with complex flavours from fresh herbs, spices and juices. For a shortcut, replace the fresh ginger, garlic and chilli with red curry paste – the fishcakes will still be tasty.

4 cloves garlic
2cm piece fresh ginger, sliced
½ fresh red or green chilli, chopped
3 tablespoons lemon juice
1 teaspoon cumin seeds
1 organic free-range egg
1½ tablespoons fish sauce
small bunch fresh coriander, chopped
600g fresh, boneless, white fish, roughly chopped
⅔ cup corn kernels or 100g green beans, finely chopped

Preheat oven to 180°C. Line a baking tray with baking paper.

Put garlic, ginger, chilli, lemon juice, cumin seeds, egg, fish sauce and coriander in a food processor and process for 30 seconds. Add chopped fish and process until mixture forms a sticky ball.

Transfer mixture to a bowl and mix in the corn kernels.

Form mixture into balls or flat rissoles about 1.5cm thick and place on prepared tray. Bake for 10-12 minutes until cooked through.

SERVES 4-6

Ceviche

This is the Spanish name for citrus-marinated fish. Versions of this dish are made in almost all tropical regions of the world, including the South Pacific. The most important consideration is that the fish is as fresh as possible.

400g fresh, firm white-fleshed fish
3 tablespoons lime juice or lemon juice
½ small red onion, finely diced
1 carrot, finely sliced or grated
½ red capsicum, deseeded and finely sliced
1 red chilli, deseeded and finely sliced
2 cloves garlic, minced
1 tablespoon fish sauce
1 cup coconut cream
sea salt
small bunch fresh coriander, roughly chopped

Slice fish into small, thin bite-sized pieces. Place in a bowl, add lime or lemon juice and mix well. Cover and leave in the refrigerator for at least 15 minutes or up to 2 hours.

To serve, combine marinated fish including juices with vegetables, chilli, garlic, fish sauce and coconut cream. Mix gently by hand.

Check seasoning and add a little salt if required.

Serve with steamed rice, avocado slices, salad leaves, taco shells or crackers.

These days most suppliers know how to provide good-quality fresh fish. As soon as you reach home, transfer the fish to a ceramic or glass container. Cover, store in the refrigerator and eat within 2 days.

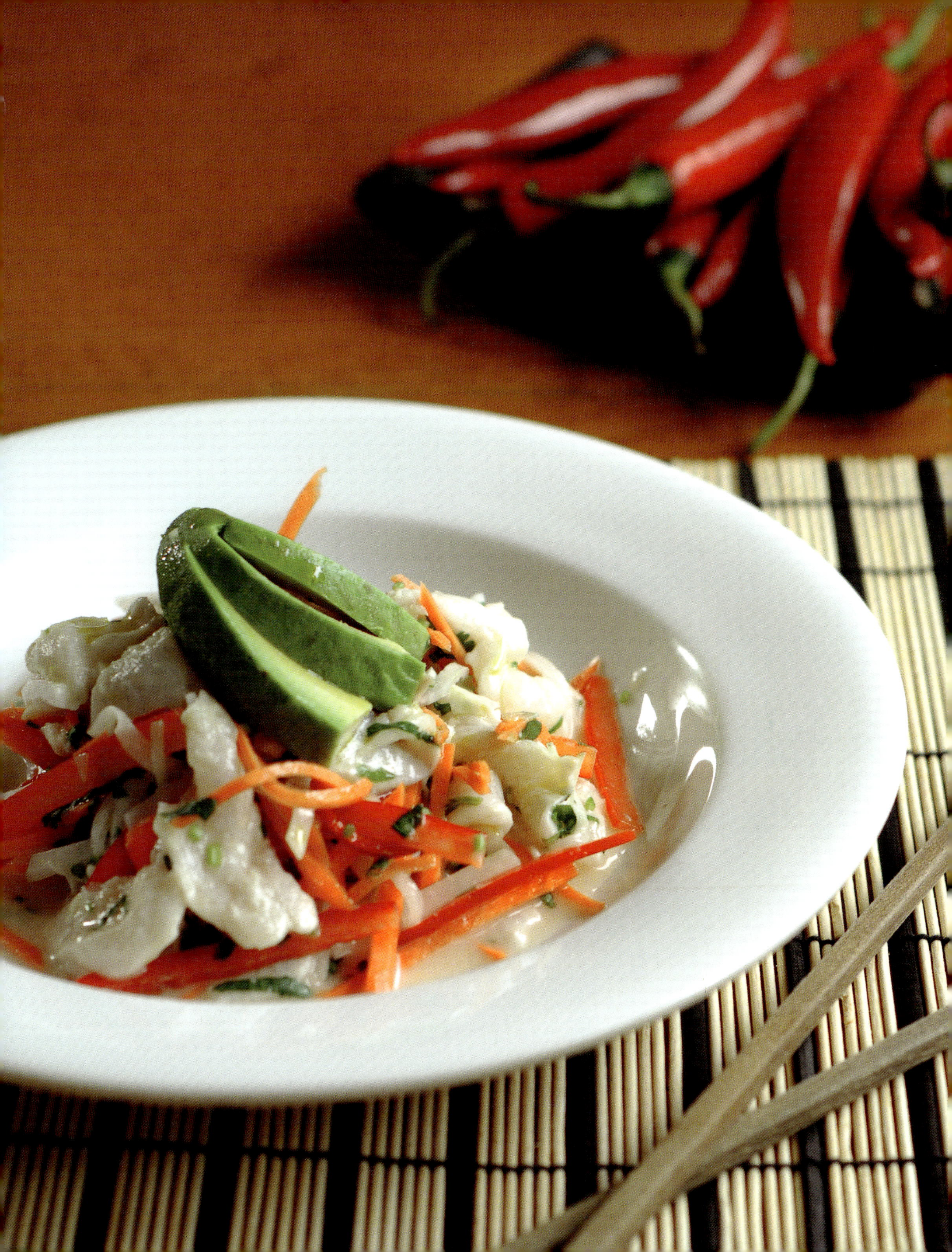

Marinated grilled fish

Mild, white-fleshed fish readily absorbs the flavours of simple marinades in just a few minutes. Cooking fish under a grill is quicker, easier and less messy than pan-frying, especially when there are more than one or two people to serve.

150–200g fresh fish fillets per person
1 tablespoon your chosen marinade per person (see *Ginger shoyu marinade* and *Lemon garlic marinade* below and *Chermoula marinade* on next page)

Portion fish into pieces about 70–100g each, to make 2–3 pieces per serve. If possible slice fish so that portions are about the same thickness, so they cook evenly.

Place portioned fish in a bowl with the marinade. Toss gently until evenly coated. Leave for 10 minutes.

Heat grill.

Transfer fish to a shallow oven tray and place under grill.

Turn fish over after several minutes and continue grilling until cooked through.

If white liquid appears out of the top of the fish, it's cooked. With practice it is possible to remove the fish before this occurs and it will complete cooking with its own heat. (Underdone fish can still be moist and delicious. Overcooked fish is dry and tough.)

When cooking for large numbers, it can be easier to bake marinated fish in an oven preheated to 220°C. In that case, there's no need to turn each portion over halfway through cooking.

Ginger shoyu marinade

1 tablespoon finely grated fresh ginger or store-bought minced ginger
1½ tablespoons shoyu
2 tablespoons olive oil

Place the ingredients in a screw-top jar and shake to combine.

SERVES 4

Lemon garlic marinade

4 cloves garlic, finely chopped
1½ tablespoons lemon juice
2 tablespoons olive oil
½ teaspoon sea salt
chopped fresh or dried herbs (optional)

Place the ingredients in a screw-top jar and shake to combine.

SERVES 4

Chermoula marinade

DF

This North African marinade can be easily made in a small blender, although the hand-chopped herbs have an appealing texture and appearance.

½ cup (packed) finely chopped fresh coriander
½ cup (packed) finely chopped Italian parsley
½ cup olive oil
2 tablespoons lemon juice
1 tablespoon ground cumin
2 tablespoons paprika
½ teaspoon cayenne pepper
4 cloves garlic, chopped
½ teaspoon sea salt

Put all the ingredients in a small bowl. Mix with a spoon to combine.

If it is too rich, add a little water or blend in a chopped fresh tomato.

Store leftover chermoula in the refrigerator for up to 2 weeks.

MAKES ABOUT 1 CUP

USE 2–3 TABLESPOONS TO SERVE 4

Pad Thai with calamari

DF

Our version of this well-known Thai dish includes plenty of vegetables. Frozen calamari rings (without crumbs) are now available at most large supermarkets. Tempeh, tofu or prawns may be used instead of calamari.

150g Pad Thai rice noodles (thin, flat noodles)
1 tablespoon sesame or coconut oil
2 eggs, lightly beaten
200g frozen calamari rings, defrosted and drained
½ cup finely sliced zucchini, red capsicum or carrot
250g mung bean sprouts
¼ cup cashews, roughly chopped
2 spring onions, sliced
small bunch fresh coriander

SAUCE
1 tablespoon tamarind paste or lemon juice
2 tablespoons fish sauce
1–2 teaspoons chilli sauce
2 teaspoons honey

Place rice noodles in a large bowl and cover with boiling water. Leave for about 7–10 minutes until soft. Drain.

Place sauce ingredients in a small bowl and whisk to combine.

Heat a wok or large frying pan and add 1 teaspoon of oil. Stir-fry the eggs until cooked through and broken into small pieces. Remove from wok and set aside until required. Clean wok if necessary.

Reheat wok and add 2 teaspoons of oil. Gently stir-fry the calamari for about 2 minutes.

Turn heat up to medium-high and add zucchini, sprouts and cashews. Cook until sprouts are slightly softened.

Add sauce and rice noodles, then heat and stir until noodles are hot. If noodles begin to burn or stick to the pan, add a little water.

Turn heat down then add fried egg, spring onion and coriander. Mix well and serve immediately in individual bowls.

SERVES 2–3

Overleaf: Pad Thai with calamari

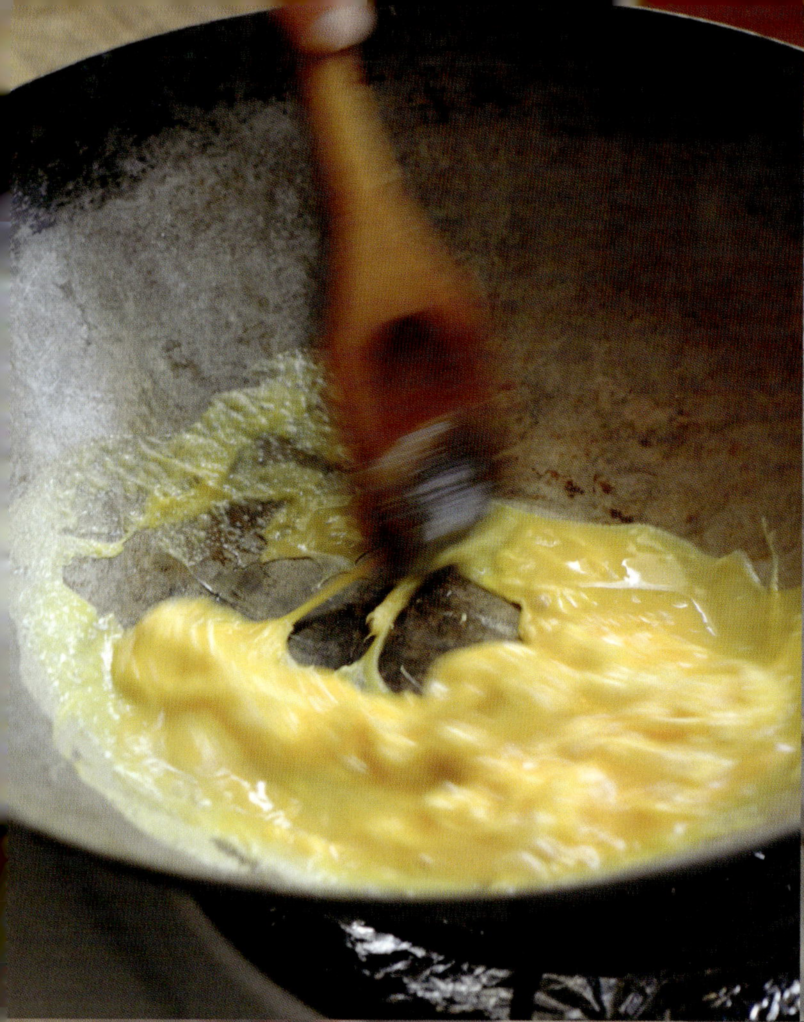
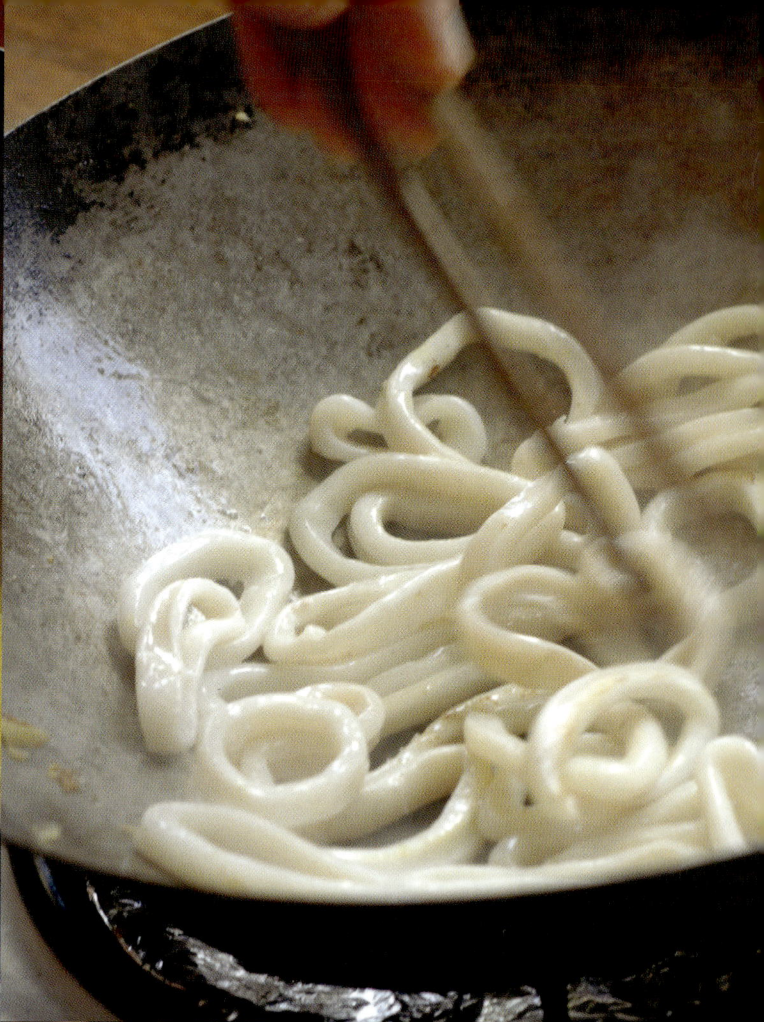
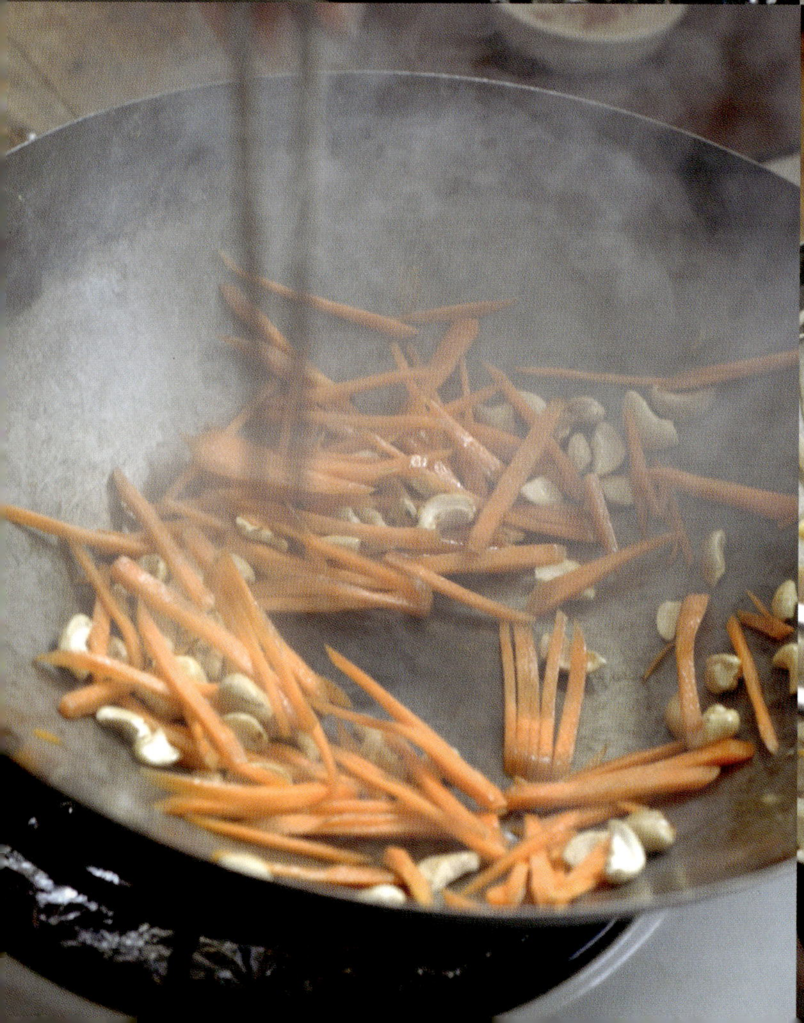
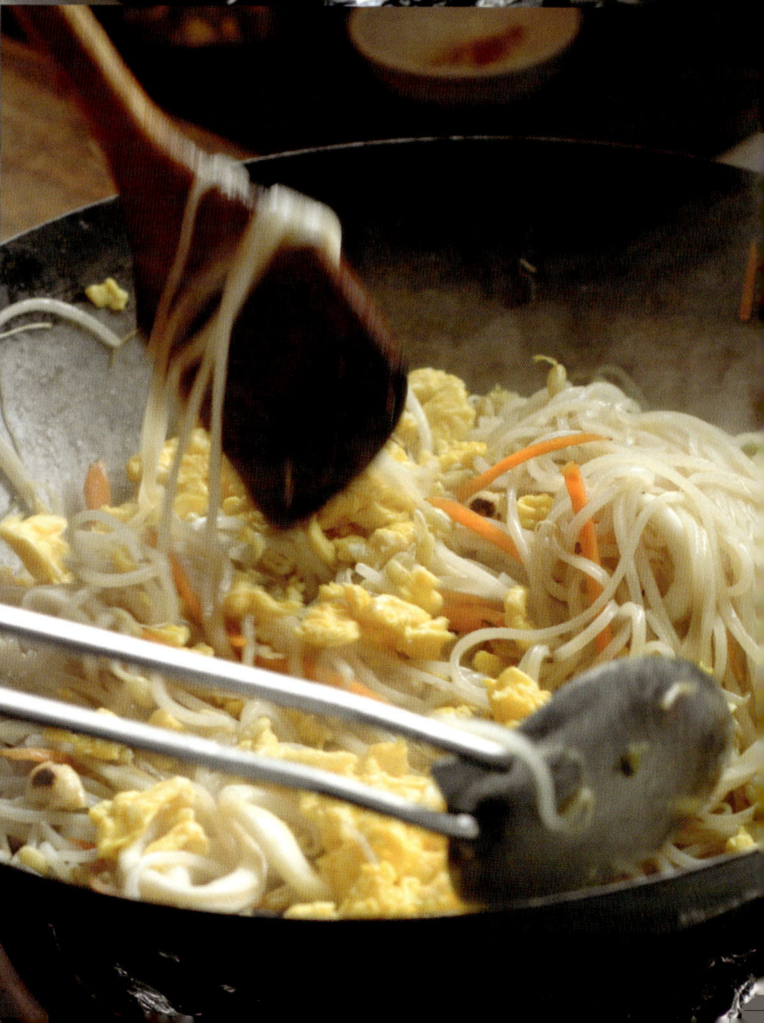

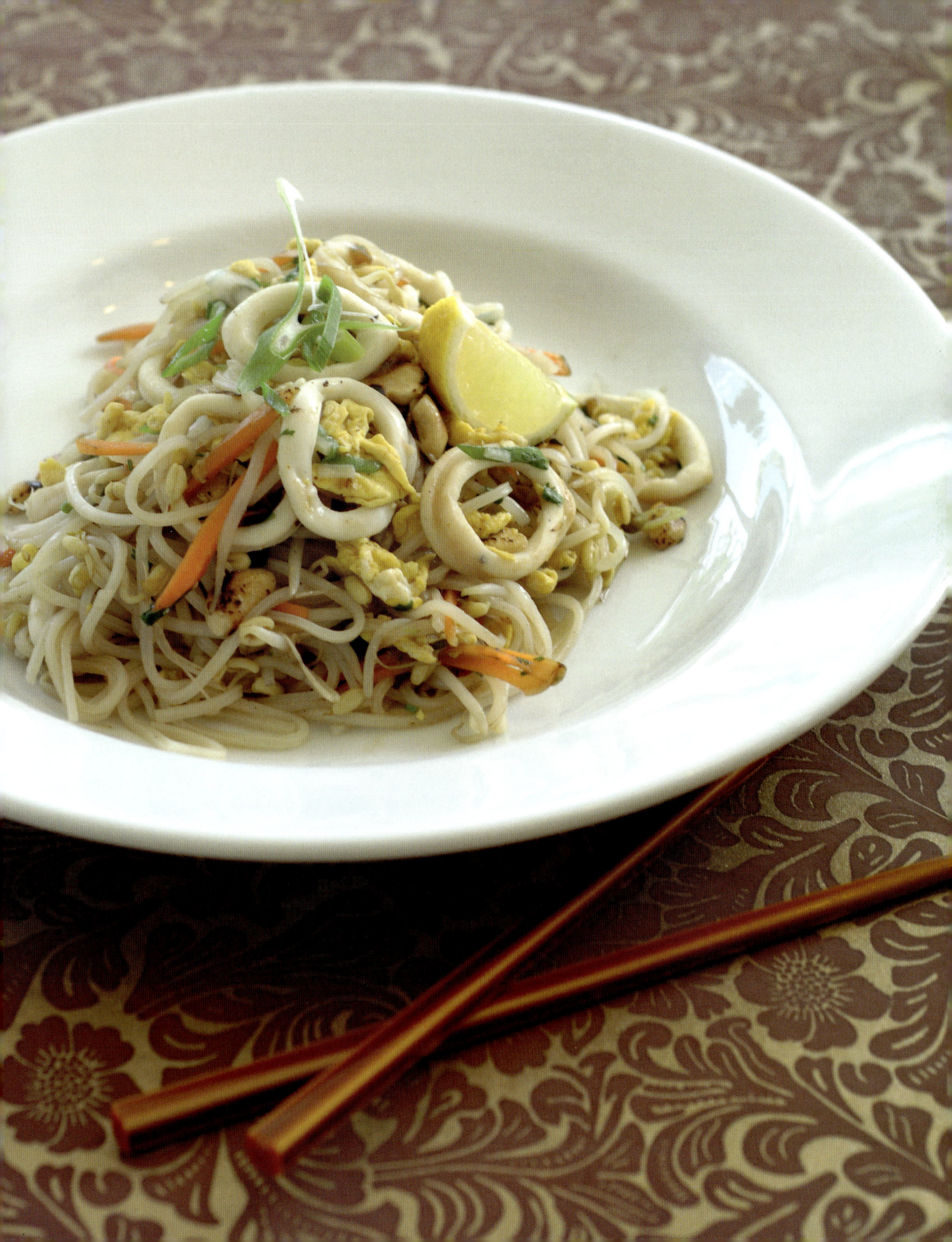

Smoked fish frittata

A rich, smoky aroma will fill the kitchen as this frittata slowly bakes.

small bunch silverbeet (400g), washed well
8 organic free-range eggs
200ml yoghurt
¼ teaspoon grated nutmeg
1 teaspoon sea salt
black pepper
3 medium-sized carrots (400g), grated
200g smoked fish, skin removed
½ red capsicum, deseeded and cut into strips (optional)

Preheat oven to 160°C. Line with baking paper or lightly oil a 20 x 30cm baking dish.

Cut silverbeet stems and leaves into 2cm strips. Place in a saucepan with about 1cm of water. Cook over high heat for several minutes until silverbeet leaves have wilted. Drain and leave to cool.

Place eggs, yoghurt, nutmeg, salt and pepper in a bowl and whisk to combine.

Press grated carrot into prepared baking dish. Pour some egg mixture over carrot and press down through carrot. Add silverbeet in an even layer. Pour rest of egg mixture evenly over top of silverbeet.

Break smoked fish into small pieces and scatter over the top. Push fish down into egg mix a little. Arrange sliced capsicum on top if desired.

Bake for about 30-40 minutes until completely cooked. Check by giving the centre of the frittata a little press with your finger. The top will feel firm and appear lightly puffed up when it is ready. Leave to cool slightly before slicing and serving.

SERVES 6–8

Be creative with your frittata filling ingredients. Try hot smoked salmon and puha (sow thistle), blue cheese and grated pumpkin or feta, mushroom and spinach. Frittata keeps for 2 or 3 days in the refrigerator and packs easily for school, office, picnic or pot-luck parties. Cut into small squares, it can be served as a finger-food.

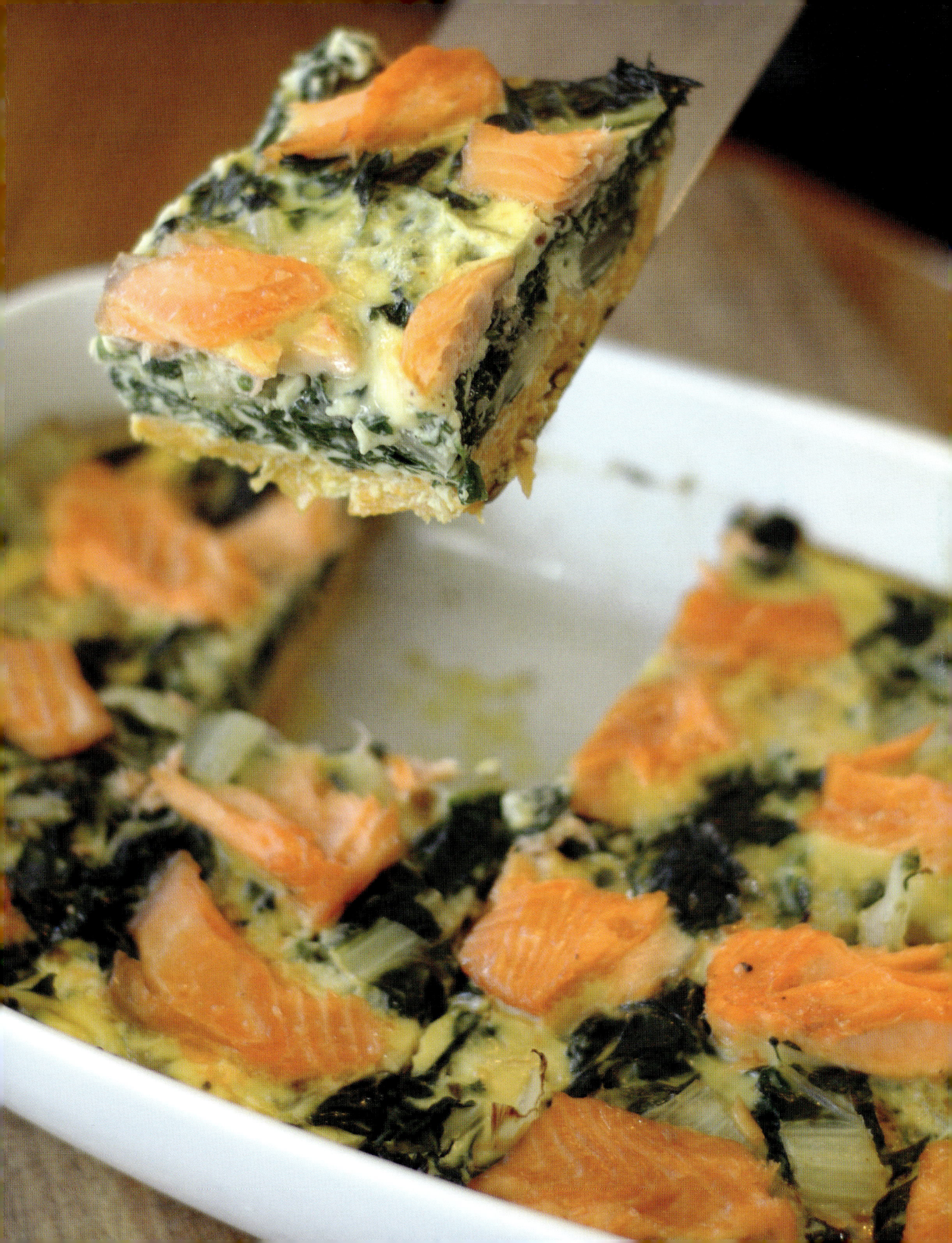

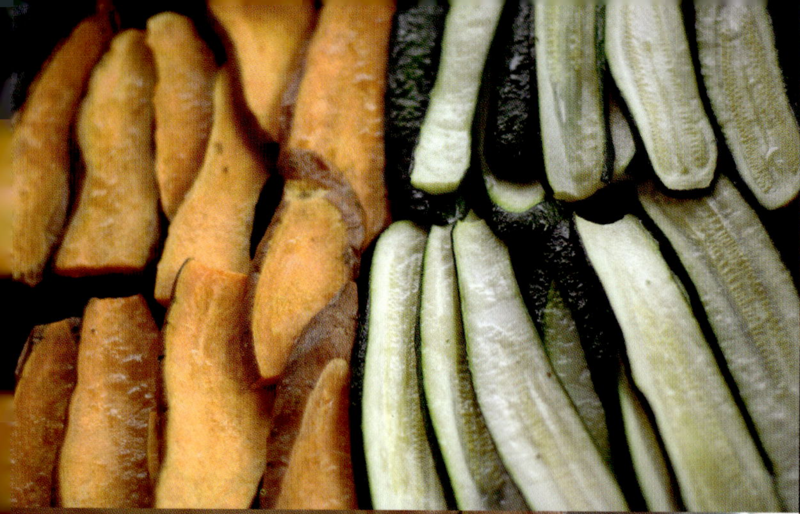

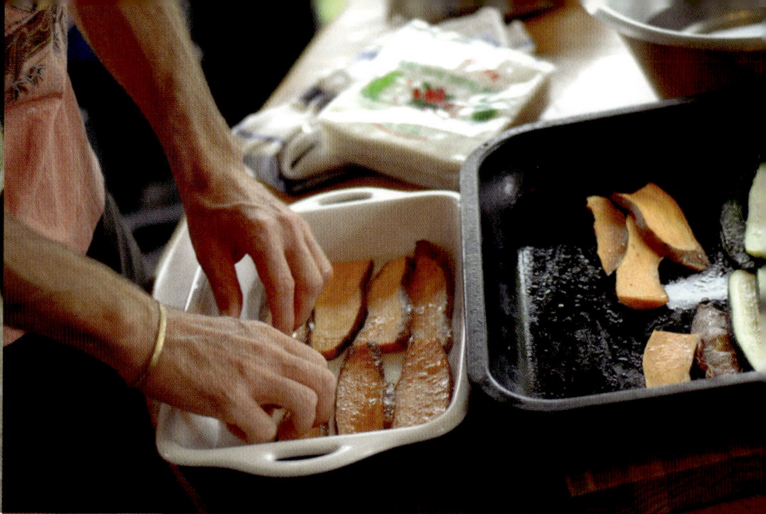

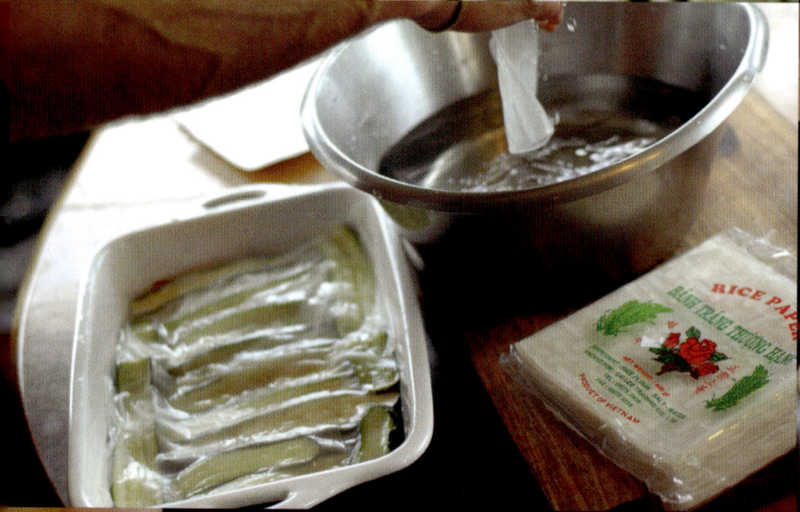
RICE PAPER

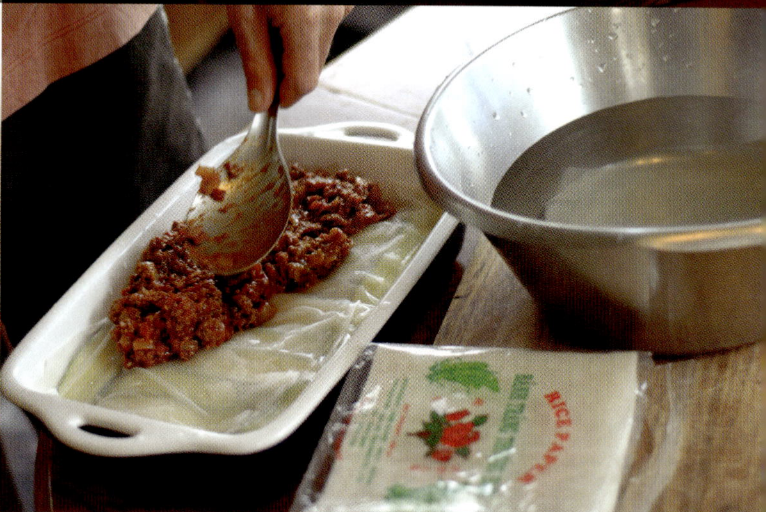

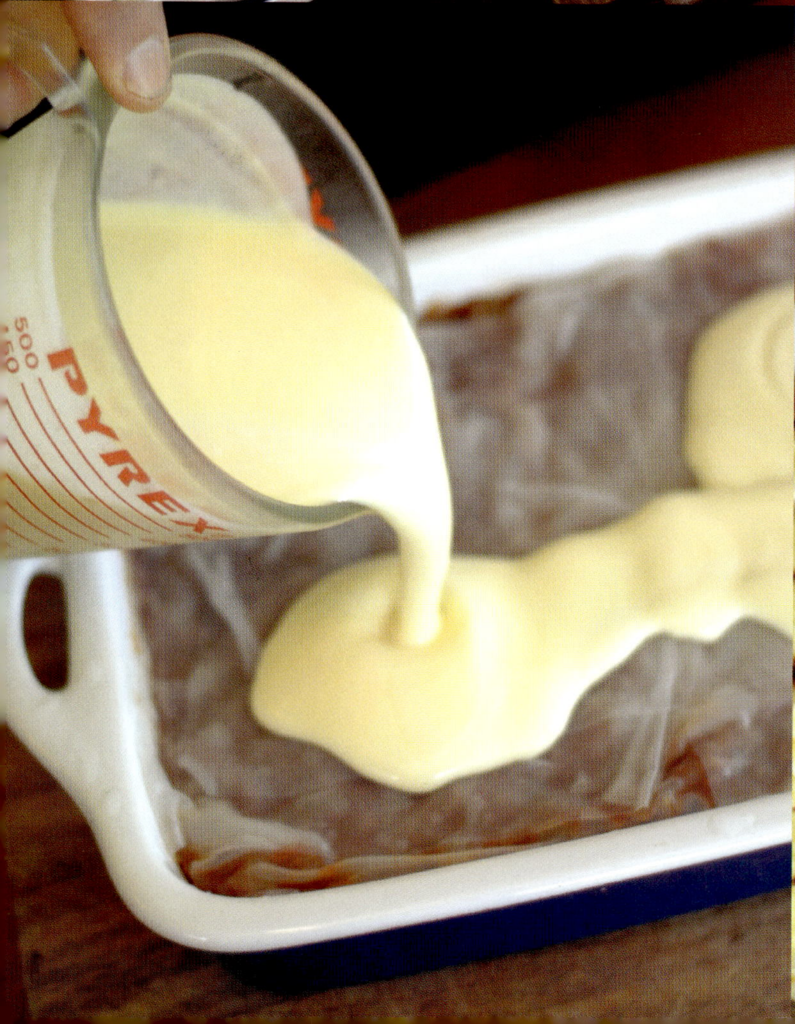
PYREX
500

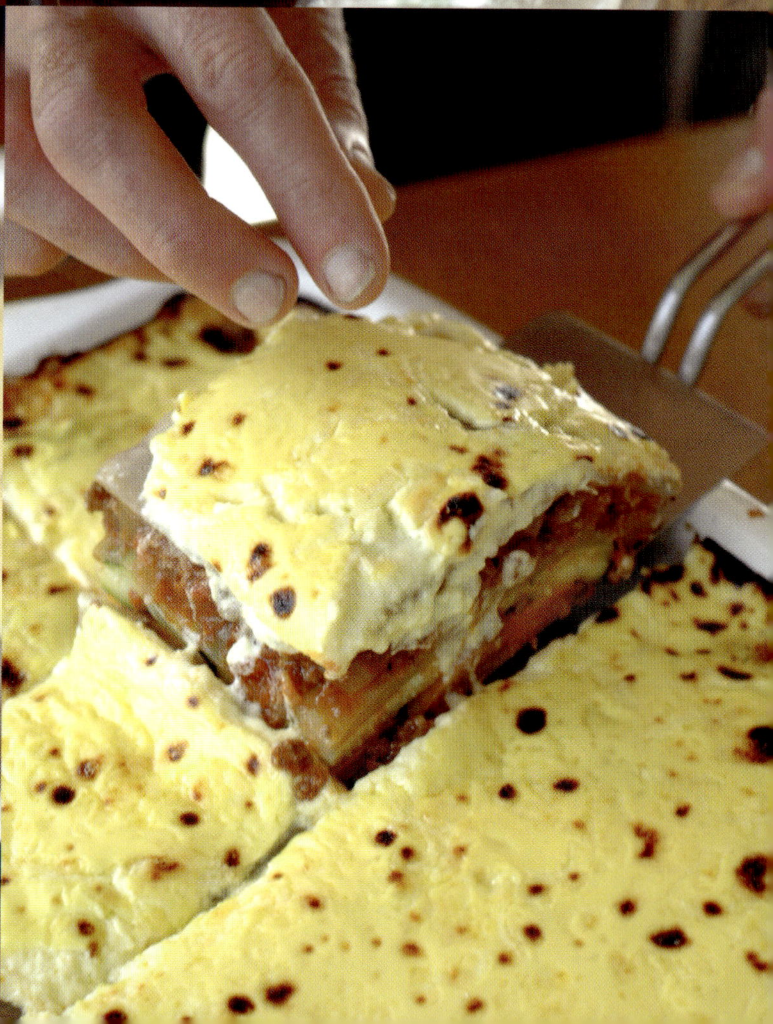

Rice paper lasagne

Rice paper sheets are available from Asian supermarkets. However, some brands include wheat flour so check the ingredients list on the packet to make sure the rice paper is gluten-free. Use this basic lasagne recipe and adapt the filling for the season.

LAMB LAYER
1 teaspoon olive oil
1 medium-sized onion, chopped
450g lamb mince
3 cloves garlic, minced
400g can tomatoes, chopped
3 tablespoons tomato paste
1 teaspoon sea salt
½ teaspoon black pepper
2 teaspoons Worcestershire sauce

GRILLED VEGETABLE LAYER
1 tablespoon olive oil
400g pumpkin or kumara (sweet potato), peeled
400g zucchini, red capsicums or mushrooms
½ teaspoon sea salt

LASAGNE
100g rice paper sheets (about 10 sheets)
2 egg yolks
2 cups yoghurt
grated Parmesan (optional)

Put oil and onion in a frying pan over medium heat and sauté until slightly softened.

Add lamb and garlic. Continue cooking until mince is browned, breaking up lumps with a wooden spoon.

Add tomatoes, tomato paste, salt, pepper and Worcestershire sauce. When boiling again, turn heat down, cover and simmer for 15–20 minutes. Remove from heat and allow to cool.

To prepare grilled vegetables, preheat oven to 180°C. Oil 2 baking trays.

Slice vegetables in 0.5cm-wide strips of even thickness and arrange on prepared trays. Season with salt. Bake about 15–20 minutes until just soft. Check as you may need to remove the softer vegetables early.

To assemble lasagne, oil a 20cm x 30cm ovenproof dish and lay the grilled vegetables evenly across the bottom.

Fill a large bowl with warm water. Put 2 sheets of rice paper in the water and soak for 30 seconds or until soft. Lift each sheet out carefully and lay on top of the vegetables. Repeat several times to create an even layer of rice paper 3–4 sheets thick. Pour lamb mixture on top. Create another layer of rice paper sheets.

Whisk egg yolks and yoghurt together in a small bowl and spread on top. Sprinkle with Parmesan, if using.

Bake in the middle of the oven at 180°C for 30 minutes or until starting to bubble at the edges.

Get into the habit of making one big main dish for your evening meal and serving a simple green salad alongside it. Casseroles, soups, stews and lasagne are ideal for this.

Wild venison rissoles

DF

Plenty of vegetables add nutrition and fibre to these rissoles, also making them deliciously soft and moist. While chopping ingredients by hand makes for an interesting texture, using a food processor can save time if you're in a hurry. As an alternative, use beef mince.

1 onion, finely chopped
350g carrot or parsnip, grated
½ cup parsley, finely chopped
1 tablespoon ground linseed
2 teaspoons dried oregano
1 teaspoon paprika
½ teaspoon sea salt
pinch of black pepper or cayenne pepper
500g wild venison mince

Preheat oven to 180°C. Oil a roasting dish.

Put everything except the mince in a large bowl and mix well.

Add mince and mash with the hands and fingers until well combined.

Form mixture into patties or balls and place in prepared dish.

Bake for about 10-15 minutes until cooked through. (Cooking time will depend on the thickness of the rissoles.)

For a variation, pour chopped tomatoes or tomato pasta sauce over the uncooked rissoles before baking.

SERVES 4

Wild venison casserole

DF

Slow-cooking renders less-expensive, tough cuts of meat into rich, comforting food that is ideal for a winter's night. This recipe requires a casserole dish with a heavy lid. It can also be made with beef using blade steak.

2 tablespoons olive oil
500g wild venison, diced
2 medium onions, chopped
1 medium leek, washed well and chopped
4-6 cloves garlic, sliced
½ cup white wine
3 carrots, chopped chunky
1 teaspoon sea salt
1 tablespoon curry powder or 1-2 teaspoons curry paste
440g can chopped tomatoes

Preheat oven to 130°C.

Put 1 tablespoon of oil in a large heavy-based frying pan and sauté venison until browned. Transfer to a casserole dish.

Return pan to the heat and add another tablespoon of oil. Sauté onions until starting to soften. Add leek and garlic and continue to cook for a few more minutes.

Add wine, bring to a boil and reduce slightly. Remove from heat and transfer vegetables and liquid to the casserole dish.

Add the chopped carrot, sea salt, curry powder or paste, and tomatoes to the casserole dish. Mix all ingredients together. Cover casserole dish with a heavy lid.

Cook for 3-4 hours, until the meat is tender. Check every hour or so that there is still sufficient liquid. Serve with rice or mashed potatoes and steamed greens.

Wild deer, goat and rabbit are a good choice for meat-eaters as they are nutritionally, ecologically and ethically superior to farmed animals. Grass-fed organic beef and lamb are good choices, too. Organic meat is still a bit more expensive than non-organic, but it is definitely worth the extra expense for so many reasons.

Braised soy ginger chicken

DF

This quick and richly flavoured semi-roasted chicken dish is a family favourite from Anna's childhood.

1 free-range chicken
500 ml chicken stock
4 tablespoons shoyu
¼ cup molasses
4 tablespoons grated fresh ginger

Preheat oven to 160°C.

Put chicken in a snug-fitting saucepan.

Put remaining ingredients in a screw-top jar and shake to combine. Pour over the chicken and cover.

Place over medium heat and simmer chicken and marinade for 10 minutes. Turn chicken over and simmer for a further 10 minutes.

Remove chicken from the liquid, place in an oven dish and bake for 30 minutes or until, when carved with a knife, juices run clear.

Carve and serve with vegetables or salad. The sauce can be made into a nice gravy if desired.

SERVES 4–6

Greek lamb stew with quinoa

DF

1 tablespoon olive oil
4–6 lamb shoulder chops (750g)
½ cup quinoa, rinsed
2 onions, chopped
2 zucchini, sliced
400g can tomatoes
8 cloves garlic, crushed
1 teaspoon sea salt
freshly ground black pepper
2 cups chicken stock
½ cup dry white wine
10–12 black olives
small handful of mint, chopped

Preheat oven to 160°C.

Heat oil in a heavy-based frying pan and brown lamb chops on both sides. Transfer to a large casserole dish.

Scatter over the quinoa, onion, zucchini, tomatoes, garlic, salt and pepper. Pour on the chicken stock and wine and cover with a tight-fitting lid or foil and cook for 1–1½ hours until lamb is tender.

To serve, sprinkle with olives and mint.

SERVES 4–6

Once the staple of Incan warriors, quinoa has become a popular gluten-free alternative to rice, bulgur wheat and pasta. It is a valuable food for vegetarians as it supplies complete protein. With its nutty flavour and fluffy texture, it adapts well to sweet and savoury recipes.

Ginger beef salad

DF

In this recipe the beef is cooked rare. Just searing the outside gives the meat a delicious texture and flavour, and leaves certain beneficial enzymes and nutrients intact.

1 teaspoon sesame or coconut oil
300g sirloin beef, cut into 1.5cm-thick steaks
2 tablespoons lemon juice
2 tablespoons olive oil
1 teaspoon toasted sesame oil
2 tablespoons shoyu
2 teaspoons grated fresh ginger
2 tablespoons sesame seeds, toasted
1 red capsicum, deseeded and sliced
200g snow peas or other greens, blanched
250g mung bean sprouts

Put sesame or coconut oil in a hot frying pan. Sear steaks briefly on each side until cooked rare or medium-rare. Transfer to a chopping board and leave for 10 minutes to cool.

Put lemon juice, olive oil, toasted sesame oil, shoyu and ginger in a medium-sized bowl and stir to combine.

Thinly slice the meat. Add to bowl and mix gently with the marinade. Place in refrigerator for at least 30 minutes to marinate.

To serve, transfer meat and marinade into a large bowl. Add sesame seeds, red capsicum, snow peas and mung bean sprouts. Toss gently together and serve in individual bowls.

SERVES 4

Chicken tagine with lemon and olives

DF

This spicy aromatic North African dish is a real crowd-pleaser. Any leftovers will freeze well for another meal.

MARINADE
⅔ cup olive oil
1 tablespoon turmeric
1 tablespoon paprika
1 teaspoon salt
pinch of cayenne pepper
½ teaspoon black pepper

2kg free-range chicken legs, trimmed of excess skin and fat
4 onions, diced
4 cloves garlic, crushed
4 large tomatoes, chopped
2cm piece fresh ginger, grated
juice of 1 lemon
1 bunch fresh coriander, chopped
1 cup green olives
4 preserved lemons (preserved in salt), cut into quarters

Mix marinade ingredients together. Add meat and stir to coat. Refrigerate all day or overnight.

Heat a large frying pan over medium heat. Using tongs, remove chicken pieces from marinade and place in frying pan. (This may need to be done in 2-3 batches.) Sauté chicken on each side until golden, then remove to a large oven dish with a tight-fitting lid and set aside. Preheat oven to 180°C.

Pour remaining marinade into frying pan, add onions and sauté until softened. Add garlic, tomatoes and ginger and simmer, stirring frequently, for 10 minutes over low heat.

Pour sauce over chicken, cover and place in oven. Cook for 20 minutes, then add lemon juice, coriander, olives and preserved lemons.

Continue cooking until olives and lemons are heated through.

Serve with quinoa or rice.

SERVES 8

Ginger is a warming spice known for improving digestion and circulation. Fresh ginger tea has been found to reduce nausea and cold symptoms. Add fresh grated ginger to oriental soups, curries, marinades, dressings and salads or try mixing it into a tropical fruit salad.

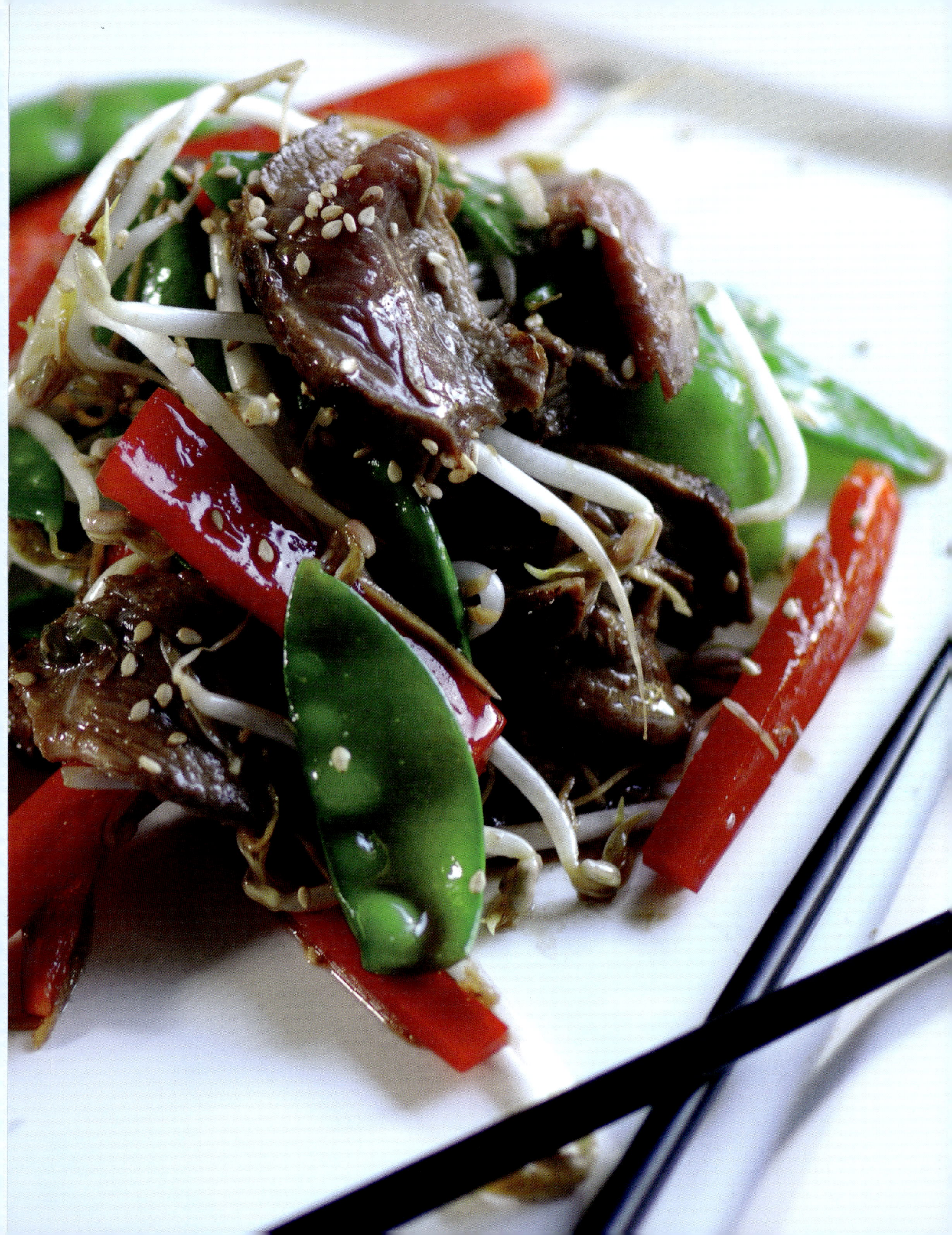

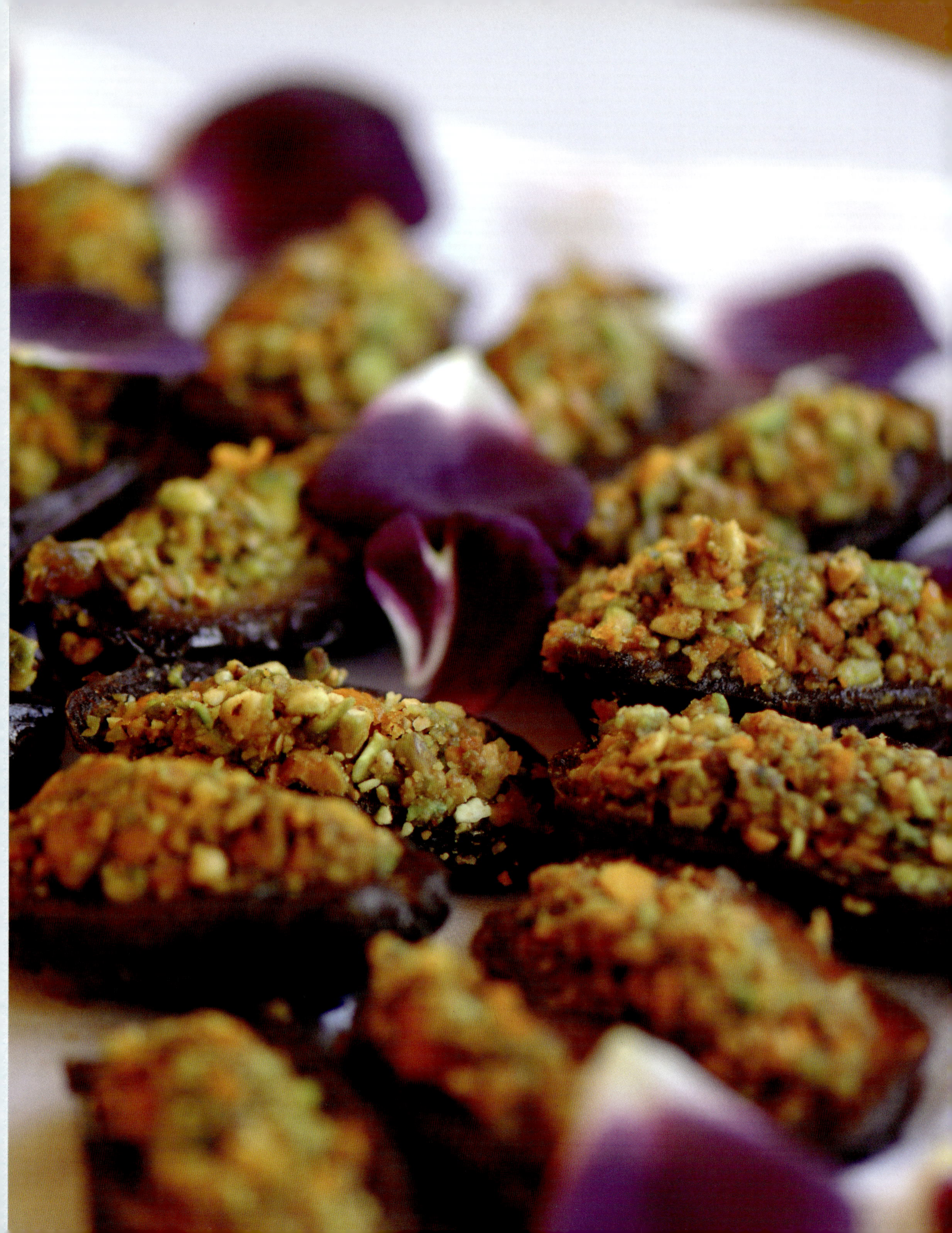

Persian delights

DF V

Plump, moist, fresh Medjool dates are a treat as they are, and this simple pistachio-nut filling makes them an exotic and elegant after-dinner surprise.

¼ cup shelled pistachio nuts
1 teaspoon honey
¼ teaspoon ground cardamom
rind of 1 orange, chopped fine
1 teaspoon rosewater or orange juice
6 fresh Medjool dates

Grind the pistachio nuts in a mortar and pestle almost to a powder, but with a few chunks remaining. Add honey, cardamom, orange zest and rosewater or orange juice. Continue to grind until it is well combined and sticks together.

With a small knife, split each date in half and remove the pit. Stuff each halved date with about 1 teaspoon of pistachio mixture.

Serve on a beautiful platter and decorate with rose petals.

MAKES 12 BITE-SIZED TREATS

Zucchini chocolate no-bake cake

DF V

A wonderful use for all those summer zucchini, this cake is raw, vegan and surprisingly delicious! It is more like a dense pudding in consistency and holds its shape well if formed in a cake tin or sculpted into shape.

½ cup walnuts
½ cup hazelnuts
4 tablespoons desiccated coconut
⅓ cup ground sesame seeds
½ cup ground flaxseed
⅓ cup cocoa powder
½ teaspoon ground cinnamon
500g zucchini, chopped
½ cup raisins
¾ cup soft dates, pitted and chopped

Line a 20cm x 20cm cake tin or casserole dish with cling film.

Put walnuts and hazelnuts in a food processor and pulse until still a bit chunky. Transfer ½ cup of these nut chunks into a large bowl and set aside until required. Continue processing remaining nuts until very fine. Add coconut, ground sesame seeds and flaxseed, cocoa and cinnamon and pulse again until well mixed. Add all this to the nuts in the bowl.

Put chopped zucchini in food processor and blend to a pulp. Add raisins and dates. Process again until well mixed.

Add zucchini mixture to nut mixture and knead together.

Spread mixture into prepared tin and press flat. Cover and refrigerate until ready to serve. It is best to leave for at least 2 hours as it will become firmer.

Remove top layer of cling film and turn cake out onto a serving dish.

Spread a layer of *Cashew cream* (see *Fresh fig tart*, page 112) on top. Garnish with flowers or dust with cocoa powder.

SERVES 10

Cinnamon not only has a lovely flavour, it also helps the heart. Research has shown ¼–1½ teaspoons of cinnamon per day can reduce cholesterol, triglycerides and blood glucose. This suggests cinnamon may be beneficial for diabetics and people at risk of heart disease. According to Ayurveda and Chinese medicine, cinnamon is excellent for improving circulation and digestion.

Fresh fig tart

DF V

Fresh local figs can only be enjoyed in late summer and autumn as they need to ripen on the tree. Therefore, in our house we call this no-bake dessert Gratitude Pie, as fresh figs remind us to be grateful for the seasons and for locally grown food!

BASE
⅔ cup almonds
½ cup dried figs, chopped
½ cup desiccated coconut
½ cup sesame seeds, ground fine in a spice grinder
pinch of sea salt

CASHEW CREAM
1½ cups cashew pieces
2 tablespoons maple syrup or honey
½ cup water

TOPPING
500g fresh figs
1 tablespoon lavender petals (optional)
2 tablespoons honey

☼ Soak almonds and cashew pieces separately overnight.

To make the base, put drained and rinsed almonds and dried figs in a food processor and process until mixture is fine and crumbly.

Add coconut, ground sesame and salt. Process until well combined. (Mixture should stick together when squeezed in your fingers.)

Press into a 20cm flan dish with removable base. Refrigerate until required.

To make the cashew cream, drain and rinse cashew nuts and put in a blender or food processor with maple syrup or honey and water. Blend until fairly smooth.

To assemble tart, spread cashew cream evenly across the base. Trim stalks from figs then slice in half or in chunky wedges. Arrange figs on top of cashew cream.

Mix lavender petals, if using, and honey together with just enough warm water to make a thick syrup. Drizzle syrup over figs. Serve at room temperature.

Leftover tart will keep for several days in the refrigerator. It can also be frozen.

SERVES 12

To make the colourful tart on page 2, use the *Fresh fig tart* recipe but replace the topping with rings of sliced stonefruit and cherries instead of fresh figs.

Spiced tamarillo compote

DF V

Tamarillos, also known as tree tomatoes, are a wonderful blend of bitter, sweet and sour. Most people find they need some sweetening. This recipe requires no cooking. The dried fruit is softened with tamarillo juice, creating a sweet, smooth blend of flavours.

6–7 tamarillos (500g)
⅓ cup pitted dates, diced
⅓ cup sultanas
1 teaspoon mixed spice
¼ teaspoon ginger powder
small pinch of sea salt

Using a small sharp knife, cut a cross in the pointy end of each tamarillo. Place in a large bowl and pour on enough boiling water to cover. Leave for 1 minute, then drain and cool. When cool enough to handle, use the small knife again to peel off the skins, which should come away easily.

Cut each tamarillo in half lengthwise, then into 3 or 4 thick slices. Place in a bowl and add remaining ingredients. Mix gently together. Cover bowl and place in the refrigerator. Leave for at least 24 hours before serving.

SERVES 4

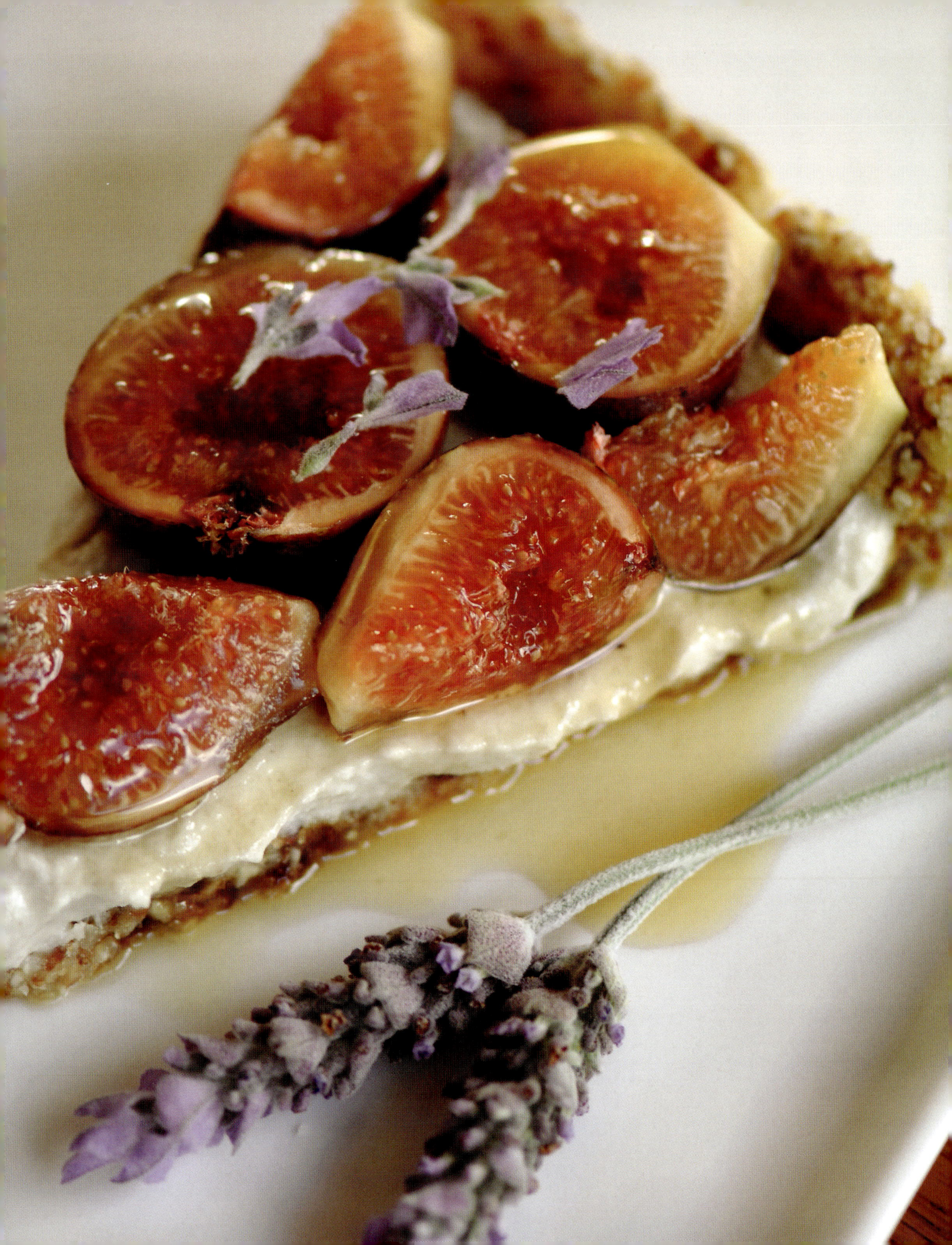

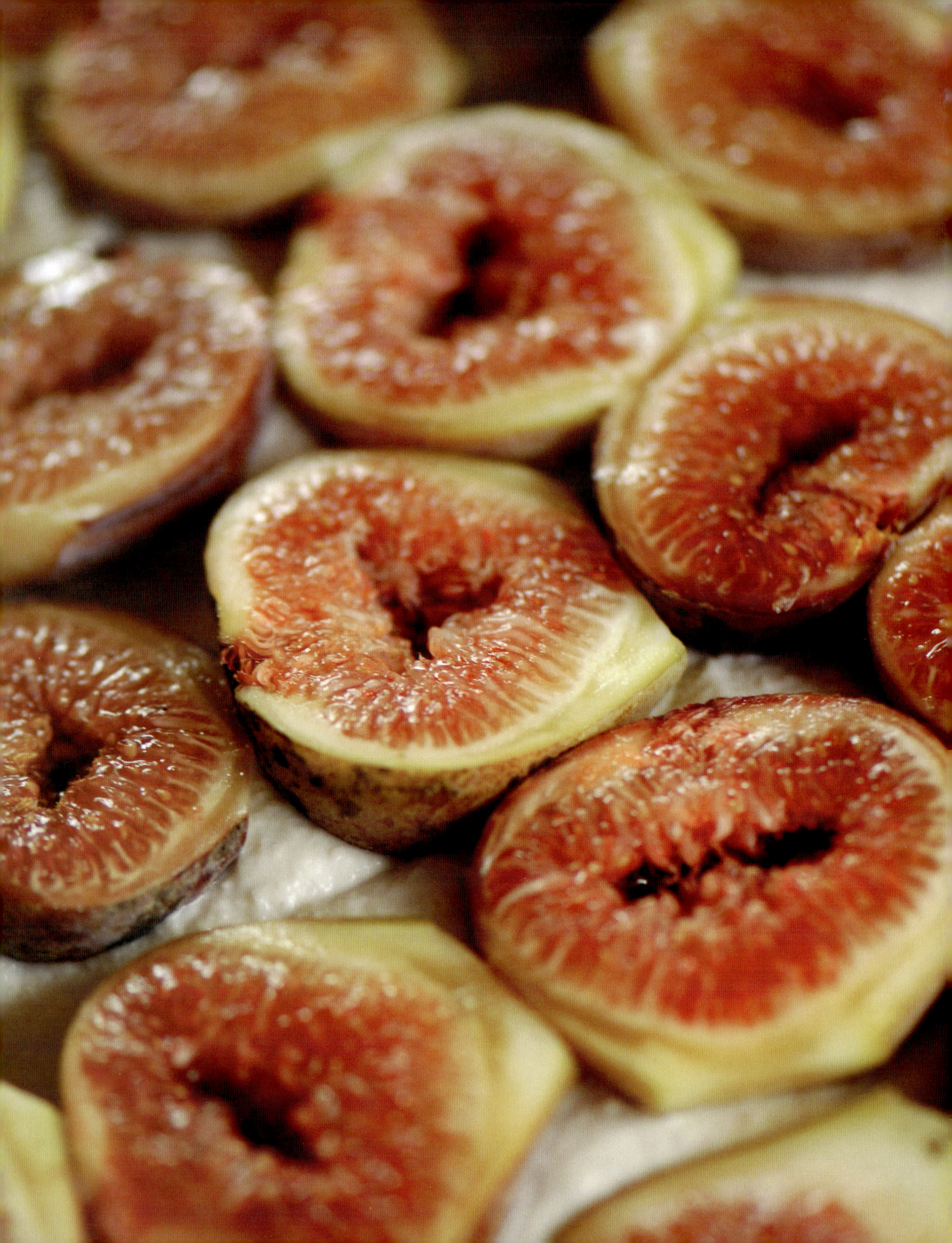

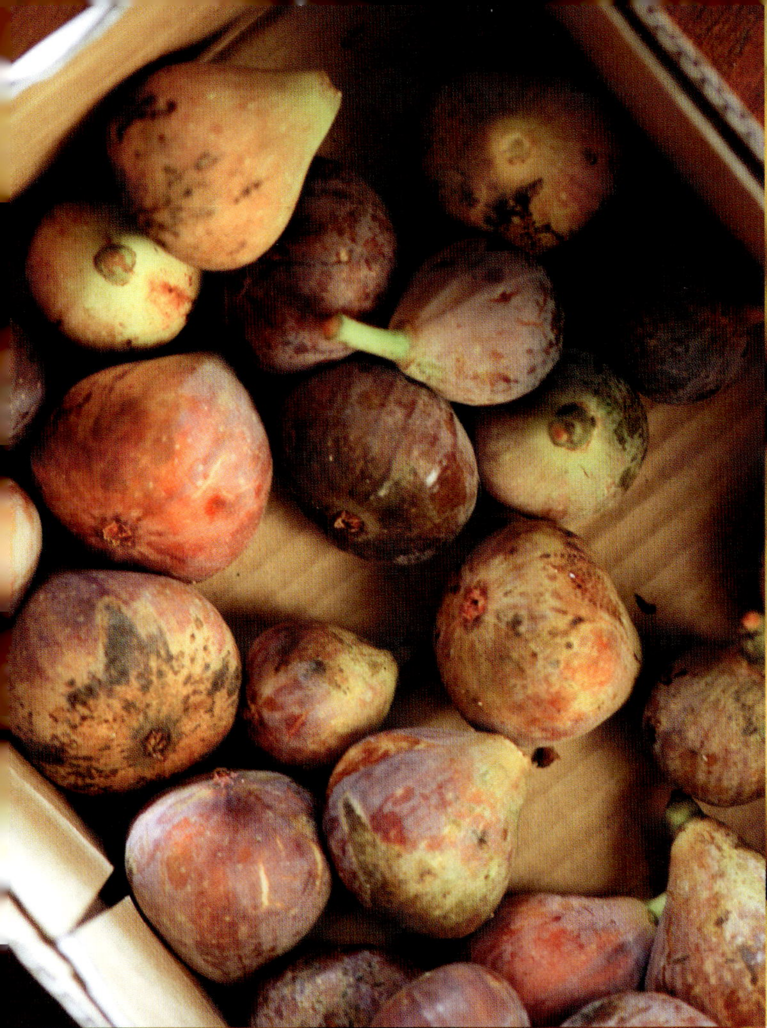
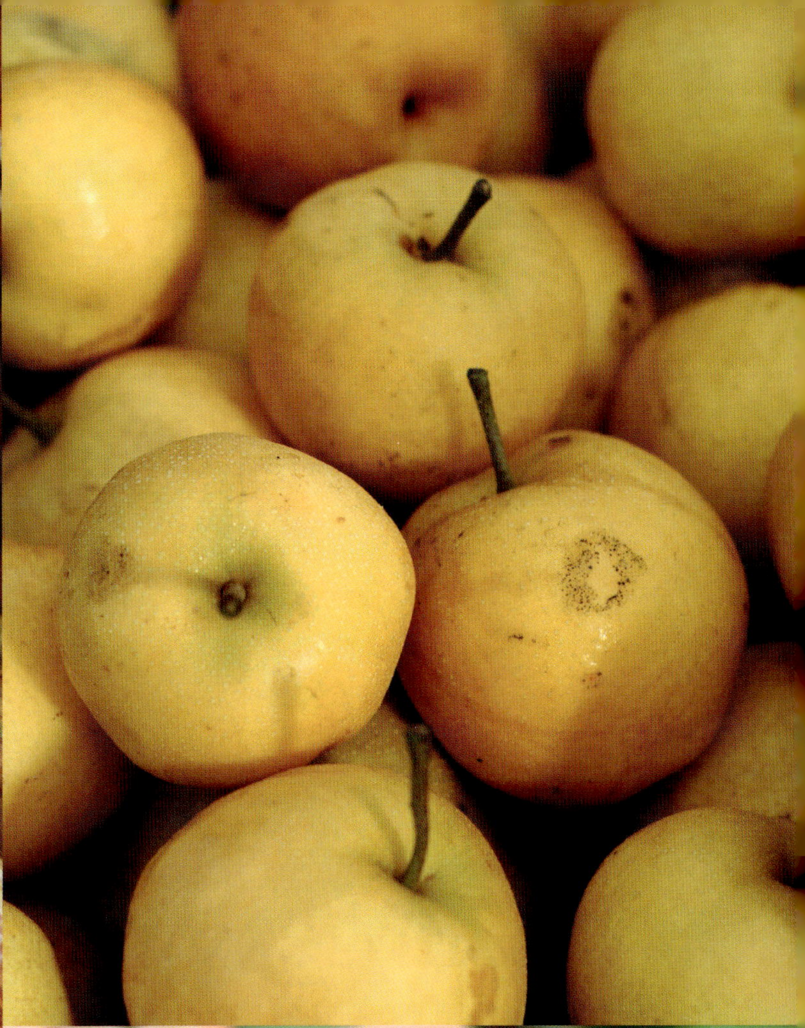
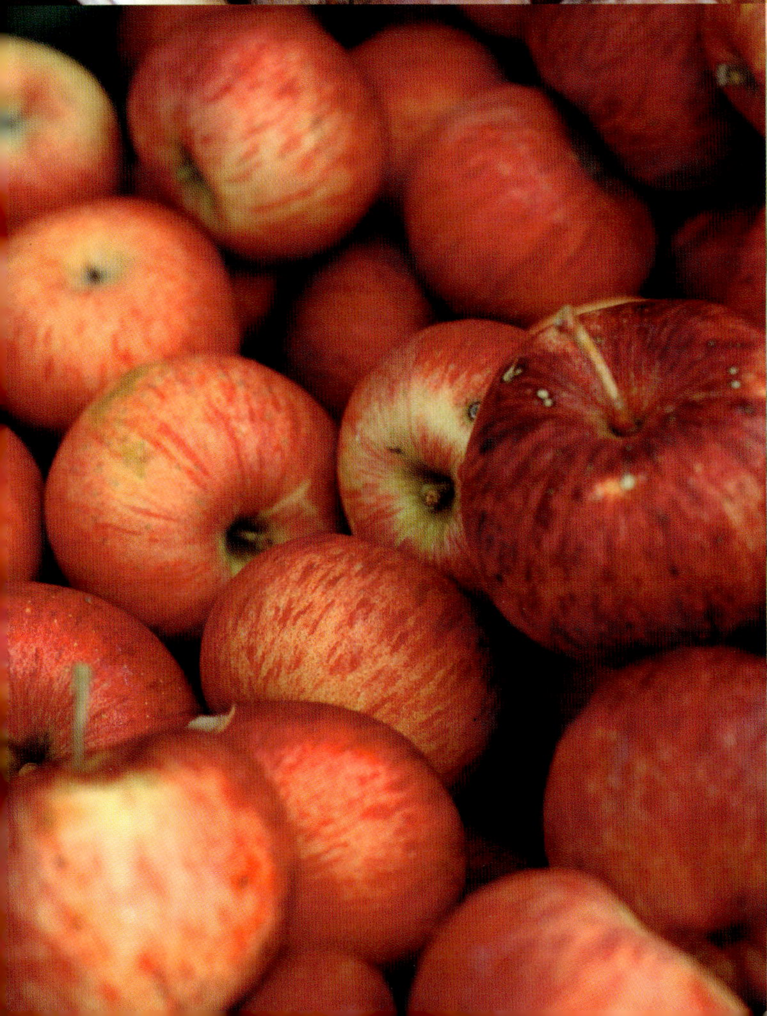
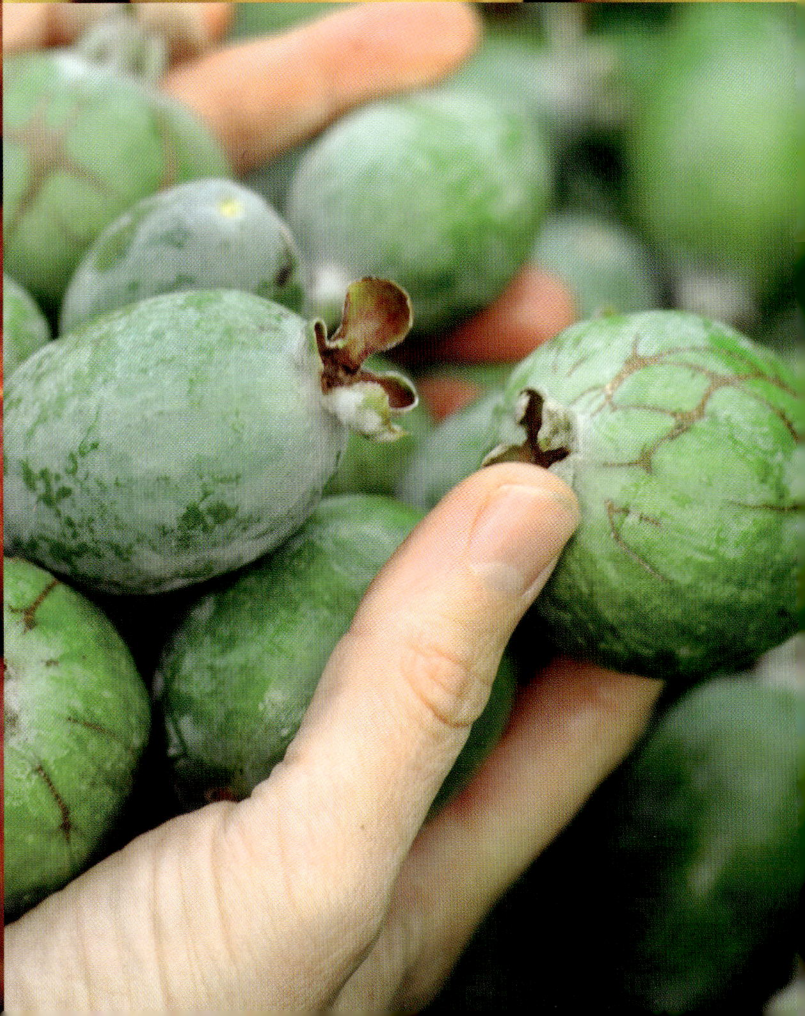

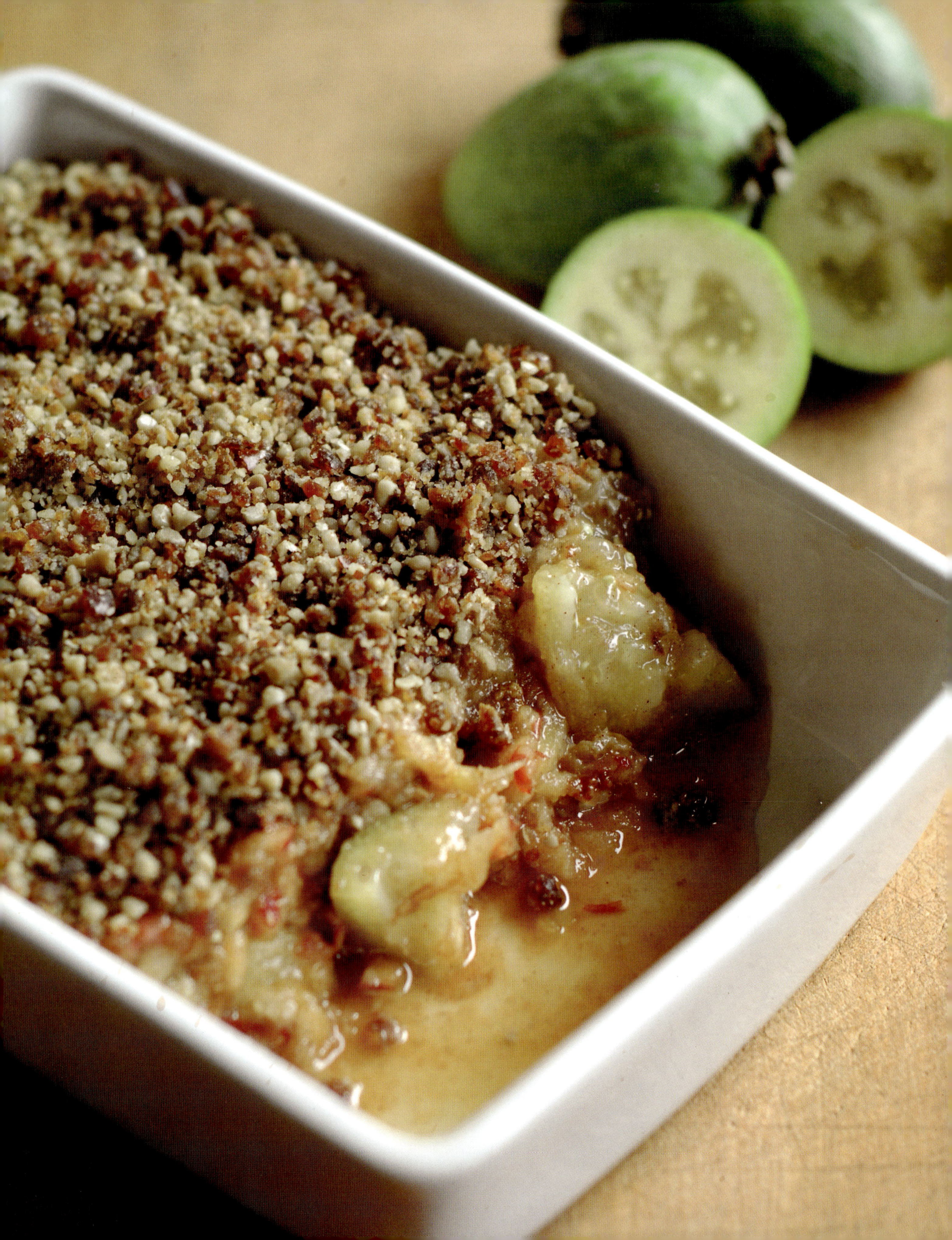

Feijoa nut crumble

DF V

This warm but raw dessert is a wonderful way to enjoy feijoas, which thrive in a subtropical climate. For an alternative, replace the feijoas with 1½ cups of frozen berries. Heat the crumble just enough to warm through to preserve the fresh flavour of the fruit.

CRUMBLE TOPPING
½ cup sunflower seeds
½ cup dates, pitted and chopped
½ cup walnuts
½ teaspoon ginger powder
pinch of sea salt

FRUIT BASE
500g feijoas
2 cups grated apple
⅓ cup raisins
1 teaspoon ground cinnamon
small pinch of ground cloves
pinch of sea salt

Preheat oven to 120°C.

To make topping, place all ingredients in a food processor and process until mixture has a fine texture. Transfer to a separate bowl until required. (There's no need to wash the food processor before making the fruit base.)

To make fruit base, halve feijoas and scoop out flesh with a spoon into a large bowl. Chop into small chunks.

Put 1 cup of grated apple, raisins, cinnamon, cloves and sea salt in a food processor and process for a few seconds until raisins are mostly puréed.

Transfer mixture to bowl containing feijoas and remaining grated apple. Mix gently with a large spoon.

Place fruit mixture into a shallow ceramic or ovenproof dish and spread out evenly. Sprinkle the crumble mixture on top.

Before serving, heat for 30–40 minutes until warmed through.

Serve with fresh whipped cream or *Soft-serve banana ice-cream* (see page 125).

SERVES 6

Coconut orange cake

DF

Once the oranges are cooked, this low-sugar cake is super-fast to put together, although a food processor is essential.

, thin-skinned oranges

ie sugar, xylitol

ted coconut
e flour (see page 18)
en-free baking powder

Scrub fruit well. Place in a saucepan over medium heat, cover with water and bring to a boil. Reduce heat to a simmer, cover with a lid and simmer for 1 hour. Change water and simmer for 1 hour further. Drain and, when cool enough to handle, cut fruit in half carefully, and remove any seeds.

Preheat oven to 175°C. Grease and line a medium-sized spring-form cake tin.

Put fruit, skin and all, in a food processor and process to a smooth purée.

Add egg, olive oil and sugar. Process at high speed until thick and lemon-coloured. Add coconut, gluten-free flour and baking powder. Gently pulse to combine. Pour into the prepared tin.

Bake for 45 minutes or until firm and a skewer inserted in the centre comes out clean. Check after 30 minutes and if the top is getting too brown, cover loosely with foil.

SERVES 10–12

Coconut cookies

DF

These soft, chewy, gluten-free cookies are simple to make. Brazil nuts, walnuts or almonds can be used instead of cashews and sunflower seeds.

½ cup cashew pieces
½ cup sunflower seeds
1 egg
1 teaspoon vanilla essence
60g melted butter or coconut oil
⅓ cup whole cane sugar, coconut sugar or raw sugar
½ teaspoon baking soda
pinch of sea salt
1 cup desiccated coconut
2 tablespoons arrowroot

Preheat oven to 180°C. Lightly grease an oven tray.

Put nuts and seeds in a food processor or spice grinder and process until finely ground.

Put egg, vanilla, butter or oil, sweetener, baking soda and salt in a bowl and whisk together. Add ground nuts and seeds, coconut and arrowroot. Mix well.

Working with 1 heaped tablespoon of mixture at a time, press gently to form into a ball and place on prepared tray, leaving about 2cm between each. When all balls are formed, flatten each one slightly so that all are of an even thickness. Bake for 10-15 minutes until brown.

MAKES ABOUT 15 COOKIES

Black rice pudding

DF V

Black rice has a delicious creamy texture and exotic, earthy flavour. The rich, white coconut cream topping is a perfect complement to the sweetened rice. This may be eaten warm or cooled and leftovers will keep in the refrigerator for several days.

1 cup glutinous black rice
4 cups water
50g palm sugar or alternative sweetener
pinch of sea salt

COCONUT CREAM TOPPING
400g can coconut cream
pinch of sea salt
1 teaspoon lemon juice
1 tablespoon arrowroot
½ cup mango, pineapple or papaya, diced (optional)

☀ Wash and rinse black rice in a sieve. Place in a saucepan with 1 litre of water. Leave to soak for at least 4 hours or overnight.

Place saucepan with drained rice and water over medium heat and bring to a boil. Cover with a lid and turn heat to low. Leave to simmer for about 45 minutes, stirring occasionally, until almost all water is absorbed; the rice should now have a creamy texture - like a pudding.

Add sweetener and sea salt to hot rice. Stir well until sugar has dissolved. Spoon rice into small individual bowls.

To make topping, put coconut cream, salt, lemon juice and arrowroot in a small saucepan over low heat and stir to combine. Slowly bring to a boil. The mixture should thicken slightly.

To serve, pour topping over black rice. Garnish with diced fruit, if using.

SERVES 6-8

There are many alternatives to using ordinary sugar in cooking and baking. Natural options include using dried fruit (like cooked puréed dates), maple syrup, honey, whole cane sugar (dehydrated sugar-cane juice), coconut sugar and molasses. Depending on what you are making and your own preferences, you can usually use the above ingredients cup for cup (at least in this cookbook). Two other alternatives are stevia and xylitol. We often use stevia liquid in drinks, and sometimes in baking. Xylitol has a very low glycaemic index; however, it is a highly processed mineral-deficient food that is best used in moderation.

Black rice pudding

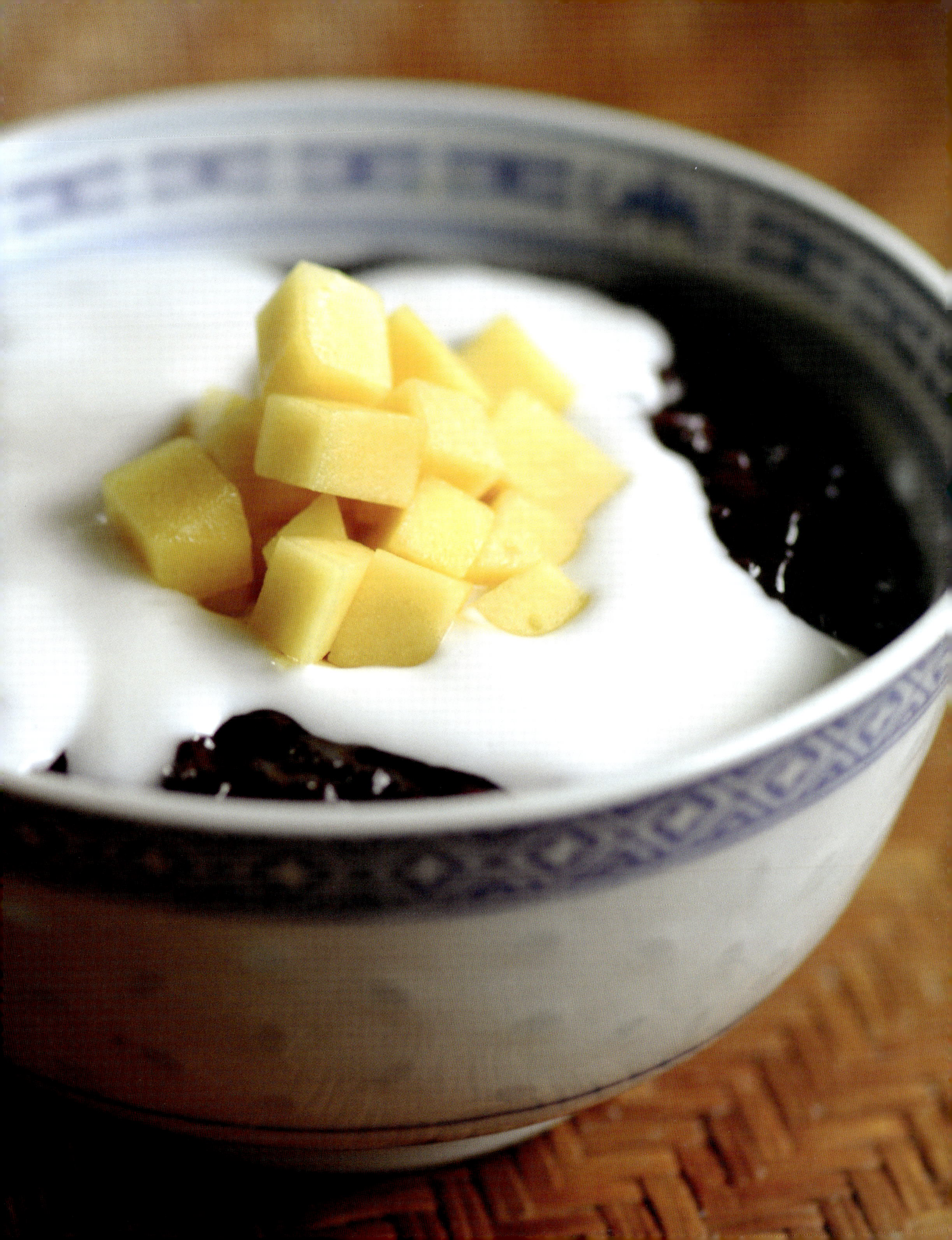

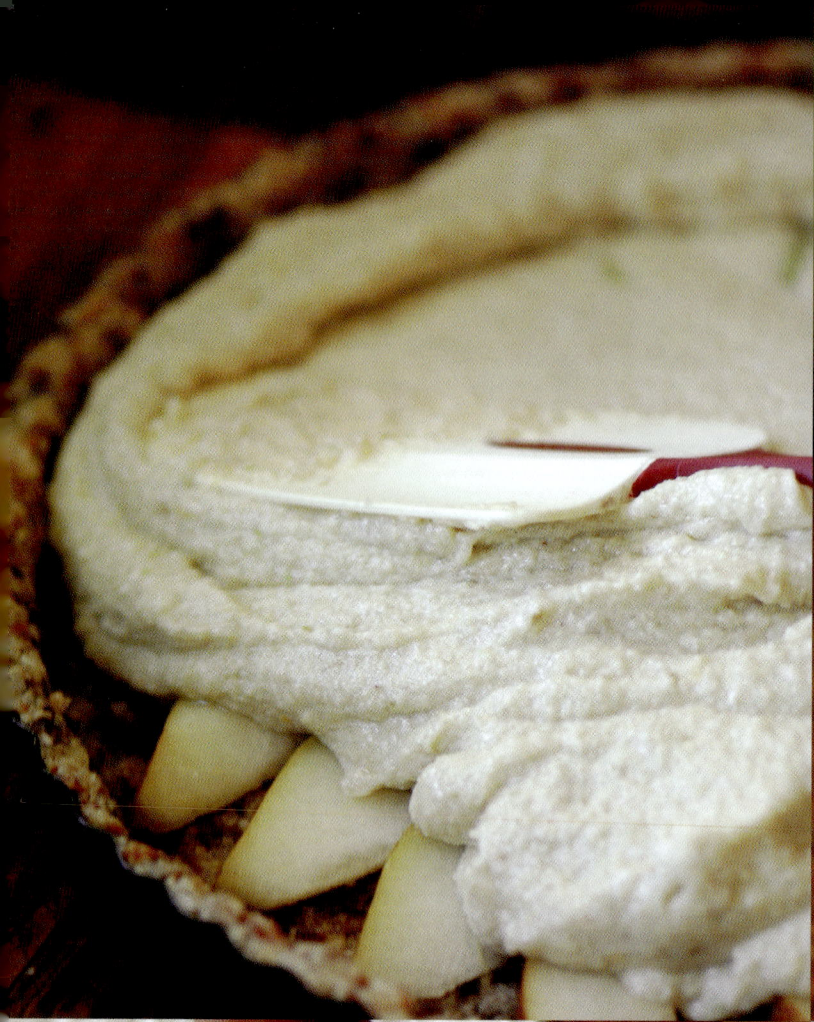
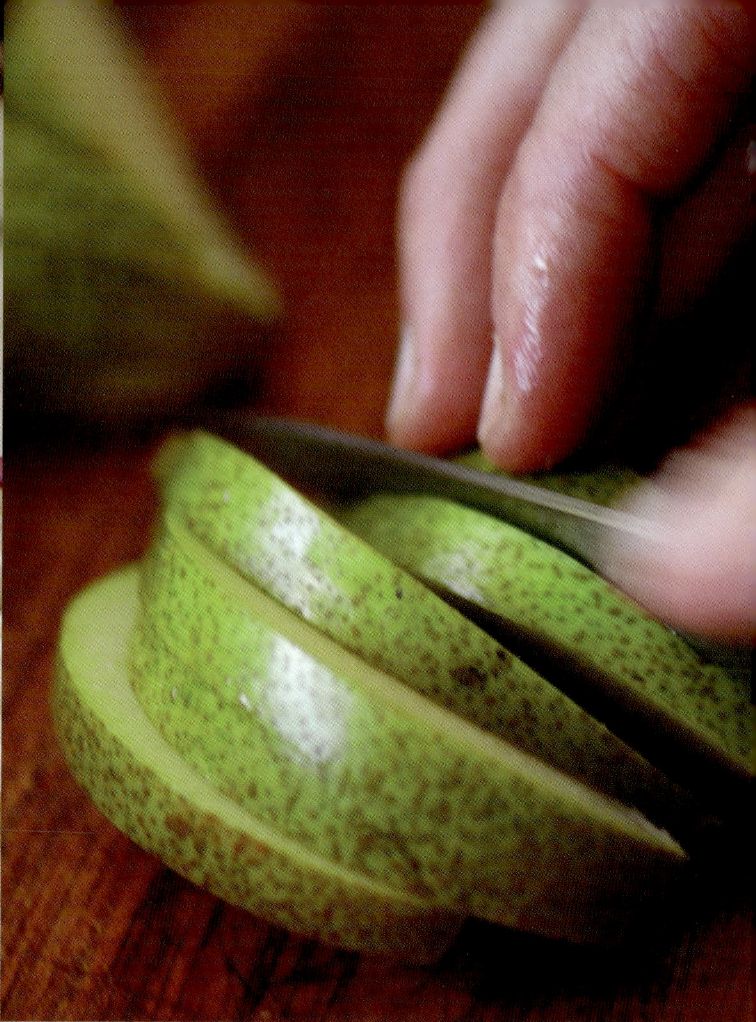
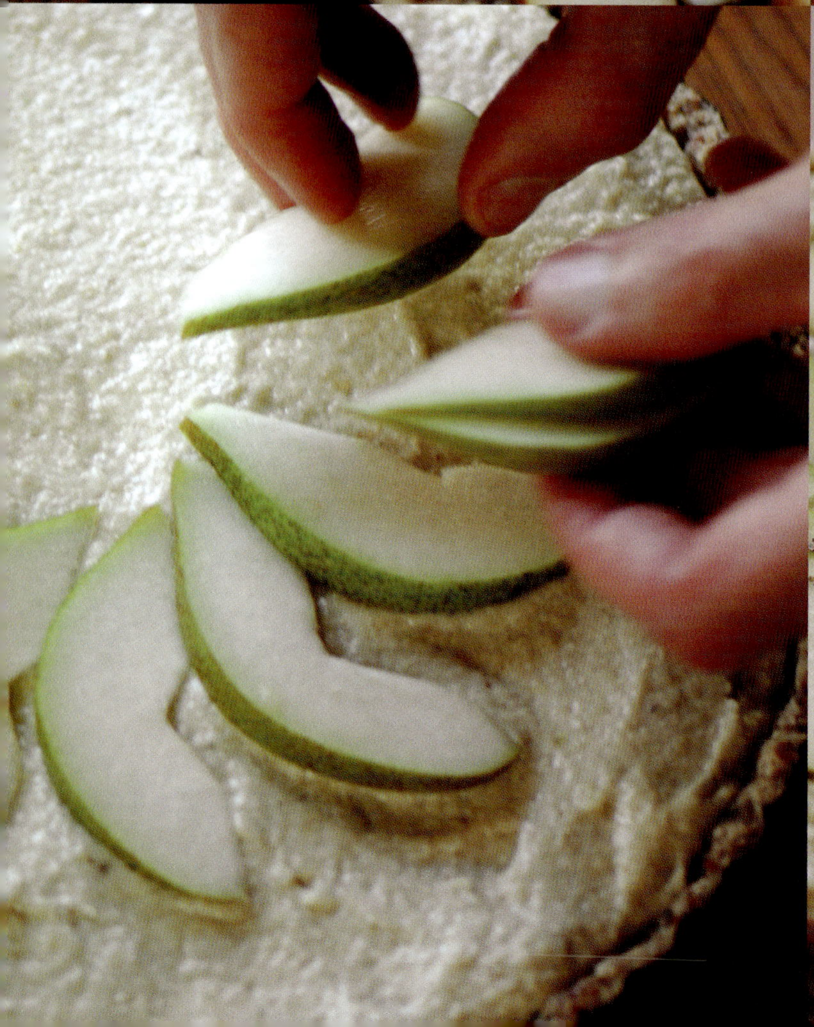
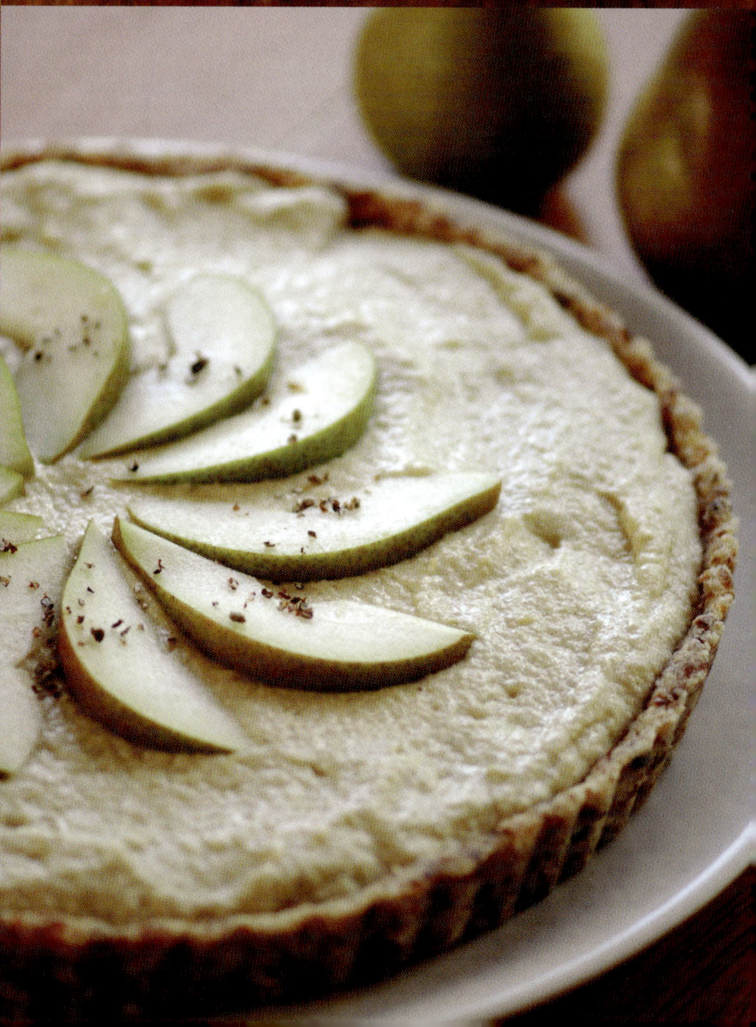

Pear and cardamom tart

DF V

This dessert looks and tastes a treat. It is simple to make, requiring no baking. Psyllium is not essential to this recipe but it does help the filling to set, making the tart easier to slice and serve.

BASE
⅔ cup almonds
½ cup dates, chopped and pitted
½ cup desiccated coconut
½ cup sesame seeds, finely ground in a spice or coffee grinder
1 teaspoon ginger powder
pinch of sea salt

FILLING
1 cup cashew pieces
100g dried apricots
1 large pear, roughly chopped
1 teaspoon ground cardamom
½ teaspoon ground cloves
2 tablespoons psyllium hulls
½ teaspoon sea salt
2–3 pears, sliced thinly

Put almonds for base and cashews for filling in separate bowls and cover with water. Soak overnight. Soak dried apricots overnight in ⅔ cup of water.

Drain almonds and put in a food processor with dates. Process until fine and crumbly.

Add coconut, ground sesame seeds, ginger and salt. Continue to process until well combined. (The mixture should stick together when squeezed in your fingers.)

Press mixture into a 20cm flan dish with a removable base. Refrigerate while making topping. (There's no need to wash food processor before making filling.)

To make filling, drain cashews and put in food processor with the roughly chopped pear, apricots (including most of the soaking liquid), spices, psyllium and salt. Process until smooth.

Remove base from refrigerator and arrange sliced pear over base, reserving a few slices to decorate the top.

Pour cashew and apricot filling over pears and spread evenly.

Decorate tart by carefully arranging reserved pear slices on top.

SERVES 8–10

Strawberry kanten

DF V

Traditional kanten jelly is regaining popularity in Japan as the agar agar – a natural setting agent derived from seaweed – moderates the absorption of sugar into the blood and supports bowel health.

3½ cups apple juice
pinch of sea salt
1 teaspoon pure vanilla essence
4½ tablespoons agar agar flakes
3 tablespoons arrowroot
300g mixed fresh or frozen berries

Choose a tray for the jelly, about 20cm x 15cm. You could also make the jelly in a bowl. If you wish to get your jelly out in one piece, line tray or bowl with cling film.

Pour 3 cups apple juice into a small saucepan. Add salt and vanilla, and sprinkle on agar agar flakes. Heat slowly until agar agar dissolves. Gradually bring to a boil, turn down heat and simmer for 5 minutes.

Mix arrowroot powder in remaining apple juice until dissolved. Pour this slowly into the saucepan, whisking continuously. Keep whisking until whole mixture thickens and returns to the boil.

Place berries in prepared tray or bowl. Carefully pour on the kanten jelly, taking care to keep the berries evenly distributed. Refrigerate until cool and set.

When set, slice into squares, or scoop out with a spoon. Serve with *Cashew cream* (see *Fresh fig tart*, page 112) or yoghurt.

SERVES 6

Pear and cardamon tart

Sunny banana walnut truffles

DF V

1½ cups walnuts
½ cup dried coconut
100g chopped dried figs (about 6-7 figs)
2 tablespoons buckwheat groats
2 tablespoons ground linseed
½ large ripe banana
1 teaspoon ginger powder
pinch of sea salt
extra desiccated coconut

Put walnuts in a food processor. Blend on high speed until they are the texture of coarse breadcrumbs. Add remaining ingredients and blend briefly until combined.

Form into little balls. Leave as they are or roll each ball in coconut, carob or sesame seeds.

MAKES ABOUT 10 SNACK-SIZED BALLS

Cashew apricot bliss balls

DF V

1½ cups cashew pieces
1½ cups dried apricots, roughly chopped
½ cup desiccated coconut
½ teaspoon ginger powder
¼ teaspoon ground cardamom
pinch of sea salt
zest of 1 orange
extra desiccated coconut

Put all ingredients in a food processor and process for several minutes until mixture can be pressed into a ball. If necessary, add a little water to help mixture combine. (Start with just 1 teaspoon of water.)

Form into little balls. Roll each ball in coconut, if desired.

MAKES ABOUT 16 SNACK-SIZED BALLS

Apricot shortcake

300g dried apricots
3 cups water
50g coconut sugar (or fine raw sugar)
2 tablespoons honey
115g butter, softened
1 egg
145g gluten-free flour (see page 18)
1 teaspoon gluten-free baking powder
¼ teaspoon sea salt

Simmer apricots in water until they are soft and the water has almost evaporated. Remove from heat. When cool blend in a food processor to a smooth purée.

Preheat oven to 170°C. Grease a 25cm springform cake tin or flan dish.

Place butter, sugar and honey into a cake mixer or food processor. Blend until smooth and fluffy. Add egg and beat in. Sift dry ingredients. Pulse gently or fold into butter mixture with a large spoon.

Dollop ⅔ of mixture into the baking pan. Use wet hands and press mixture into the base and slightly up the sides. It doesn't need to be smooth, just roughly the same thickness across the base.

Spread the apricot mixture on top. Then drop teaspoonfuls of remaining mix across the top of the apricot spread and, using wet hands, spread them out slightly. There will be gaps in the topping - that's OK!

Bake for about 25 minutes or until the topping is turning golden brown.

Serve warm or cold with yoghurt, cream or *Cashew cream* (see *Fresh fig tart*, page 112)

SERVES 8-10

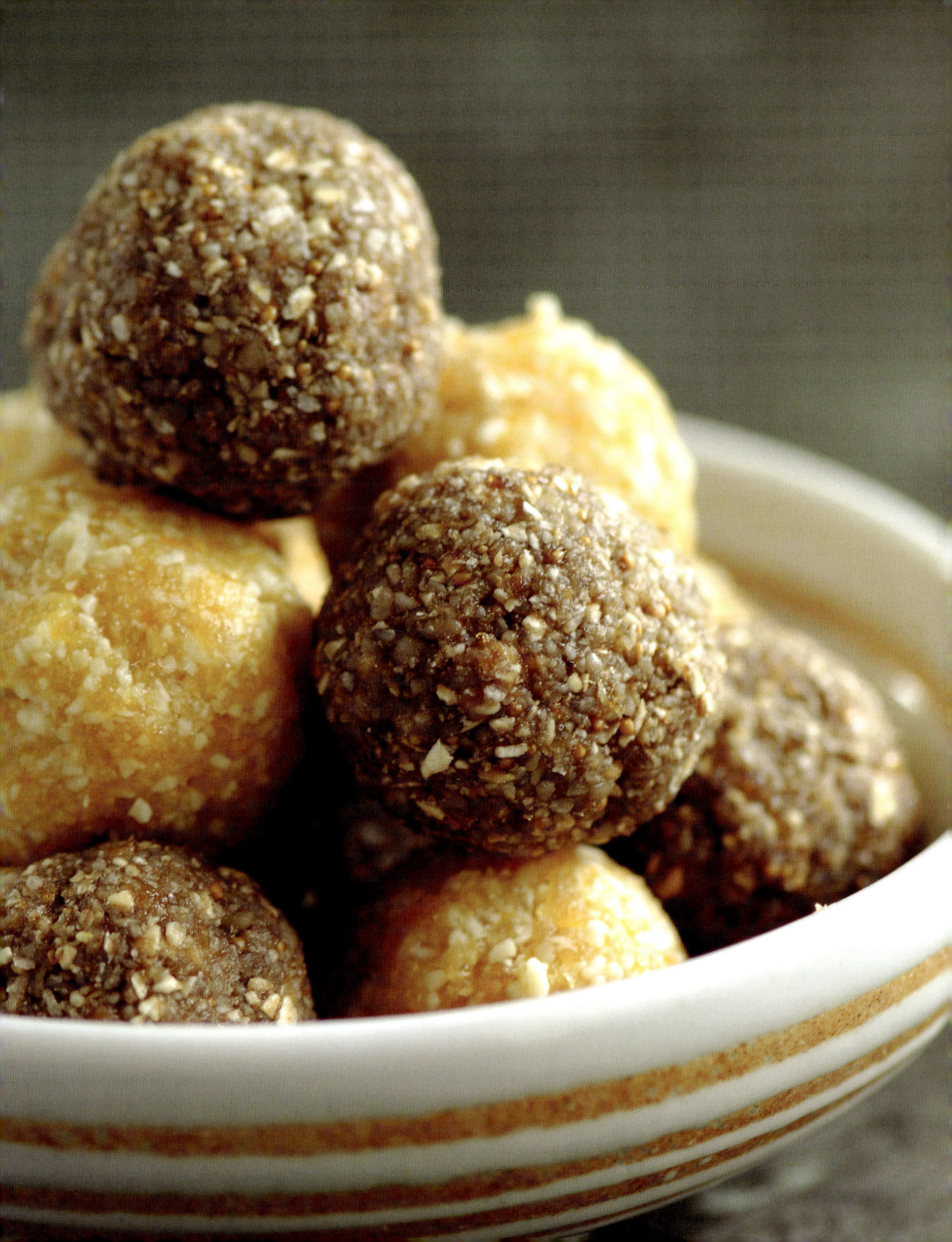

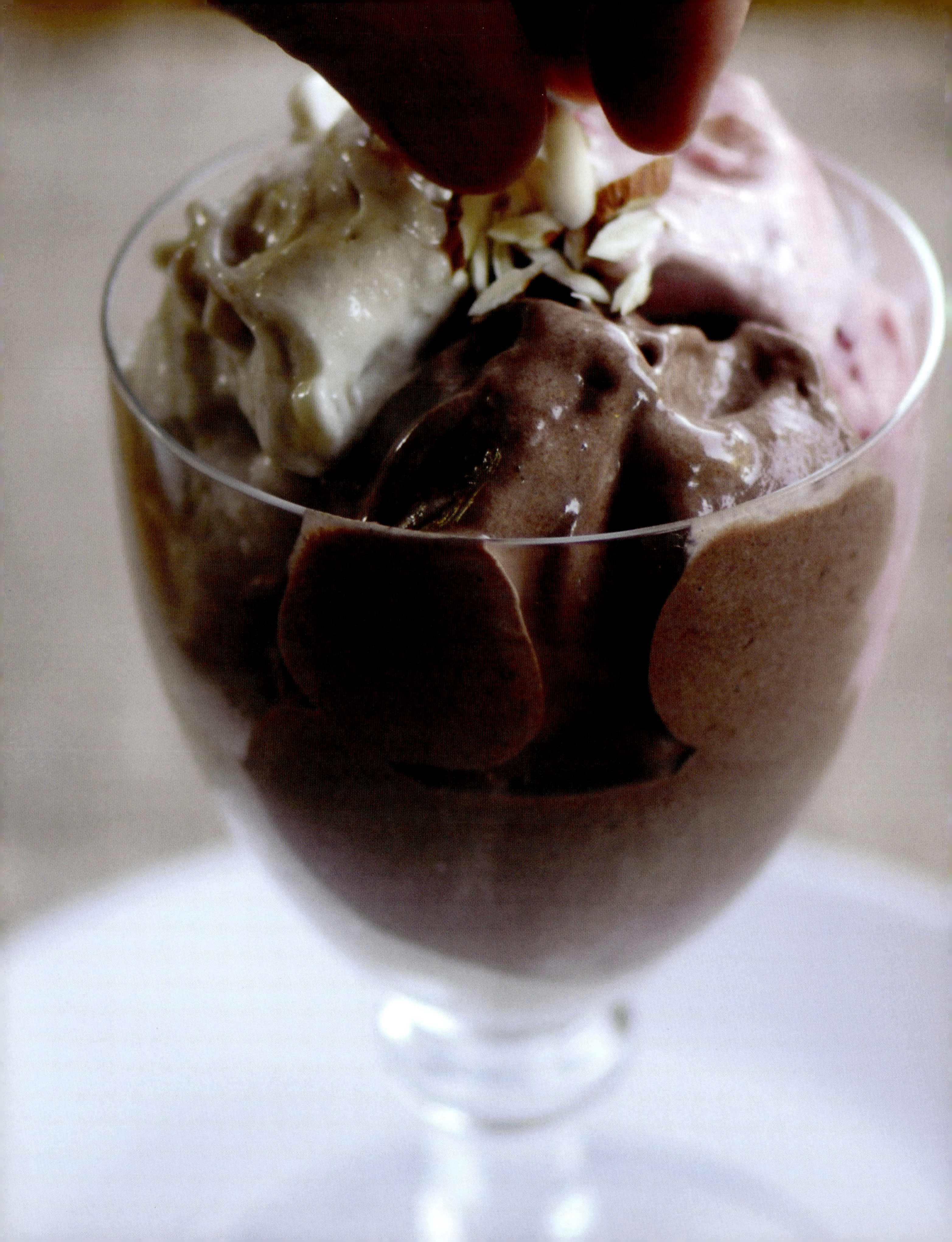

Soft-serve banana ice-cream

DF V

These banana-based ice-creams have a soft, creamy consistency and need to be consumed immediately, but that is seldom a problem! Dairy-free and without added sugar, they are perfect for people with dietary restrictions.

VANILLA BANANA ICE-CREAM
3 bananas
⅓ cup cashew pieces
150ml coconut cream, rice milk or soy milk
1 teaspoon pure vanilla essence

CHOCOLATE BANANA ICE-CREAM
3 bananas
⅓ cup cashew pieces
150ml coconut cream, rice milk or soy milk
3 tablespoons cocoa powder or carob
1 teaspoon ginger powder
½ teaspoon pure vanilla essence

RASPBERRY BANANA ICE-CREAM
3 bananas
⅓ cup cashew pieces
150ml coconut cream, rice milk or soy milk
½ cup frozen raspberries

☀ Prepare bananas at least 8 hours in advance. Chop bananas into bite-sized pieces and freeze. Soak cashew pieces overnight and drain.

Put all ingredients except bananas in a food processor and process until well puréed. With the food processor still running, gradually add frozen banana pieces.

Serve immediately, as it goes very hard when frozen.

EACH RECIPE SERVES 4

Piña colada ice-cream

DF V

When we have surplus fruit we chop it into small pieces and freeze it ready to make this delicious frozen dessert. The ice-cream will go completely solid if placed back in the freezer, so only make as much as you need.

½ pineapple
½ fresh banana
¼ cup coconut cream

Prepare pineapple at least 8 hours in advance. Remove skin and tough core, chop flesh into bite-sized pieces and freeze.

Put banana and coconut cream in a food processor or strong blender. Blend until smooth.

With the food processor still running, gradually add frozen pineapple pieces, then blend until mixture is smooth.

Spoon into 4 small bowls and eat immediately.

SERVES 4

For some, food is merely a fuel, used to top up energy levels when required. For others, food and emotions are bound up in a complex relationship of pleasure and guilt. Judging yourself for 'being naughty' in relation to food or worrying about getting fat when eating is more damaging to your health than the occasional piece of cake! If you do struggle with food issues, we recommend you seek help from an experienced therapist, a 12-step programme, or try EFT (Emotional Freedom Technique).

Soft-serve banana ice-cream

Chocolate mint squares

DF V

Here's our delicious gluten-, dairy- and sugar-free alternative to chocolate fudge. Serve these squares with fresh strawberries, all piled up together for dramatic effect.

½ cup almonds
½ cup sesame seeds
⅓ cup desiccated coconut
⅓ cup cocoa powder
8 large dried figs (150g), sliced
½ cup dates, pitted and chopped
2 drops pure peppermint essence
2 tablespoons water

☀ Soak almonds in water overnight, then drain.

Line a 10cm x 20cm loaf tin with cling film.

Grind sesame seeds in a spice grinder or coffee mill until fine. (Do this in 2-3 batches if necessary.)

Put all ingredients in a food processor and process on high speed until mixture has a fine, crumbly texture. Squeeze some of the mixture in your fingers - it should be just moist enough to hold together. Add a little bit more water if necessary.

Press mixture into the bottom of prepared loaf tin and refrigerate for 30 minutes until firm.

To serve, remove from tin and slice into squares.

MAKES ABOUT 18 SQUARES

Beetroot chocolate cake

DF

This may sound like an odd combination for a cake, but most people are amazed when they try it. The beetroot keeps the cake moist, just as carrots do in a carrot cake. What a great way to eat vegetables, nuts and seeds!

¼ cup flaxseed
⅓ cup almonds
⅓ cup sunflower seeds
300g beetroot, trimmed and scrubbed
¾ cup olive oil or melted butter
1 cup whole cane sugar or brown sugar
2 free-range eggs
½ teaspoon pure vanilla essence
1 cup gluten-free flour (see page 18)
2 teaspoons gluten-free baking powder
½ cup cocoa

Preheat oven to 180°C. Grease and flour a 23cm round cake tin.

Grind flaxseed fine in a spice grinder or mortar and pestle. Transfer to a large bowl.

In a food processor, grind almonds and sunflower seeds as fine as possible using the S blade. Add to the flaxseed.

Grate beetroot using the fine grating attachment of a food processor. Add to nuts and seeds.

Fit blending blade to food processor. Place oil, sugar, eggs and vanilla into food processor. Blend on high for a couple of minutes. Transfer to a large bowl. Sift flour, baking powder, and cocoa onto the wet mix. Add grated beetroot, ground nuts and seeds. Stir everything together until just combined. (The mixing can be completed in the food processor if it is large enough.)

Pour into prepared tin and bake for 35-40 minutes until an inserted skewer comes out clean.

SERVES 8-12

We make *Beetroot chocolate cake* in a food processor. There's a bit of juggling with the blending and grating attachments, but there's no need to wash out the processor bowl between any of these steps.

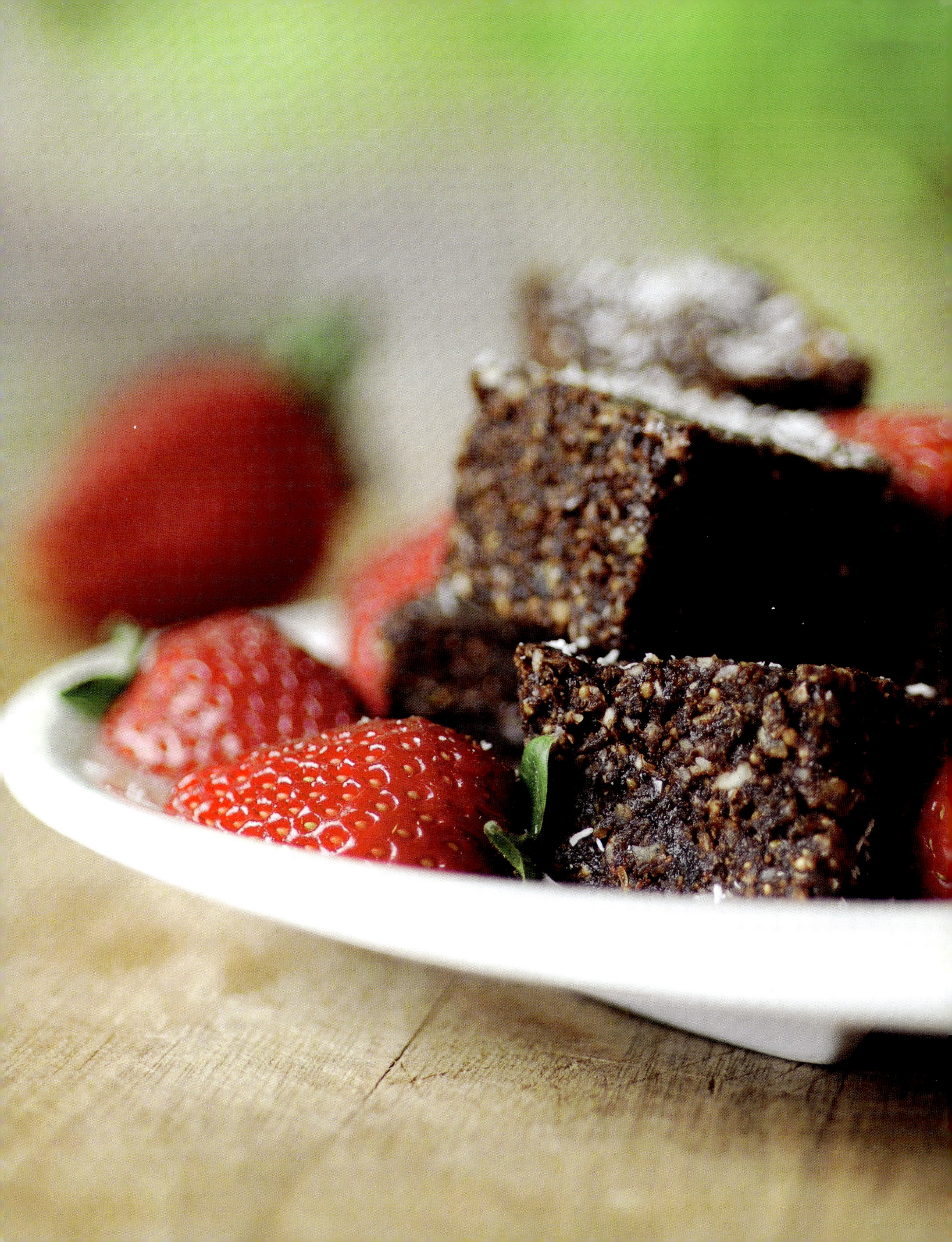

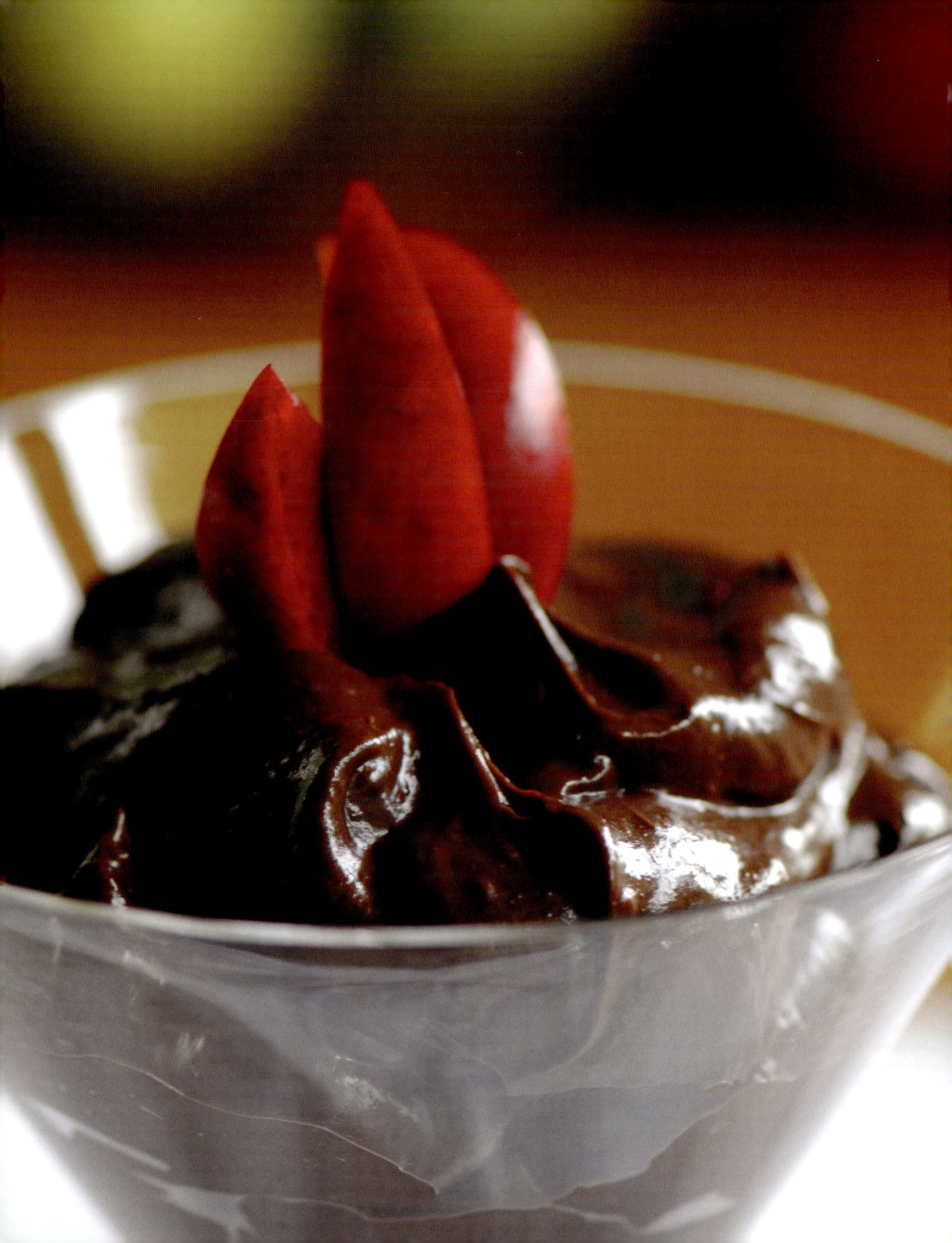

Avocado chocolate mousse

DF V

This surprisingly rich, smooth mousse is dairy-free. Avocado is the magic ingredient – its healthy oils create a luscious creamy texture. It keeps well in the refrigerator for more than 10 days – if you can resist dipping into it!

½ cup dehydrated sugar cane juice or honey
½ cup water
2 medium-sized avocados (300g flesh)
1 teaspoon pure vanilla essence
¼ teaspoon ground cinnamon
½ cup good quality cocoa powder
juice of ½ small lemon

Put all ingredients in a food processor and process to combine.

Refrigerate until required.

SERVES 8

Apricot muesli bar

DF V

Many store-bought muesli bars contain high levels of sugar, hydrogenated oils and preservatives. Some also contain artificial colouring. This recipe is a much healthier (and tastier) alternative. Many thanks to Nicola Galloway for providing the original inspiration behind the recipe.

Note: This bar is not especially sweet, so if you want it sweeter add 4 tablespoons of honey or 20 drops of stevia extract to the wet ingredients.

200g apricots, chopped
1 cup fruit juice
2 eggs
75g butter, melted, or coconut oil
1 cup buckwheat flakes
½ cup buckwheat groats
½ cup millet flakes
1 cup desiccated coconut
⅓ cup gluten-free flour (see page 18)
½ teaspoon ground cinnamon
1 teaspoon gluten-free baking powder
pinch of sea salt

Preheat oven to 180°C. Grease and line a 15cm x 25cm slice tin.

Put chopped apricots in a bowl with the fruit juice.

Whisk together eggs and butter. Add to fruit mixture.

Combine dry ingredients in a separate bowl. Add wet ingredients and mix until well combined.

Press into prepared tin and bake for 20–25 minutes until firm and starting to colour.

Slice when cool and store in an airtight container.

MAKES ABOUT 15 BARS

Avocado chocolate mousse

Drinks

Once while hiking a remote track in the hills behind Nelson, we rested beside a stream before beginning a long steep climb. Anna suggested we fill our water bottles but I resisted, sure we'd pass plenty of other streams and adamant we wouldn't want the extra weight. Many hours later, hot, thirsty and anxious, we were so relieved to find a small pond. Anna graciously forgave me. I have since learned to be more cautious. - **ROGER**

Just like a garden, we also need regular watering to be at our best! Limiting your fluid intake can lead to fatigue, dry skin, headaches and constipation. When we become dehydrated the first thing to suffer is our clarity of thought.

WATER
Drinking sufficient water is even more important than eating. With plenty of water and no food, people can survive for at least 30 days. However, without water you could die within five days.

How much water do you need? You can get 20-40 per cent of your required daily fluids from eating fresh fruit and vegetables. The remainder must come from drinking and water is always the best choice to quench a thirst. Most experts agree that approximately eight glasses of water per day is sufficient to maintain proper hydration. Begin your day with a glass of water because you lose a lot of water during the night due to respiration and metabolic processes.

To carry water for drinking, we recommend using bottles made of stainless steel, strong glass with a padded carrier case or stable plastic. Look for plastic bottles marked with recycling number 1. Avoid PVC (marked with a number 3) and polycarbonate (marked with a number 7). Never leave plastic water bottles in a car - heat degrades plastic which can cause chemicals to leach into the water.

SOFT DRINKS

Fizzy drinks, energy drinks and fruit-flavoured drinks contain plenty of sugary energy and have minimal nutritional value. Studies clearly show a strong link between soft-drink consumption and childhood health issues, such as obesity, tooth decay, caffeine dependence and weak bones, indicating that soft drinks are completely unsuitable for children.

FRUIT JUICE

Fruit juice is often promoted as a healthy alternative to sugary drinks. Pure fruit juice is a relatively natural product and contains none of the additives found in soft drinks. However, it is high in fructose (fruit sugar) and can cause the same extreme response in blood-sugar and insulin levels as sucrose (white sugar). If you drink fruit juice in any quantity it is best to drink it diluted with water. This is especially important for young children.

CAFFEINE

A fit, healthy person can safely enjoy one daily coffee. However, regularly drinking several cups a day can cause a range of problems including difficulty losing weight, anaemia and sleep problems. Anyone with compromised physical or mental health should avoid caffeine completely. Both black and green teas contain caffeine too – although many varieties of tea also have some health benefits. There are many satisfying substitutes for caffeinated drinks, such as herbal teas and dandelion root coffee.

ALCOHOL

Some researchers believe a glass of alcohol per day may have positive heart-health benefits. Red wine is regarded as a healthier choice due to antioxidant phenolic compounds. However, alcohol is an addictive substance that contributes to widespread health issues and social distress. Try going without alcohol for several days – withdrawal symptoms or cravings are a sure sign of addiction.

MILK

Our experience and research has led us to believe that pasteurised and homogenised milk does not contribute to optimum health. However, the process of fermenting milk into yoghurt and other cultures can reduce the lactose content by 30–40 per cent, which is why people who have difficulty digesting milk may feel fine after eating yoghurt.

Here is our list of the most easily digested and nourishing milks to drink or use in cooking:
- fresh raw goat's and cow's milk
- homemade nut and seed milk
- packaged almond milk, rice milk and oat milk
- whole (unhomogenised) cow's milk.

Mango cardamom lassi

This is an exotic, healthy treat – it's refreshing, nourishing and balancing. It may be enjoyed at breakfast, as a snack, or as a dessert, and is the perfect way to finish a curry meal.

Acidophilus yoghurt contains probiotics that help create healthy intestines.

1 fresh ripe mango, peeled and stone removed
1½ cups unsweetened acidophilus yoghurt
2 teaspoons honey
pinch of sea salt
¼ teaspoon ground cardamom

Put all ingredients in a blender and blend until smooth and creamy.

Pour into 2 glasses and serve immediately.

SERVES 2

Probiotics are supplements of beneficial intestinal bacteria. Within your intestine are about 2 kilograms of bacteria! Probiotics assist the body to keep a balanced ecology of gut flora. When things get out of balance, due to things like overeating sugary foods or taking antibiotics, *Candida* infections and bowel problems can manifest themselves. Probiotics come from eating non-digestible foods like fibre. They help good bacteria thrive and stay healthy. Eating a diet rich in wholefoods ensures we get plenty of probiotics.

Chocolate almond smoothie DF V

1 banana, peeled and chopped
1½ tablespoons cocoa powder
⅓ cup almonds, soaked overnight, drained and rinsed ✹
1 tablespoon honey
½ teaspoon pure vanilla essence
1 cup water

Put all ingredients in a blender and blend until smooth and creamy.

Pour into 2 glasses and serve immediately.

SERVES 2

Raspberry avocado smoothie DF V

1 banana, peeled and chopped
1 small avocado, peeled and stone removed
1 cup frozen raspberries
1 tablespoon honey
1 cup water
small pinch of sea salt

Put all the ingredients in a blender and blend until smooth and creamy.

Pour into 2 glasses and serve immediately.

SERVES 2

Make *Raspberry cream* by omitting the water from the *Raspberry avocado smoothie*. In this thicker form, it can be used as an alternative to yoghurt for breakfast or with sliced fresh fruit for dipping.

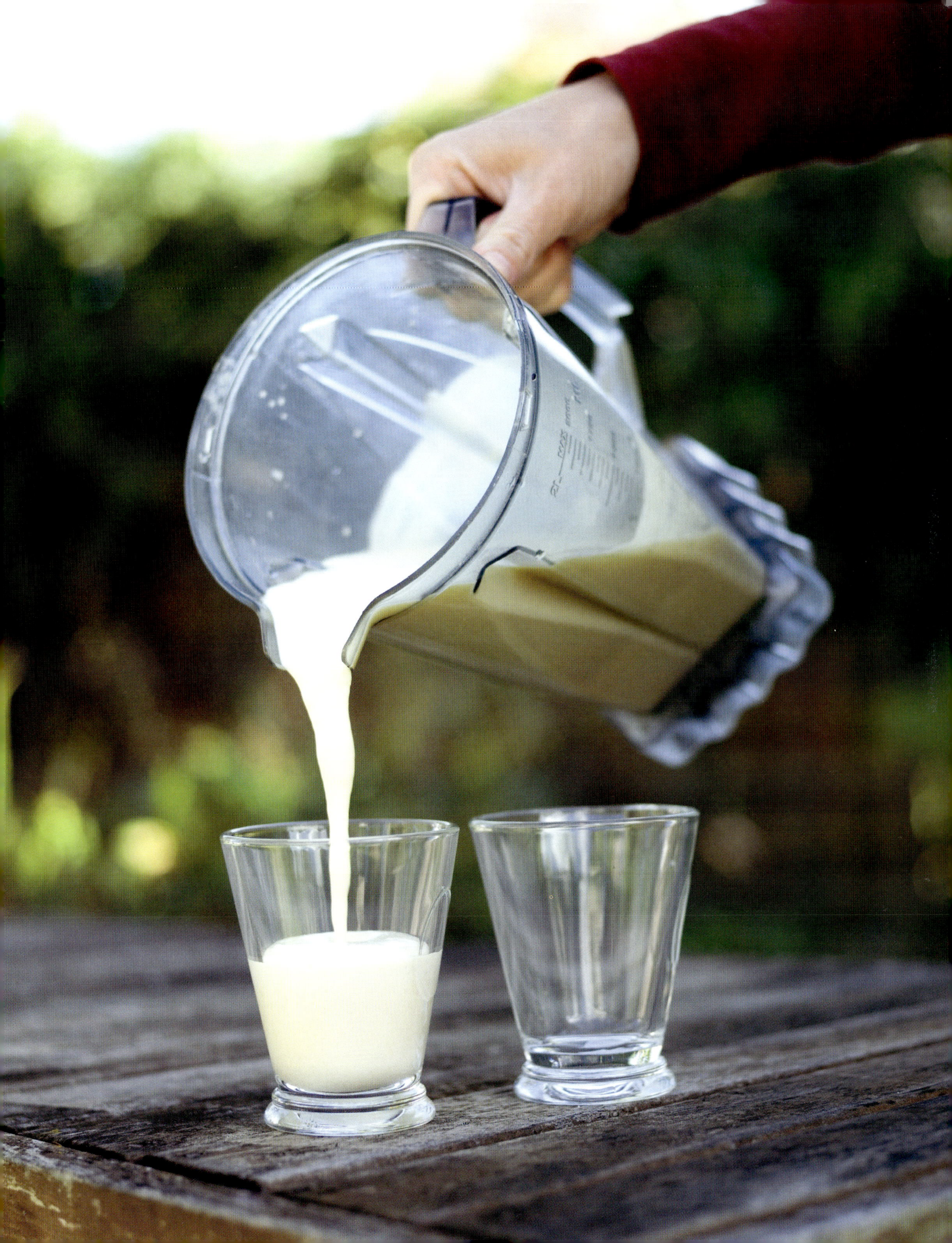

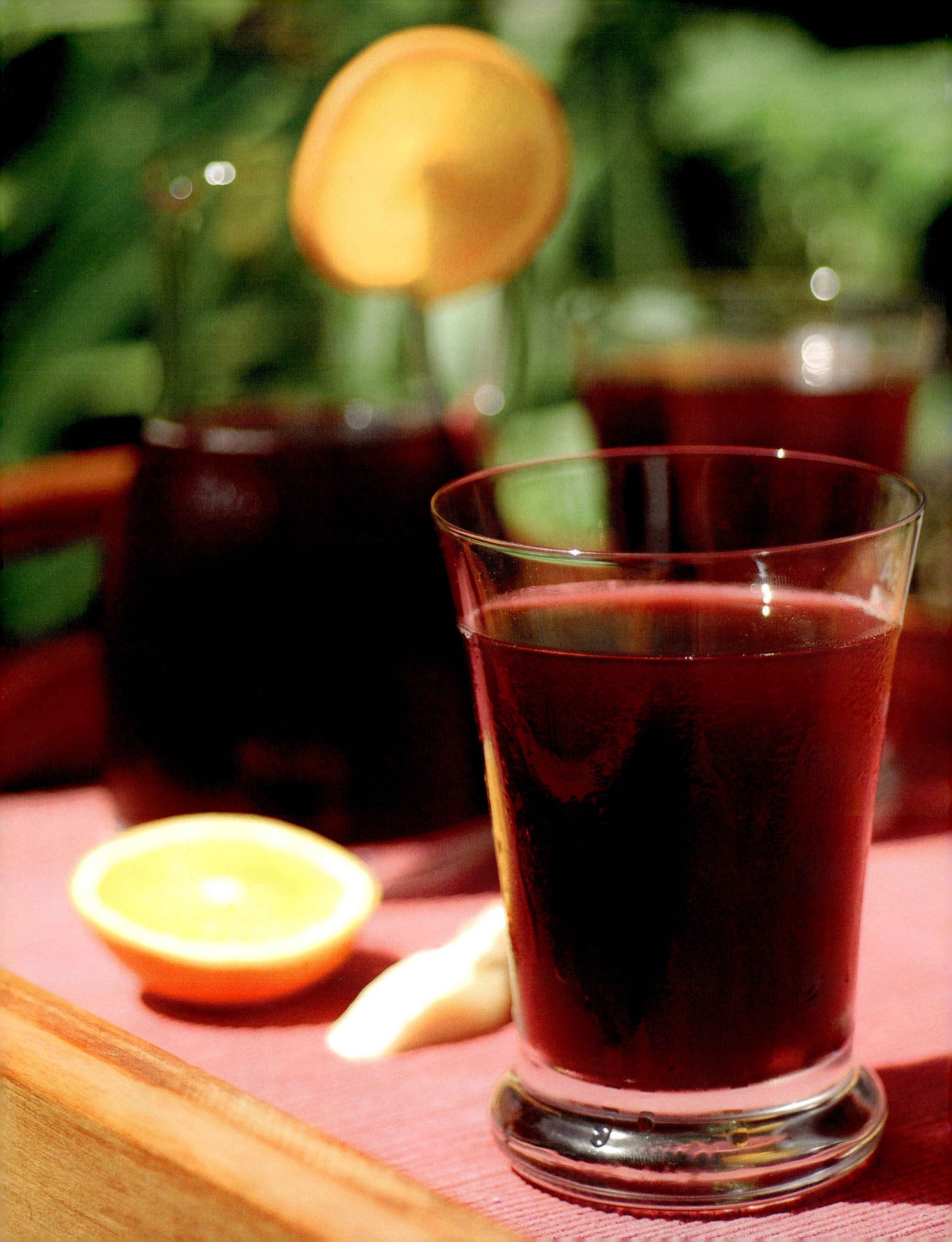

Pineapple mint cocktail

DF V

For a taste of summer, pineapple is hard to beat.

½ pineapple
10 medium-sized mint leaves
small piece of fresh ginger, sliced or grated
pinch of sea salt
1 cup water
honey (optional)

Peel pineapple and remove any tough spikes, hollows or bumps. Remove core and chop flesh into chunks.

Put all ingredients except honey in a blender and blend until smooth.

Taste and add honey if required.

Serve immediately or refrigerate until ready to serve.

SERVES 4

Iced berry tea

DF V

Get the flavour of summer berries all year round with this refreshing berry tea.

2 cups water
3 berry-flavoured herbal tea bags
6 slices fresh ginger
½ orange, sliced
4 tablespoons honey
500ml dark grape juice, chilled
1 litre sparkling or still water, chilled

Combine 2 cups water, teabags, ginger, orange slices and honey in a large saucepan on medium heat and slowly bring to a boil. Simmer for 10 minutes. Leave to cool for 30 minutes then chill in the refrigerator.

When ready to serve, mix this concentrate with chilled grape juice and chilled sparkling or still water.

To serve, pour over ice in individual glasses.

SERVES 6

Lemon iced tea

DF V

In the hottest days of summer take time to relax and sip on a glass of iced tea.

3 cups boiling water
3 black tea bags
2 tablespoons honey
juice of 2 lemons
lots of ice cubes
lemon slices

Pour water onto the tea bags. Leave tea to steep for about 5 minutes. Do not squeeze out the tea bags as these last traces can be very bitter. Discard tea bags.

Stir honey into hot tea.

Pour lemon juice into 4 glasses.

Three-quarters fill each glass with ice.

Pour tea over ice in each glass.

Stir well. Garnish with slices of lemon.

SERVES 4

Add fresh mint or lavender flowers to each glass along with the ice, but before pouring the tea.

Left: Iced berry tea
Overleaf left: Lemon iced tea. Overleaf right: Sweet spiced tea

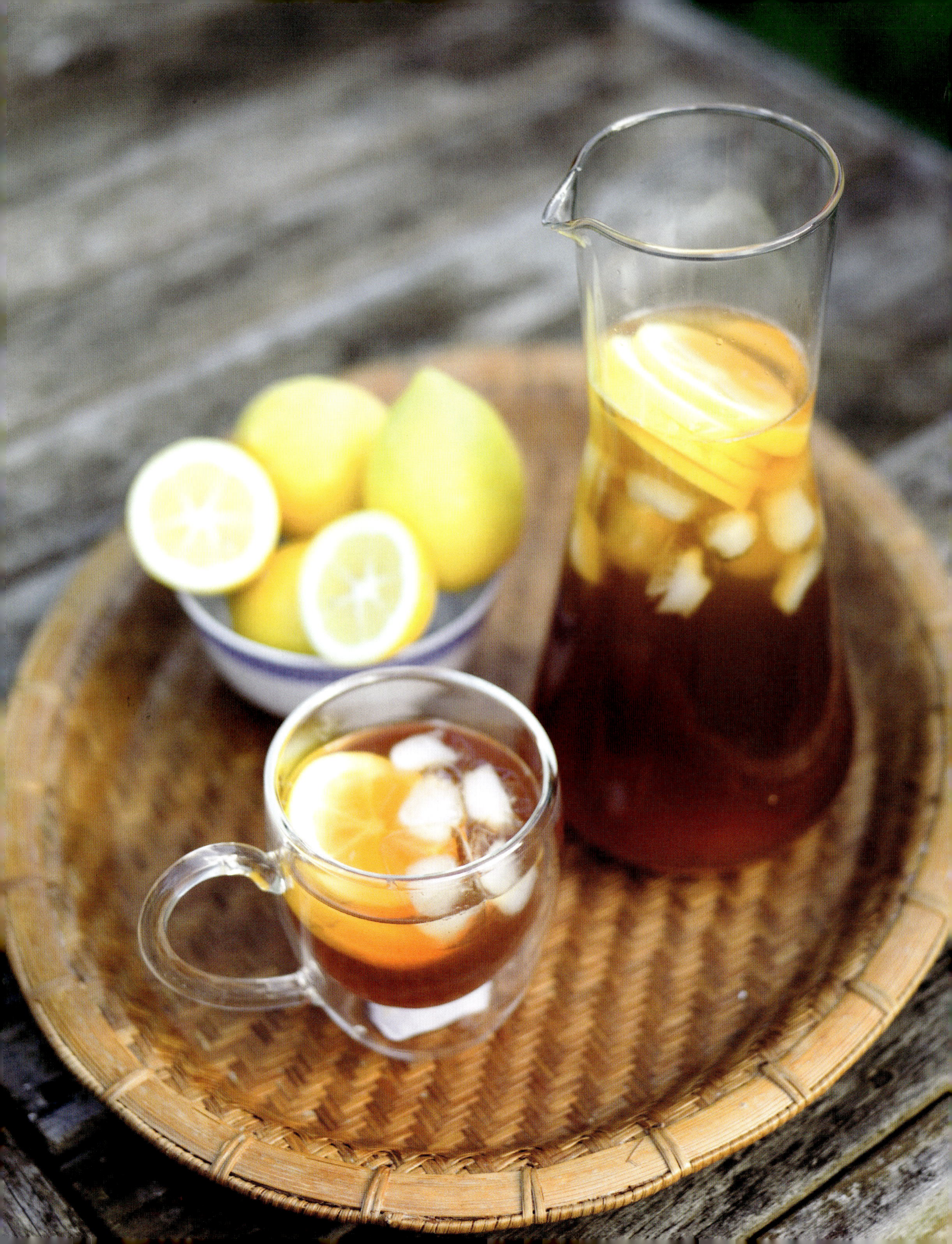

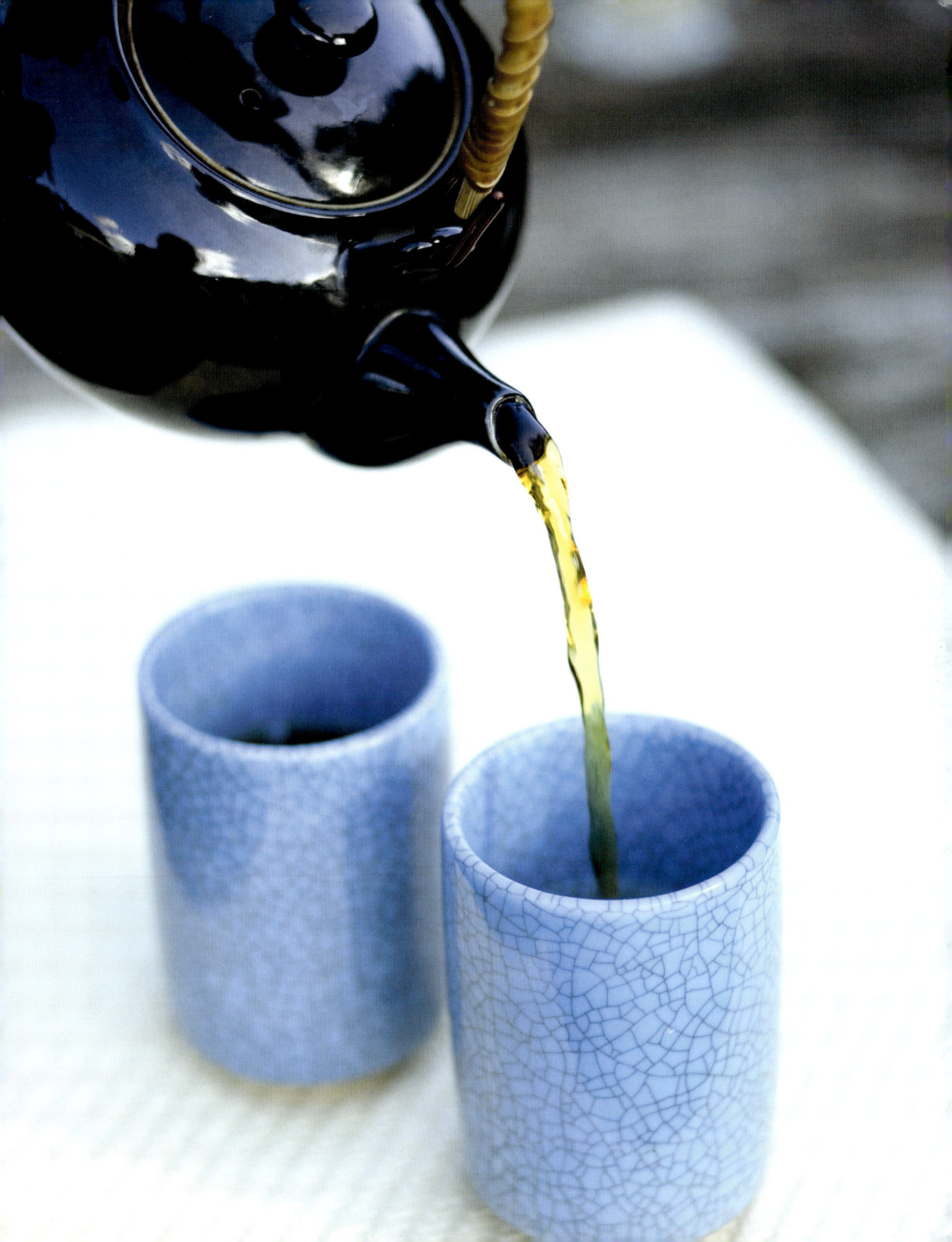

Sparkly fruit punch

DF V

The zesty flavour of fresh fruit makes this punch a real crowd-pleaser. It is also easy to multiply the recipe for a large party.

2–3 oranges (250g), peeled and flesh roughly chopped
1 litre apple or pear juice
500ml sparkling mineral water
1 cup frozen mixed berries
handful of fresh mint leaves

Blend orange flesh with 1 cup of fruit juice.

In a large bowl, mix blended orange and remaining fruit juice and all other ingredients.

MAKES 8 GLASSES

Ginger rooibos tea

DF V

Rooibos (red bush) tea from South Africa has a robust satisfying flavour. It is also caffeine- and tannin-free. In winter, try adding fresh ginger for a warming drink with extra zing.

3 rooibos tea bags
fresh ginger slices
1.5 litres cold water

Put all the ingredients in a saucepan over medium heat and bring slowly to a boil. Simmer for 5 minutes. Alternatively, use a coffee plunger and simply leave to steep for 5 minutes.

Strain and serve immediately.

MAKES 6 CUPS

Sweet spiced tea

DF V

Share this wonderful warming drink with friends on special winter occasions. Omit any of the spices that are not easy to obtain – it will still be delicious.

2 liquorice tea bags
½ teaspoon fennel seed
½ teaspoon aniseed
½ teaspoon star anise
1 teaspoon cardamom pods
8 dried dates
fresh ginger slices
2 fresh orange slices
1.5 litres cold water
small pinch of sea salt

Put all ingredients in a saucepan over medium heat and gradually bring to a boil. Turn heat down and simmer for about 15 minutes.

Strain and serve immediately.

MAKES 6 CUPS

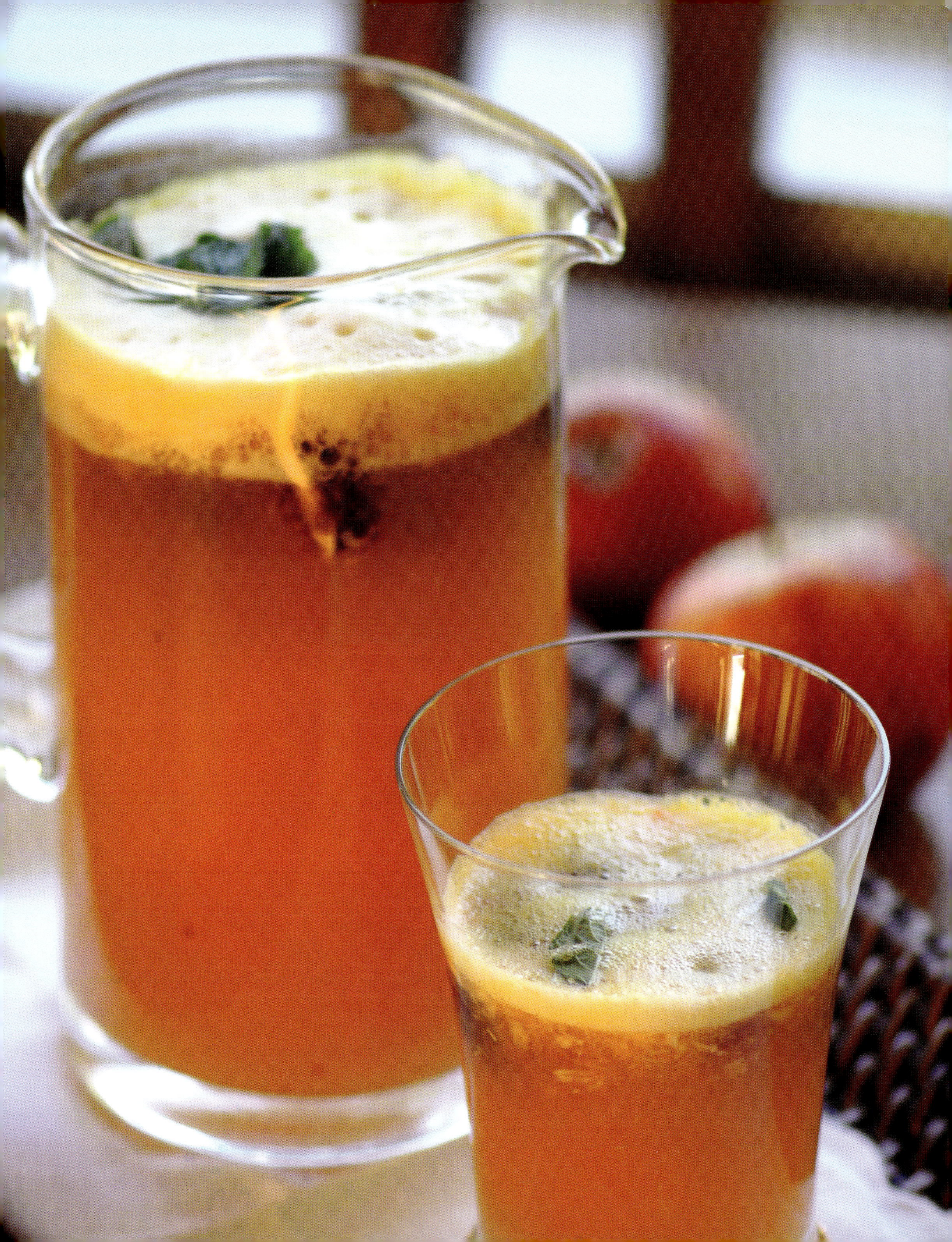

Glossary

ARAME
This Japanese sea vegetable has a fine, firm texture with a mild flavour that can enhance many salads and soups. Soak for 30 minutes before use.

BEE POLLEN
Bee pollen is flower pollen that is collected from bees' bodies as they enter a hive. Pollen is a nourishing food, containing essential amino acids and many vitamins and minerals.

BLACK RICE
A deep purple when cooked, black rice has a nutty taste and soft texture, and is high in iron and other nutrients. Available from Asian food stores.

BOK CHOY
A dark green variety of the mustard family, it comprises bunches of firm-textured leaves with thick, crunchy white stems.

BUCKWHEAT
This gluten-free triangular seed is often referred to as a grain, but is actually a small dried fruit. Buckwheat is native to Central Asia and a significant food in Russia. Traditionally cooked whole or ground into a flour it can also be sprouted and eaten raw.

CAROB
The carob tree is native to the Mediterranean. The dried ground flesh of the pod has a flavour similar to sweetened cocoa. It contains no caffeine and is often used as a non-allergenic cocoa substitute.

CHIA SEED
A South Amercian superfood high in omega 3 oil, minerals and fibre. Chia contains all eight amino acids, making it a complete protein source.

CHINESE FIVE-SPICE
A balanced mixture of ground spices designed to combine the five flavours of Chinese cooking. A typical mix includes cinnamon, black pepper, cloves, fennel seed and star anise.

CHLORELLA
A dark-green single-celled freshwater algae, chlorella is a great source of protein and micronutrients. It is a valuable detoxification aid and is excellent mixed with a little juice or in a smoothie.

COCONUT OIL
Coconut oil is very stable at higher cooking temperatures and rarely goes rancid. The saturated fat in coconut oil is in a form that is easy to assimilate and does not have the same adverse effect as the saturated fat in animal products. It is anti-bacterial and can speed up the metabolism.

DAIKON
The literal translation of daikon is 'large root'. It is a long, fat, white root-vegetable with crisp texture and mild radish flavour; delicious grated in salads and wraps. It is also known as Chinese radish.

DEHYDRATED SUGAR CANE JUICE
The texture, golden colour and caramel flavour lend well to baking. It retains minerals that are stripped away to make white sugar. Rapadura is the Portuguese word for unrefined dehydrated sugar cane juice and a brand that we recommend.

FEIJOA
A relative of the guava, feijoa is an egg-shaped fruit with a green skin and a pulpy, deliciously aromatic flesh. Originally from the Brazilian highlands, this small tree grows well in a subtropical climate.

FLAXSEED
Consumed as an oil or as freshly ground seed, flaxseed is becoming popular as a nutritional supplement, mainly for its omega-3 content. Sometimes called linseed, it can be ground and used in baking or pancakes to replace eggs.

GLUTEN
A protein found in some grains, including wheat, rye and barley. Gluten gives wheat dough its elasticity. An allergy to gluten causes the digestive disorder known as coeliac disease. Gluten may also be found in many additives to processed food.

HIJIKI
This Japanese sea vegetable is ink-black in colour with a firm texture and strong taste of the sea. It brings a dramatic dimension to salads.

KALE
A member of the brassica family, kale has dark-green leaves that do not form a head. It is the closest form of cultivated brassica to wild cabbage. It is very hardy, pest-resistant, easy to grow and, possibly, has even more nutritional benefits than broccoli.

KARENGO
This sea vegetable, harvested in the South Island of New Zealand, is very closely related to Japanese nori. It is purple and becomes soft and slimy when soaked.

KOMBU
This wide flat seaweed is a good source of calcium, iron, protein, and vitamins A, B1 and B2. We add it to cooking beans to bring out the flavour and increase digestibility. It is also delicious soaked and cooked in miso soup but needs to be removed and sliced, then added back before serving.

KUMARA
The Maori word for New Zealand sweet potato, kumara can be used in the same way as the American sweet potato or yam.

MEDJOOL DATES
Originally from Morocco, these large, succulent dates are grown in the USA and are often labelled California dates.

MILLET
A mineral-rich gluten-free grain, small and round in shape. Millet is a staple food in Africa.

MISO
Fermented soya bean paste. Some varieties are made with added grains. Although a cooked product, miso is alive with healthy enzymes.

MIZUNA
This mild-tasting leafy Chinese green, a member of the mustard family, has feathery leaves with a white stem.

NORI
A variety of seaweed from Far-East Asia most commonly seen in its processed form, as sheets for making rolled sushi.

POMEGRANATE MOLASSES
Made from concentrated pomegranate juice, this dark-brown liquid has a versatile sweet-and-sour flavour. It can be found at specialty stores.

PSYLLIUM HULLS
Psyllium is a native Mediterranean plant. The seed hulls are most commonly used as a bulking and lubrication aid for the digestive system. When moistened, psyllium hulls expand, becoming jelly-like, and as such make an excellent thickener in some desserts.

PUHA
A nutrient-rich leaf vegetable also known as sow thistle which, when cooked, tastes similar to chard.

RAW HONEY
In its raw form, honey contains many valuable enzymes, vitamins, minerals and other factors. Most commercial honeys are pasteurised to guarantee long storage; however, the processing destroys many of the micronutrients. Buy raw honey from the farm gate or at farmers' markets.

QUINOA
This small round white fruit of the goosefoot plant is a native to the Andes. It can be eaten sprouted, ground to be used as a flour or cooked in a similar way to rice. It is very high in protein.

SEA SALT
Salt produced simply by the evaporation of sea water contains a broad range of minerals and has a more rounded, complex taste than refined salt. Some of the better varieties of sea salt actually have a dirty-grey appearance.

SHOYU
Shoyu is Japanese for 'soy sauce' and is now used in the West to distinguish good-quality fermented soy sauce from inferior unfermented versions.

SPELT
A highly nutritious and ancient grain from the wheat family, spelt can replace standard wheat flour in baked goods, white sauces and pastas.

SPIRULINA
This dehydrated powder made from freshwater algae is one of the richest known sources of complete protein. It is also an excellent source of vitamins, minerals, anti-oxidants, chlorophyll and essential fats.

STEVIA
A sweetener derived from a tropical plant native to South America, stevia contains compounds which are 250–300 times sweeter than table sugar. However, it does not significantly alter blood glucose, and so can be safely consumed by diabetics. In our view, there are no health concerns with moderate use of stevia.

TAHINI
Ground sesame seed paste, and a traditional Middle-Eastern ingredient, tahini is a good alternative to butter and peanut butter. Unhulled tahini is darker and a useful source of calcium and other minerals.

TAMARI
This Japanese word describes the rich liquid that leaches out of miso. In the West, however, the term usually refers to wheat-free fermented shoyu.

TAMARIND PASTE
From the South-East Asian tamarind tree, this sticky pulp surrounds the seeds inside the fruit pods. It has a sweet and sour taste. Available in Asian food stores either as a block (in which case you need to check there are no seeds in it) or as a concentrated liquid (easy to use but has been processed).

TEMPEH
A food made from fermented soya beans. Originally from Indonesia, tempeh has a richer heavier texture and flavour than tofu.

UMEBOSHI VINEGAR
This sour, salty liquid is derived from making Japanese pickled plums (umeboshi paste) and is perfect in Asian-style salad dressings. The paste imparts a tangy, salty flavour to many dishes. Lovely on warm brown rice, in sushi rolls or with tahini on toast.

WAKAME
This Japanese sea vegetable is most often used in traditional miso soup. It has silky firm-textured fronds with a mild flavour. Usually sold as 'fueru wakame', cut into small pieces that only need to be soaked, sometimes it may be found whole in a dried form with the tough stems intact – in which case it needs to be soaked, then de-stemmed and chopped.

XYLITOL
This non-nutritive tooth-friendly sweetener has minimal impact on blood sugar. Found in many fruits and vegetables, it is most commonly made from maize.

Recipe index *(numbers in bold indicate recipe photographs)*

Adzuki pumpkin casserole 90
Almond pilaf **84**, 85
Apple ginger dressing 77
apricot bliss balls, Cashew 122, **123**
Apricot muesli bar 129
Apricot shortcake 122
artichokes, Roast Jerusalem 68
Asparagus and mushroom salad 70
Avocado chocolate mousse **128**, 129
avocado soup, Beetroot and 49, **50–51**
avocado salsa, Mango and 69
avocado smoothie, Raspberry 132
Baba ghannouj 40
bacon stir-fry, Cabbage and 69
Balsamic-roasted beetroot with goat's cheese and rocket **60**, 61
Banana berry muffins **24**, 25
banana ice-cream, Soft-serve **124**, 125
banana walnut truffles, Sunny 122, **123**
beef salad, Ginger 106, **107**
Beetroot and avocado soup 49, **50–51**
Beetroot chocolate cake 126
Beetroot tamarind dip 40
beetroot with goat's cheese and rocket, Balsamic-roasted **60**, 61
Bircher-style breakfast 22, **23**
Black rice pudding 118, **119**
blueberry apple compote, Buckwheat pancakes with 28, **29**
Bok choy stir-fry 60
Braised soy ginger chicken 105
Broccoli and cauliflower salad 63
Brown rice and pomegranate muesli 22
brown rice, Pressure-cooked 81
Buckwheat kasha 85
Buckwheat pancakes with blueberry apple compote 28, **29**
Cabbage and bacon stir-fry 69
Cakes
 Apricot shortcake 122
 Beetroot chocolate cake 126
 Coconut orange cake 117
 Zucchini chocolate no-bake cake 111
calamari, Pad Thai with 97, **98–99**
cannellini and spinach salad, Warm **88**, 89
carrot dip, Curried 36
Cashew apricot bliss balls 122, **123**
Cashew cheese 41

casserole, Adzuki pumpkin 90
casserole, Wild venison 104
Cauliflower mash 62
Cauliflower salad with anchovy dressing 72
cauliflower salad, Broccoli and 63
Ceviche 94, **95**
Chermoula marinade 97
Chicken tagine with lemon and olives 106
Chicken, rice and lemon soup 49
chicken, Braised soy ginger 105
chilli beans, Mexican 80
Chocolate almond smoothie 132
chocolate cake, Beetroot 126
Chocolate mint squares 126, **127**
chocolate mousse, Avocado **128**, 129
chocolate no-bake cake, Zucchini 111
cocktail, Pineapple mint 135
Coconut cookies 118
Coconut orange cake 117
Coconut spinach dip 37
compote, Spiced tamarillo 112
cookies, Coconut 118
Coriander pesto 36
corn and green bean salad, Tempeh, **64**, 65
Corn fritters 45
crumble, Feijoa nut **116**, 117
Cucumber dill soup 48
Curried carrot dip 36
curry, Tempeh and kumara 80
Dips
 Baba ghannouj 40
 Beetroot tamarind dip 40
 Coconut spinach dip 37
 Coriander pesto 36
 Curried carrot dip 36
 Wild weed pesto 34, **35**
Dressings
 Apple ginger dressing 77
 Green goddess creamy dressing 77
 Lemon tahini dressing 77
 Orange soy dressing 76
 Toasted sesame dressing 76
 Umeboshi dressing 76
egg-fried rice, Karengo 45
Farinata 42, **43**
Fave feta fiesta 37
Feijoa nut crumble **116**, 117
fig tart, Fresh 112, **113**
fish cakes, Indonesian 94
fish frittata, Smoked 100, **101**

fish, Marinated grilled 96
Fresh fig tart 112, **113**
Fresh fruit quinoa muesli 27
Fresh mustard 76
frittata, Smoked fish 100, **101**
fruit punch, Sparkly 138, **139**
Gado-gado 82, **83**
Ginger beef salad 106, **107**
Ginger rooibos tea 138
Ginger shoyu marinade 96
Gluten-free flour 18
goat's cheese and rocket, Balsamic-roasted beetroot with **60**, 61
grapefruit salad with mint dressing, Lentil and 90, **91**
Greek lamb stew with quinoa 105
Green goddess creamy dressing 77
Hearty miso soup 52, **53**
hummus, Roast pumpkin 34
ice-cream, Pina colada 125
ice-cream, Soft-serve banana **124**, 125
Iced berry tea **134**, 135
iced tea, Lemon 135, **136**
Indonesian fish cakes 94
Kale and roasted pumpkin salad **66**, 67
kanten, Strawberry 121
Karengo egg-fried rice 45
karengo with pumpkin seeds, Pan-roasted 44
kasha, Buckwheat 85
kimchi salad, Korean **74**, 75
Korean kimchi salad **74**, 75
kumara curry, Tempeh and 80
kumara with shiitake, Sweet and sour 63
lamb stew with quinoa, Greek 105
lasagne, Rice paper **102**, 103
Lemon garlic marinade 96
Lemon iced tea 135, **136**
Lemon tahini dressing 77
Lentil and grapefruit salad with mint dressing 90, **91**
lentil stew, Red 89
Mango and avocado salsa 69
Mango cardomom lassi 132, **133**
Marinades
 Chermoula marinade 97
 Ginger shoyu marinade 96
 Lemon garlic marinade 96
Marinated grilled fish 96
mash, Cauliflower 62
Mexican chilli beans 80
Migas **26**, 27

Millet with pumpkin and nori 81
miso soup, Hearty 52, **53**
muesli bar, Apricot 129
muesli, Brown rice and pomegranate 22
muesli, Fresh fruit quinoa 27
muffins, Banana berry **24**, 25
mushroom rissoles, Tofu and **38**, 39
mushroom salad, Asparagus and 70
mustard, Fresh 76
Orange soy dressing 76
Oven-baked savoury wedges 62
Pad Thai with calamari 97, **98–99**
pancakes with blueberry apple compote, Buckwheat 28, **29**
Pan-roasted karengo with pumpkin seeds 44
parsnip soup, Pea and 52
pasta sauce, Zucchini and olive 68
Pea and parsnip soup 52
Pear and cardomom tart **120**, 121
Pear and walnut salad 70, **71**
pears and feta, Red quinoa salad with 86, **87**
Persian delights **110**, 111
pesto, Coriander 36
pesto, Wild weed 34, **35**
pickles, Red radish 73
pilaf, Almond **84**, 85
Pina colada ice-cream 125
Pineapple mint cocktail 135
pomegranate muesli, Brown rice and 22
ponzu, Wakame cucumber salad with 72
porridge, Three-grain 25
Pressure-cooked brown rice 81
pudding, Black rice 118, **119**
pumpkin and nori, Millet with 81
pumpkin casserole, Adzuki 90
pumpkin hummus, Roast 34
pumpkin salad, Kale and roasted **66**, 67
punch, Sparkly fruit 138, **139**
quinoa salad with pears and feta, Red 86, **87**
radish pickles, Red 73
Raspberry avocado smoothie 132
Red lentil stew 89
Red quinoa salad with pears and feta 86, **87**
Red radish pickles 73
Rice balls 44
Rice noodle and watercress salad 73
Rice paper lasagne **102**, 103
rice pudding, Black 118, **119**

General index

rice, Karengo egg-fried 45
rice, Pressure-cooked brown 81
Roast Jerusalem artichokes 68
Roast pumpkin hummus 34
rooibos tea, Ginger 138

Salads
   Asparagus and mushroom salad 70
   Balsamic-roasted beetroot with goat's cheese and rocket 60, **61**
   Broccoli and cauliflower salad 63
   Cauliflower salad with anchovy dressing 72
   Ginger beef salad 106, **107**
   Kale and roasted pumpkin salad 66, **67**
   Korean kimchi salad **74**, 75
   Lentil and grapefruit salad with mint dressing 90, **91**
   Pear and walnut salad 70, **71**
   Red quinoa salad with pears and feta 86, **87**
   Rice noodle and watercress salad 73
   Simple pressed salad 75
   Spinach salad with walnut pesto dressing 67
   Tempeh, corn and green bean salad 64, **65**
   Wakame cucumber salad with ponzu 72
   Warm cannellini and spinach salad **88**, 89

Salmon salsa 41
salsa, Mango and avocado 69
salsa, Salmon 41
Satay sauce 82
sauce, Satay 82
seeds, Tamari roasted 42
sesame dressing, Toasted 76
sesame, Wild greens with 64
shiitake, Sweet and sour kumara with 63
Silky spinach soup 48
Simple pressed salad 75
Smoked fish frittata 100, **101**
smoothie, Chocolate almond 132
smoothie, Raspberry avocado 132
smoothie, Superfood breakfast 28
Soft-serve banana ice-cream **124**, 125

Soups
   Beetroot and avocado soup 49, **50–51**
   Chicken, barley and lemon soup 49
   Cucumber dill soup 48
   Hearty miso soup 52, **53**
   Pea and parsnip soup 52
   Silky spinach soup 48
   Tomato and coconut soup with fish dumplings **54**, 55

Sparkly fruit punch 138, **139**
Spiced tamarillo compote 112
spinach dip, Coconut 37
Spinach salad with walnut pesto dressing 67
spinach salad, Warm cannellini and **88**, 89
spinach soup, Silky 48
Strawberry kanten 121
Sunny banana walnut truffles 122, **123**
Superfood breakfast smoothie 28
Sweet and sour kumara with shiitake 63
Sweet spiced tea **137**, 138
tagine with lemon and olives, Chicken 106
Tamari roasted seeds 42
tamarillo compote, Spiced 112
tamarind dip, Beetroot 40
tea, Ginger rooibos 138
tea, Iced berry **134**, 135
tea, Lemon iced 135, **136**
tea, Sweet spiced **137**, 138
Tempeh and kumara curry 80
Tempeh, corn and green bean salad 64, **65**
Three-grain porridge 25
Toasted sesame dressing 76
Tofu and mushroom rissoles **38**, 39
Tomato and coconut soup with fish dumplings **54**, 55
Umeboshi dressing 76
venison casserole, Wild 104
venison rissoles, Wild 104
Wakame cucumber salad with ponzu 72
Warm cannellini and spinach salad **88**, 89
watercress salad, Rice noodle and 73
wedges, Oven-baked savoury 62
Wild greens with sesame 64
Wild venison casserole 104
Wild venison rissoles 104
Wild weed pesto 34, **35**
Zucchini and olive pasta sauce 68
Zucchini chocolate no-bake cake 111

alcohol 131
arthritis 57
beans 16, 17, 78–79, 81, 89, 90
   cooking 79
   sprouting 82
blood 57, 75
blood-sugar levels 16, 25, 27, 78, 90, 111, 121, 131, 141
bowels 109, 121, 132
breathing 11
butter 41
caffeine 131
   alternatives to caffeine 131, 140
cancer 11, 12, 25, 57, 67, 109
cancer-preventing foods 25, 57, 67
Candida 109, 132
carbohydrates 16, 33, 42, 57, 78, 109
cholesterol 111
circulation 106, 111
cleaning products, natural 12
coeliac disease 6, 79, 140
complex carbohydrates 16
cooking oils, healthy 16, 60, 76
cooking oils, polyunsaturated 17, 77
cosmetics, natural 12
detoxification 11, 36, 47, 140
diabetes 16, 36, 42, 57, 78, 109, 111, 141
digestion 19, 86, 106, 111
eggs 16, 21, 27
energy levels 33, 34, 45, 78, 109, 118, 125
exercise 10, 12
farmers' markets 17
fats 16, 76, 109, 141
flour 16, 17, 73, 78, 109
food intolerances 45, 73 (see also gluten intolerance)
free-radicals 76
gluten intolerance 28, 103, 117, 140
grains 16, 17, 22, 25, 78–79
   cooking 79
heart disease 16, 25, 42, 57, 75, 109, 111
heart, strengthening 57, 78, 111, 131
immune system 16, 25, 49, 57, 63, 109
intestines 132
iodine 75
margarine 41
meat 92, 93, 104
   organic 104
meditation 13
melatonin 11

milk
   cow's 86, 131
   goat's 86, 131
nervous system 11, 16, 25, 57
non-starchy vegetables 16
nuts 17, 18
   soaking 18
obesity 16, 25, 42, 131
oils, see *cooking oils*
omega oils 27, 41, 140
organic food 17, 48, 60, 78, 90, 93, 104
polyunsaturated cooking oils 17, 77
potatoes 62
pressure cookers 81
protein 16, 18, 21, 27
pulses 78, 79, 89, 93
quinoa 27, 105
refined sugar 17, 109
salt 75
seafood 92, 93
seasoning, natural 18
seaweed, edible 44, 72, 73, 76
seeds 17, 18
serotonin 11
shiitake mushrooms 63
shopping, grocery 17
skincare 12
sleep 12
soft drinks 131
soy products 18, 77, 82, 93, 131
soya beans 80
stir-frying 60
stevia 109, 118, 129, 141
sugar, refined 17, 109
sweeteners, natural 109, 118
veganism 93
vegetables 16, 56–57, 62, 68
   non-starchy 16, 57
   starchy 16
   storing 62, 68
vegetarianism 93
water 130
wheat intolerance 73, 79
xylitol 109, 118, 141
yeast infections/problems 109, 132
yoga 10, 11

Weights & measures

The following amounts have been rounded up or down for convenience. All have been kitchen-tested.

ABBREVIATIONS

g	gram
kg	kilogram
mm	millimetre
cm	centimetre
ml	millilitre
°C	degrees Celsius
tsp	teaspoon
tbsp	tablespoon

WEIGHT CONVERSIONS

METRIC	IMPERIAL/US
25g	1 oz
50g	2 oz
75g	3 oz
100g	3½ oz
125g	4½ oz
150g	5 oz
175g	6 oz
200g	7 oz
225g	8 oz
250g	9 oz
275g	9½ oz
300g	10½ oz
325g	11½ oz
350g	12½ oz
375g	13 oz
400g	14 oz
450g	16 oz (1 lb)
500g	17½ oz
750g	26½ oz
1kg	35 oz (2¼ lb)

LENGTH CONVERSIONS

METRIC	IMPERIAL/US
0.5cm	¼ inch
1cm	½ inch
2.5cm	1 inch
5cm	2 inches
10cm	4 inches
20cm	8 inches
30cm	12 inches (1 foot)

LIQUID CONVERSIONS

METRIC	IMPERIAL	US
5ml (1 tsp)	¼ fl oz	1 tsp
15ml (1 tbsp)	½ fl oz	1 tbsp
30ml (⅛ cup)	1 fl oz	⅛ cup
60ml (¼ cup)	2 fl oz	¼ cup
125ml (½ cup)	4 fl oz	½ cup
150ml	5 fl oz (¼ pint)	⅔ cup
175ml	6 fl oz	¾ cup
250ml (1 cup)	8 fl oz	1 cup
300ml	10 fl oz (½ pint)	1¼ cups
375ml	12 fl oz	1½ cups
500ml (2 cups)	16 fl oz	2 cups
600ml	20 fl oz (1 pint)	2½ cups

NOTE: The Australian metric tablespoon measures 20ml.

TEMPERATURE CONVERSIONS

CELSIUS	FAHRENHEIT	GAS
100°C	225°F	¼
125°C	250°F	½
150°C	300°F	2
160°C	325°F	3
170°C	325°F	3
180°C	350°F	4
190°C	375°F	5
200°C	400°F	6
210°C	425°F	7
220°C	425°F	7
230°C	450°F	8
250°C	500°F	9

CAKE TIN SIZES

METRIC	IMPERIAL/US
15cm	6 inches
18cm	7 inches
20cm	8 inches
23cm	9 inches
25cm	10 inches
28cm	11 inches

This revised and updated edition published in 2014 by New Holland Publishers (NZ) Ltd

Auckland • Sydney • London • Cape Town

www.newhollandpublishers.co.nz

218 Lake Road, Northcote, Auckland 0627, New Zealand
Unit 1, 66 Gibbes Street, Chatswood, NSW 2067, Australia
The Chandlery, Unit 114, 50 Westminster Bridge Road, London, SE1 7QY, United Kingdom
Wembley Square, First Floor, Solan Road, Gardens, Cape Town 8001, South Africa

First published in 2009 as *Real Fresh Food: Healthy meals for busy people* by New Holland Publishers (NZ) Ltd

Copyright © 2009 in text: Anna and Roger Wilde
Copyright © 2009 in photography: Daniel Allen
Copyright © 2009 New Holland Publishers (NZ) Ltd
Anna and Roger Wilde have asserted their right to be identified as the authors of this work.

Publishing manager: Christine Thomson
Commissioning editor/project manager: Louise Armstrong
Editor: Fiona McRae
Designer: Keely O'Shannessy

National Library of New Zealand Cataloguing-in-Publication Data

Wilde, Anna, 1974-
Real fresh gluten-free food : simple healthy meals for everyone / Anna & Roger Wilde ; with photography by Daniel Allen.
Revision of 2009 edition.
Includes index.
ISBN 978-1-86966-417-6
1. Gluten-free diet—Recipes. 2. Cooking (Natural foods) I. Wilde, Roger, 1965- II. Allen, Daniel, 1975- III. Title.
641.56318—dc 23

10 9 8 7 6 5 4 3 2 1

Colour reproduction and printing by Craft Print Pte Ltd, Singapore.

All rights reserved. No part of this publication may be reproduced, stored in a retrieval system, or transmitted in any form or by any means, electronic, mechanical, photocopying, recording or otherwise, without the prior permission of the publishers and copyright holders.

The recipes in this book have been carefully tested by the authors. The publishers and the authors have made every effort to ensure that the recipes and instructions pertaining to them are accurate and safe but cannot accept liability for any resulting injury or loss or damage to property whether direct or consequential.